BLACK CITIZENS AND AMERICAN DEMOCRACY

UNIVERSITY PRESS OF FLORIDA

Florida A&M University, Tallahassee
Florida Atlantic University, Boca Raton
Florida Gulf Coast University, Ft. Myers
Florida International University, Miami
Florida State University, Tallahassee
New College of Florida, Sarasota
University of Central Florida, Orlando
University of Florida, Gainesville
University of North Florida, Jacksonville
University of South Florida, Tampa
University of West Florida, Pensacola

Black Citizens and American Democracy

Fighting for the Soul of a Nation

Edited by

Reginald K. Ellis,
Jeffrey L. Littlejohn,
and Peter B. Levy

UNIVERSITY PRESS OF FLORIDA

Gainesville/Tallahassee/Tampa/Boca Raton
Pensacola/Orlando/Miami/Jacksonville/Ft. Myers/Sarasota

Special thanks to the Florida A&M University Department of History and the Center for African and African American Studies for their financial support in the production on this publication.

This book will be made open access within three years of publication thanks to Path to Open, a program developed in partnership between JSTOR, the American Council of Learned Societies (ACLS), University of Michigan Press, and The University of North Carolina Press to bring about equitable access and impact for the entire scholarly community, including authors, researchers, libraries, and university presses around the world. Learn more at https://about.jstor.org/path-to-open/

References to internet websites (URLs) were accurate at the time of writing. Neither the author nor University Press of Florida is responsible for URLs that may have expired or changed since the manuscript was prepared.

Copyright 2025 by Reginald K. Ellis, Jeffrey L. Littlejohn, and Peter B. Levy
All rights reserved
Published in the United States of America

30 29 28 27 26 25   6 5 4 3 2 1

Library of Congress Cataloging-in-Publication Data
Names: Ellis, Reginald K., editor. | Littlejohn, Jeffrey L., 1973- editor. | Levy, Peter B., editor.
Title: Black citizens and American democracy : fighting for the soul of a nation / edited by Reginald K. Ellis, Jeffrey L. Littlejohn, and Peter B. Levy.
Other titles: Fighting for the soul of a nation
Description: 1st. | Gainesville : University Press of Florida, 2025. | Includes bibliographical references and index. | Summary: "This collection examines the important work of Black men and women to shape, expand, and preserve a multiracial American democracy from the mid-twentieth century to the present"—Provided by publisher.
Identifiers: LCCN 2024035556 (print) | LCCN 2024035557 (ebook) | ISBN 9780813079301 (hardback) | ISBN 9780813080987 (paperback) | ISBN 9780813070988 (pdf) | ISBN 9780813073729 (ebook)
Subjects: LCSH: African Americans—Politics and government. | Democracy—United States. | African Americans—Social conditions. | United States—Politics and government. | BISAC: HISTORY / African American & Black | POLITICAL SCIENCE / Political Ideologies / Democracy
Classification: LCC E185.615 .B54143 2025 (print) | LCC E185.615 (ebook) | DDC 973/.0496073—dc23/eng/20241228
LC record available at https://lccn.loc.gov/2024035556
LC ebook record available at https://lccn.loc.gov/2024035557

DOI: https://doi.org/10.5744/9780813079301

The University Press of Florida is the scholarly publishing agency for the State University System of Florida, comprising Florida A&M University, Florida Atlantic University, Florida Gulf Coast University, Florida International University, Florida State University, New College of Florida, University of Central Florida, University of Florida, University of North Florida, University of South Florida, and University of West Florida.

University Press of Florida
2046 NE Waldo Road
Suite 2100
Gainesville, FL 32609
http://upress.ufl.edu

CONTENTS

Introduction: Fighting for the Soul of a Nation 1
   Reginald K. Ellis, Jeffrey L. Littlejohn, and Peter B. Levy

1. Toward a Real United States Patriotism: Black Americans' Centrality to the Pursuit of a Multiracial Democracy 7
   Kristopher Bryan Burrell

2. Black Women: The Backbone of Democracy 35
   Sharlene Sinegal-DeCuir

3. Constructing a Way Forward: Civil Rights and the National Council of Negro Women 47
   Cassandra Newby-Alexander

4. "I Don't Believe This Has Anything to Do with the Alleviation of Poverty": Voting Rights, Economic Justice, and the Struggle for Democracy in Houston 71
   Wesley G. Phelps

5. Overcoming the American Lie: HBCUs' Role in Advancing Democracy 90
   Reginald K. Ellis

6. The Seamstress and the Counselor: Evelyn T. Butts, Joseph Jordan Jr., and *Butts v. Harrison* (1966) 106
   Jeffrey L. Littlejohn and Charles H. Ford

7. Who Killed Ralph Featherstone? A Case Study in the Repression of the Long Black Freedom Struggle 123
   Peter B. Levy

8. A Movement of Movements: The Making of the Maryland Anti-Lynching Federation and the Fight for Democracy in the Free State   158
   Charles L. Chavis Jr.

Epilogue   179
   Jacqueline Jones

List of Contributors   187

Index   189

Introduction

Fighting for the Soul of a Nation

REGINALD K. ELLIS, JEFFREY L. LITTLEJOHN,
AND PETER B. LEVY

On January 6, 2021, moments after President Trump spoke at the "Stop the Steal" rally, thousands of his devotees stormed the U.S. Capitol. While pundits and historians will debate whether he was criminally liable for this insurrection, there can be little doubt that he played an oversized role in inspiring one of the most serious threats to the American republic since the Civil War. This insurrection was set against the backdrop of the worst public health crisis in modern American history, which disproportionately impacted men and women of color, and Trump's negative response to the wave of protests that followed the murder of George Floyd, a Black man, by a white police officer. Coming on top of Trump's long-standing use of racial tropes to win the support of white voters, from his call to "Build the Wall" to his proclamation that some of the white supremacists who staged a deadly rally in Charlottesville, Virginia, were "good people," there could be little doubt that Trump sought to win reelection by galvanizing whites around the idea that they were losing "their" country.

Despite these efforts, the incumbent president lost his bid for reelection because people of color and like-minded white citizens turned out in record numbers. As the votes trickled in, it became clear to both Trump and the nation that Black America was sending a clear message that change was needed, not now but Right Now! From Detroit, Michigan, to Philadelphia, Pennsylvania, to Phoenix, Arizona, and Atlanta, Georgia, Black voters delivered the presidency to Joseph R. Biden. Are the years of "The American Carnage" over, or is this just another brief pause until the next antidemocratic leader emerges to reclaim the American presidency? Whether this is a pause or not, what is clear is that Black folk demonstrated, once again, their commitment to the United States and the ideal of democracy.

This anthology considers the long history of Black women and men fighting to preserve the ideals of American democracy. Collectively, its authors show that 2020 was not a watershed moment but rather a continuation of Martin Luther King Jr's. challenge to America to "live up to who she said she was on paper." We examine the role that Historically Black Colleges and Universities (HBCUs) played in developing "race leaders" focused on pressing the nation on its democratic values; we consider how the national media often neutralized Black progress by underreporting or misrepresenting the repression of Black dissent; and we analyze the long history of the struggle for the Black franchise and the interconnections between the fight for economic, gender, and racial equality. We also explore the ideas of the greatest intellectuals of their day—Frederick Douglass, W.E.B. Du Bois, Mary McLeod Bethune, James Baldwin, and others—to consider how they challenged America to fully embrace its founding principle of equality for all.

For instance, in his powerful essay "Toward a Real United States Patriotism," Kristopher Burrell highlights James Baldwin's observation that Black folk, in spite of the history of racism, retained a faith in democracy despite America's failure to live up to its ideals. They did so, Baldwin wrote, because they "never believed that collection of myths to which white Americans cling: that their ancestors were all freedom-loving heroes, that they were born in the greatest country the world has ever seen, or that Americans are invincible in battle and wise in peace, that Americans have always dealt honorably with Mexicans and Indians and all other neighbors or inferiors, that American men are the world's most direct and virile, that American women are pure." Recognizing her faults, Black activists and intellectuals have "perpetually" criticized America, holding onto the hope that such criticism would compel their country to redeem itself.[1]

At the same time, as Sharlene Sinegal-DeCuir demonstrates in her essay "Black Women: The Backbone of Democracy," Black women insisted on an inclusive democracy when many others, including Black men and white women, did not. Abolitionists, from Sojourner Truth and Maria Stewart, to post–World War II freedom fighters, such as Ella Baker and Dorothy Height, "were the torch bearers, spreading the word that neither racism nor sexism had a place in our democracy." One of the Black women who was handed this torch was Kamala Harris, who in her first speech as vice president of the United States paid tribute to the women of color who had "fought and sacrificed so much for equality and liberty and justice for all."[2]

In her richly detailed study of the National Council of Negro Women (NCNW), "Constructing a Way Forward," Cassandra Newby-Alexander echoes and expands on Sinegal-DeCuir's argument. The NCNW, she explains, differed from most mainstream male-led civil rights organizations in two fundamental ways. First, it was built from the grassroots up. Second, it demanded an end to both racial and gender inequalities. As such, the NCNW created a vision for how an inclusive democracy should be achieved and what this democracy would look like. Put somewhat differently, it showed that the end goal was to eradicate all racially and gender-based barriers to equality and that the means to achieving this goal was to build a movement from the bottom up, not the top down.

In "I Don't Believe This Has Anything to Do with the Alleviation of Poverty"—a title taken from an assertion that newly elected Republican congressman George H. W. Bush made in 1967—Wesley Phelps explores the relationship between voting rights, grassroots antipoverty activism, and democracy. Focusing on local antipoverty activists in Houston, who sought to take advantage of the federal government's maximum feasible participation rules, Phelps shows that Houston's African Americans understood all too well that access to the ballot and economic justice were two sides of the same coin. Both were essential to the American democratic experiment, and the failure to achieve one would undermine the ability to achieve the other, Bush's statement, that voter registration and fighting poverty had nothing to do with one another, notwithstanding.

Similarly, in "Overcoming the American Lie," Reginald Ellis explores the crucial role that HBCUs played in fighting for democracy. Building on the work of Jelani Favors, among others, and his own research on the founders of several HBCUs, Ellis shows that Black colleges and universities served as bastions of "black political and social development." That W.E.B. Du Bois, John Hope Franklin, Martin Luther King Jr., and Thurgood Marshall were all HBCU graduates was no accident. On the contrary, they sprouted up from the fertile soils that Black institutions of higher learning provided them because, in most cases, for them, as well as for Black non-activists, HBCUs were the only option available.

In "The Seamstress and the Counselor," Jeffrey Littlejohn and Charles Ford remind us that the struggle for voting rights did not end with the enactment of the Voting Rights Act of 1965. They do so via a rich description of the legal battle to strike down Virginia's poll tax, which culminated in a landmark victory in the U.S. Supreme Court. As in the essays by Newby-Alexander and Phelps, Littlejohn and Ford demonstrate that this victory emerged from the grass roots, as Evelyn Butts, a seamstress, and Joseph Jordan Jr., her legal counsel, teamed up to combat Virginia's (and by extension other southern states') efforts to maintain white political power, despite the Voting Rights Act, a lesson as relevant today as it was nearly fifty years ago.

Peter Levy's "Who Killed Ralph Featherstone?" explores the unsolved death of a lesser-known Black activist who was killed when a bomb exploded in the car he was driving on March 9, 1970. State and federal authorities claimed he killed himself when a bomb he was carrying, allegedly to disrupt the forthcoming trial of the prominent Black militant H. Rap Brown, inadvertently exploded. Virtually everyone who knew Featherstone well countered that he had been assassinated by those who thought Brown was in the car. In reviewing Featherstone's case, Levy explores the long history of repression of Black dissenters, the amnesia that many whites have about this history, and the efforts of Black activists, including Featherstone, to construct an alternative and more truthful understanding of America's past and its failings.

In the final essay of this collection, "A Movement of Movements," Charles L. Chavis Jr. examines the rise of the Anti-Lynching Federation of Maryland (MALF). Galvanized by the Depression-era lynchings of Matthew Williams (1931) and George Armwood (1933) on Maryland's Eastern Shore, MALF became one of the pioneering forces in Maryland's early civil rights movement. Bringing together notable politicians, educators, attorneys, activists, and religious leaders, MALF combatted lynching and the racist hypocrisy and practices of the so-called Free State.

All of these essays reveal a central paradox in American history, namely, that those who have been denied their rights have fought perpetually for those rights, not just for themselves but for all Americans. This point became abundantly clear on January 20, 2009, the date of the inauguration of Barack Obama, the first Black person to be elected president of the United States. That day, a record number of Americans poured into the nation's capital to mark the momentous occasion. Besides the bitter cold and the hope on everyone's faces, what stood out at the time were the tens of thousands of Black women, many quite elderly, all elegantly dressed, who streamed in by train, bus, car, and subway, not simply to celebrate Obama's election but to display for the world to see their commitment to democracy, in spite of all of the hardships and slights they had received since the nation's birth.

Twelve years after Obama's election, many of these same women rescued Joe Biden's campaign for the Democratic nomination, and then turned out in record numbers to defeat Donald Trump in November. At Biden's inauguration, a young Black woman, Amanda Gorman, stole the show with her reading of her poem "The Hill We Climb." Resisting the temptation to make the attempted takeover of the U.S. Capitol the focus of her oration, she captured the paradoxical faith that Black women have displayed in fighting to get America to live up to its ideals. "Somehow we weathered and witnessed a nation that isn't broken, but simply unfinished," she remarked in an allusion to the Trump-inspired insurrection. "We, the successor of a country and a time where a skinny Black girl descended from slaves and raised by a single mother can dream of becoming president, only to find herself reciting for one," she continued, further illuminating this paradox. Not simply to preserve the union, she added, but "to compose a country committed to all cultures, colors, characters and conditions." Unfortunately, in a reminder that the struggle to keep America's democracy alive did not end with Biden's swearing in, all five of President Trump's children issued a joint press release trashing Gorman's poem. "Amanda Gorman is more dangerous than the mythological Sirens," they proclaimed. "She is an unwitting foil for a fake president." Her "so-called poem" didn't even rhyme. A little over two years later, Gorman's poem was banned by a Florida school, a by-product of Florida governor and GOP presidential candidate Ron DeSantis's crusade against what he termed "woke" history.[3]

Thus, *Black Citizens and American Democracy: Fighting for the Soul of a Nation* attempts to move the national conversation beyond the present regressive political climate by highlighting key moments and movements in American history where Black folk supported the ideals of democracy and challenged those who would deny them to all Americans. This anthology speaks to the overall hopes and dreams of generations of Black folk, both past and present, in the great American experiment. Ultimately, this study suggests that in spite of the systemic barriers erected to ensure that only a subset of American society reaped the benefits of being American, underrepresented minorities in general and Black folk specifically pushed the nation and its leaders to ensure that all of her inhabitants secured the rights outlined in the U.S. Constitution, including all twenty-seven of its amendments.

Notes

1 James Baldwin, *The Fire Next Time* (New York: Vintage, 1963), 101.
2 Kamala Harris, "Vice President-Elect Acceptance Speech," *New York Times,* November 8, 2020, https://www.nytimes.com/article/watch-kamala-harris-speech-video-transcript.html.
3 Dan Boxer, "Trump Children Savagely Attack Amanda Gorman," Medium, January 22, 2021, https://medium.com/the-haven/trump-children-savagely-attack-amanda-gorman-d5f977c525dd; "Amanda Gorman's Inauguration Poem Banned by Florida School," PBS News Hour, May 24, 2023, https://www.pbs.org/newshour/education/amanda-gormans-inauguration-poem-banned-by-florida-school.

1

Toward a Real United States Patriotism
Black Americans' Centrality to the Pursuit of a Multiracial Democracy

KRISTOPHER BRYAN BURRELL

> I had a black friend. I liked her and I think she liked me, too. But now she is hostile and unpleasant. I am sure I didn't do anything to her, except be white. Is that what teachers and our political leaders really want for our society? Divide us because of our skin color? #CRT
>
> Patricia Morgan, Rhode Island state representative, Twitter, December 28, 2021

This chapter intends to reorient our popular conception of patriotism toward an understanding that protesting for greater societal equality is the ultimate expression of patriotism.[1] In demonstrating that the tradition of dissent in service of bringing about a genuine and enduring multiracial democracy is indeed patriotic, this chapter builds on a rich literature to argue that Black American protest movements should be central to discussions of American patriotism and democracy. To save the American democratic experiment and create a genuine multiracial democracy, a more accurate narrative of U.S. history needs to become predominant in schools and the basis for legislation and policy. A more accurate narrative of U.S. history considers patriotism in terms of protest to bring about the "American" ideals of equality and meritocracy, a genuine multiracial democracy, and a more economically equitable society. Among the people who have done the most throughout American history to make these ideals real have been Black protest leaders. Black protest leaders also continue to be the vanguard of creating American democracy in the present day.[2]

We are currently in an existential struggle for the survival of American democracy. In the streets, in statehouses, and on cable news, battles are occurring over who will control the story the United States tells about itself through the teaching, memorialization, and omissions of American history. Right-wing figures and their supporters are fighting to preserve "the propaganda of history": the creation and use of history for "pleasure and amusement, for inflating our national ego, and giving us a false but pleasurable sense of accomplishment,"[3] as W.E.B. Du Bois termed the largely fictional narrative of U.S. history that lauds white American achievements above those of others and congratulates white Americans for allowing non-white Americans (eventually) to share in the nation's bounty, over a century ago. Today's right-wing politicians and activists, in their efforts to secure support from white Republican primary voters, are trying to accomplish at least three major goals in advocating the prohibition of teaching U.S. history through interpretive lenses that help explain current racial inequalities. One goal is to further accelerate the rolling back of legislative protections of historically marginalized groups secured during the 1960s. A second goal is to make public discussions about contemporary structural racial discrimination no longer salient. A third goal is to justify the unprecedented economic inequality in U.S. society.

The elimination from school curricula of historical episodes in which laws, policies, and social customs were intentionally aligned against Black Americans; the prohibitions on teachers to explain historical processes as choices people made to produce racially unequal outcomes; and the framing of protest as antithetical to American ideals are dangerous to a genuine, multiracial democracy. These are all methods being employed on the political Right to create generations of Americans who will be poorly equipped to accurately explain our current social ills.[4] Rather, they will default to blaming the individual failings of those being victimized by economic and political policies that prioritize the white supremacist, capitalist status quo over the radical notion of a genuine multiracial democracy. The generations of Americans to be reared under this inaccurate, mythical, neo-Confederate, historical education would also be deprived of the very intellectual and practical tools necessary for creating and protecting genuine democracy in America: knowledge of those who have dissented from the white supremacist status quo in the pursuit of a more inclusive and equitable society.[5] Consequently, these generations of Americans would come to regard the economic, gender, and racial disparities within American society as "inevitable," "natural," and "destined," and themselves as powerless to help bring about societal change that could improve their conditions or those of others around them.

The Bastardization of Critical Race Theory

Since the start of 2021, conservative politicians and activists have launched another war on teaching about the inability of our nation to live up to the ideals espoused in its foundational documents, that "all men are created equal and are endowed by their creator with certain inalienable rights" and that all Americans have the right to "life, liberty, and the pursuit of happiness." By extension, this has also been a war on teaching about the struggles of historically marginalized groups to combat discrimination and help create a more just American democracy. Conservative politicians, activists, and pundits have, once again, worked to stir up a sense of aggrievement in white parents that learning about the ways in which nonwhite Americans have been systematically discriminated against throughout the United States' past has victimized their children. This most recent iteration of the battle over the narrative of American history, the definition of who can be a "real American," the definition of patriotism, and the creation of a multiracial democracy has manifested itself in various ways, but the roots of this struggle go back much further in American history.

During 2021 and 2022, there were numerous videos of dramatic and tense school board meetings across the country in which white parents decried lessons about racial injustice that supposedly made their children feel bad about themselves and "their country," evincing a sense of exclusive proprietorship over the nation. Far right "parental rights" groups such as Moms for Liberty have tried to overtake school boards in various places in efforts to ban books that discuss systemic racism (among other topics) from school curricula, and they attack both teachers' unions and the idea that public schools are a positive good for the nation.[6] In the tradition of the United Daughters of the Confederacy from more than a century earlier,[7] Moms for Liberty has an agenda to radically transform school curricula across the country toward a Christian, nationalist, Eurocentric, heteronormative standard that would ultimately dismantle public education and dramatically narrow the definitions of who is an American, what is patriotic behavior, and how our political system would function.

For his part, former president Donald Trump has characterized "critical race theory" as "twisted" and "completely antithetical to everything that normal Americans of any color would wish to teach their children." In his words, "the left's vile new theory" teaches white children "that *they* are evil."[8] Trump issued an executive order on September 22, 2020, banning diversity and inclusion trainings that promoted "divisive concepts" involving any form of "race or sex stereotyping" or "race or sex scapegoating" in any federal agency or among federal contractors.[9] Florida governor Ron DeSantis, following Trump's lead, banned the teaching of "critical race theory" in the state's public schools, although there was no evidence of it being done in the state. Then, on December 15, 2021, DeSantis introduced proposed legislation, the Stop the Wrongs to Our Kids and Employees Act or the Stop WOKE Act, which would allow parents to sue school districts if they believe their children are being taught "critical race theory," while invoking Rev. Dr. Martin Luther King Jr.'s "I Have a Dream" speech, no less.[10] Conservative opinion host Tucker Carlson of the Fox News Channel spent much of 2021 arguing on his highly rated nightly program that white children were being taught to hate America and hate themselves, only to admit in early November, just after the Virginia governor's election that brought Republican Glenn Youngkin (thought to be a potential bellwether for the fortunes of the Democratic Party in the 2022 midterm elections) to office—that he "never figured out what critical race theory is, to be totally honest, after a year of talking about it." After perhaps the only honest thing he had said about "critical race theory" since popularizing this newest right-wing bogeyman in his ongoing efforts to stabilize a white supremacist cultural, political, and economic status quo, Carlson demonstrated his malevolent ignorance in his very next utterance to Fox News anchor Brit Hume: "They're teaching that some races are morally superior to others. That some are inherently sinful, and some inherently saintly, and that's immoral to teach that because it's wrong."[11]

As Carlson's willingness to deliberately malign a theory he admittedly knew nothing about makes clear, the ire toward "critical race theory" has never actually been about critical race theory; most conservatives cannot accurately define it, nor have they really tried. Rather, the furor generated over "critical race theory" has really been about "rally[ing] the Republican base—to push back against the recent reexaminations of the role that slavery and segregation have played in American history and the attempts to redress those historical offenses."[12] This was part of Glenn Youngkin's campaign strategy as he ran for governor of Virginia in 2021. He tapped into frustrations among white Virginian parents toward the public schools and joined the chorus of Republican candidates asserting, without evidence, that "critical race theory" was being taught in Virginia public schools. Once elected, his very first act as governor was to sign an executive order banning the teaching of "critical race theory" in the state's primary and secondary schools.¹³ Another purpose for caricaturing "critical race theory" has been to suppress the "hard history,"¹⁴ to use Ohio State University history professor Hasan Kwame Jeffries's term, that educates about the structural and enduring ways Black people, people of color, and poor people have been persistently disadvantaged throughout U.S. history in their pursuit of the full exercise of American citizenship rights and a genuine multiracial democracy. A third goal of the coordinated right-wing effort has also been stabilizing the current economic and political order by crafting a narrative of American development that eliminates discussion of structural or systemic racial discrimination.¹⁵ In this formulation, racism, to the extent that it existed at all, was exemplified by individual acts of discrimination and largely "solved" by the civil rights movement of the 1960s, only to be totally "finished off" by the election of the nation's first Black president Barack Obama in 2008 *and* 2012. How could a country suffering with structural racism have possibly elected a Black man to be president, not once, but twice?¹⁶

The most recent example of this conservative formulation of American history that suppresses "hard history" is the 2023 Florida Social Studies Standards for African American History. In sixth grade, "instruction includes how slaves developed skills which, in some instances, could be applied for their personal benefit."¹⁷ This "Benchmark Clarification" not only flattens the economic disparities inherent in the commodification of slavery, incorrectly placing enslaved person and slaveholder on equal economic terms, but just as insidiously, this "clarification" implies that slavery was a "civilizing institution" that gave Black people skills they never would have gained otherwise, as if enslaved Blacks had no prior knowledge or skills before being brought to North America, or that it would not have been inherently better for Black people to acquire vocational skills as free people. This framing of slavery as almost a benign institution in some ways harkens back to the neo-Confederate historical narratives created, promoted, and disseminated by the United Daughters of the Confederacy (UDC) and prominent professional historians, such as William Dunning and Ulrich B. Phillips, during the early twentieth century. The Daughters understood that if they could control the narrative of southern history, they could maintain the racial status quo most effectively. So they wrote and disseminated their own local and regional histories of the Civil War and Reconstruction eras. Leaders of the UDC also mandated edits to school textbooks across the country that characterized Confederate leaders and soldiers as patriots and fighters for a just cause, and Reconstruction as an unfortunate period of corrupt Black and white Republican rule that necessitated "redemption" for white southerners.[18]

While Florida's high school standards are more detailed, relatively few mention the structural and legal barriers to African American freedom, equality, and more that illustrate how the country incrementally, but almost inexorably, moved toward emancipation and later racial equality during the civil rights movement of the 1950s and 1960s. The phrase "Jim Crow Laws" is used once as an example of how prejudice and racism curtailed individual freedoms, and the word "segregation" is used twice, once as a factor that caused the "Great Migration" of Blacks from the South and another time in reference to those who fought to break down segregation in the military during World War II.[19] The backgrounding of the structural racism omnipresent throughout U.S. history, combined with the foregrounding of interracial partnership to combat prejudice and the focus on individual African American achievements, has the potential to present a narrative of American history that atomizes everyone, makes the Black people that ascended the social, political, or economic ladder the norm, and renders those who are unable to achieve those same heights individual failures and culturally defective, rather than part of a group ensnared in a capitalist and white supremacist political structure designed to make it impossible to fully participate in the country's democratic system. The Florida standards appear to avoid structural discussion of formal politics between 1968 and 2008, so as to be able to continue making the conservative argument that the United States has entered a "post-racial" era, in which it is legitimate to take "antiwhite racism" seriously.

Proponents of a "post-racial United States" narrative conflate structural racism with individual racist acts, and acting in racist ways with benefiting from a racist political and economic system. Denying structural racism allows conservatives to blame Black Americans, people of color, and the poor of all races for the social ills their communities disproportionately experience, characterizing "those people" as personally defective or suffering from a "culture of poverty" that renders them unable to behave in ways "normal" (read: white, middle-class) Americans do.[20] So, as historian Jeanne Theoharis and others argue, by disingenuously co-opting the words of civil rights movement leaders to support exclusionary ends, and in eliminating instruction about instances that illustrate the structural racial, economic, gender, and sexual discrimination codified into our political system, conservative politicians, activists, and commentators deliberately "misuse civil rights history" in order to sap it of its radical and transformative power.[21] Conservative politicians and activists today, harkening back to those who opposed the Black freedom struggle of the 1950s and 1960s, employ an "ethos of colorblindness" to undermine efforts at creating a genuine multiracial democracy. This ethos attempts to provide conservatives with a way to "feign ignorance about the unequal effects of their policies on black citizens," as well as to use the words of civil rights figures toward anti-democratic—and thereby, anti-patriotic—ends.[22]

Some conservative politicians, activists, and pundits claim that merely mentioning racial discrimination in discussions of the country is, in fact, "racist," not to mention "unpatriotic," and teaching young people that white Americans treated nonwhite Americans in discriminatory ways through the creation of laws and policies is "divisive" and teaching children to "hate their country." The tweet from Rhode Island state representative Patricia Morgan referenced in the chapter's epigraph manages in fewer than 280 characters to encapsulate the reductive conservative view of (1) how the concept of "race" functions in the United States; (2) how conservatives continue to identify themselves as the aggrieved party in discussions of racial discrimination; and (3) how Black Americans are really the ones at fault for the "division" present in the country. The tweet is problematic for many reasons, but it is worth focusing on the last two sentences in which Representative Morgan maligns teachers and characterizes discussions of race as "divisive." The struggle our society is engaged in over how U.S. history will be taught and what constitutes patriotism underscores the fact that we all understand that what children are taught matters. Representative Morgan, Ron DeSantis, Moms for Liberty, and other conservatives seek to control educational curricula to censor teaching methods that decenter white, patriarchal, and triumphalist narratives of U.S. history. And as I previously stated, a corollary goal is to weaken teacher controls over their classrooms, teachers' unions, and ultimately public education writ large.

Representative Morgan's tweet failed to mention that back in March 2021 she had been a co-sponsor of a state bill to prohibit "teaching divisive concepts and . . . making any individual feel discomfort, guilt, anguish or any distress on account of their race or sex."[23] This deliberately vaguely worded bill was in line with right-wing efforts occurring across the country to constrict discussions of historical structural racism that truthfully depicted white supremacist oppression of nonwhite Americans—not because it is inaccurate, but because knowing this information necessitates changes in law, policy, and custom at every level of society. Essentially, white Americans' feelings were more important than historical facts. Even though this bill failed to pass the Rhode Island legislature on June 30, 2021, similar bills are moving toward passage (or have passed) in other states, and our national conversations about education, race, and democracy roil on.[24]

To begin countering right-wing disinformation, it is necessary to articulate an accurate definition of critical race theory (CRT), then provide historical examples of the ways Black Americans have consistently pushed the nation toward becoming better versions of itself, which will offer lessons for how we can continue building a true multiracial democracy today. CRT, developed by legal scholars Derrick Bell, Kimberlé Crenshaw, and others in the 1970s and 1980s, is a legal theory that provides a lens through which to see structural discrimination in American law. Taught in law schools and sometimes in colleges, CRT "challenges the ways race and power are constructed and represented in American legal culture and, more generally, in American society as a whole." Practitioners are united by at least two fundamental principles: to understand how white supremacy and its subordination of people of color have been created and maintained in the laws of the United States, and to change the "vexed bond between law and racial power."[25] Critical race theorists wanted to understand how and why racial inequalities persisted decades after the legal and legislative accomplishments of the 1950s and 1960s. Rejecting the "culture of poverty" thesis, over the past four decades critical race theorists have worked to develop legal theories for identifying and combating structural racism in the law, and lenses through which to analyze the construction and impacts of race in the United States.

Right-wing politicians and activists, such as Manhattan Institute for Policy Research senior fellow Christopher Rufo, have deliberately bastardized CRT and turned it into a catch-all phrase to get conservatives' support for completely rewriting K–12 U.S. history curricula.[26] As of April 11, 2023, twenty-eight states had introduced bills or taken other steps to restrict teaching "critical race theory" or otherwise limit how teachers could discuss racism and sexism in their classrooms.[27] These efforts allow white parents and the broader conservative public to ignore the structural racism that has existed (and continues to exist) throughout American history (and in the present).

This right-wing movement to protect white supremacist conceptions of U.S. patriotism and democracy, though not new, is incredibly dangerous for several reasons. Besides the perversion of U.S. history promoted in projects such as former president Trump's 1776 Commission, anti–"critical race theory" legislation in various states, the modification of some U.S. history textbooks, and the censorship of others will produce generations of Americans who have false conclusions as to why current inequities in our society exist, if not stopped. This will make it easier to continue blaming the victims of historical inequality, strengthening beliefs that there are inherent and irremediable deficiencies in certain groups of people that make them less intelligent, lazier, and more prone to crime, for example, than white Americans. These future generations will be unaware that such erroneous and stereotypical tropes also have histories stretching back centuries. Conservative politicians, activists, and commentators are also promoting a definition of U.S. patriotism that is racialized and uncritical; assumes a white, Christian nation; and pays blind obeisance to the American flag, rather than the egalitarian ideals the nation is supposed to represent. Consequently, as this anti-democratic movement becomes increasingly mainstreamed, anyone who protests injustice is derisively labeled a "radical" and "divisive," and told they are not "real" Americans.[28]

The "Perfecters" of American Democracy

Despite the attacks from the right wing, the very groups of Americans historically most derided have often been the people who have committed and sacrificed the most to make real the rhetorical democratic ideals of the United States. They have worked to breathe life into what otherwise would wither as a dead letter. As journalist and scholar Nikole Hannah-Jones has written, "Black Americans have ... been, and continue to be, foundational to the idea of American freedom. More than any other group in this country's history, we have served, generation after generation, in an overlooked but vital role: it is we who have been the perfecters of this democracy."[29] That role of "perfecter" has meant dreamer, designer, advocate, and in some instances defender. Therefore, in the framing and teaching of U.S. history there needs to be a reorientation of the public view of what makes someone a patriot and the United States a democracy.

Traditional tropes of "patriotism" or the characterization of certain people as "real Americans" have long been used to assert native-born white American ownership over (1) the physical territory of the United States, (2) the idea of American equality, and (3) the visual representation of who counts as an "American" and thereby deserves to participate in the democracy. Whether it be the "Redeemers" of the Reconstruction era who needed to "save" the nation's political system from African Americans' corrupt natures, which would ruin American civilization and shatter the "natural" order of white domination; or the opponents of civil rights and Black Power who, viewing the massive mobilization of Americans, argued that the country needed "law and order"; or contemporary Republicans and the efforts to promote "patriotic education,"[30] in the words of Donald Trump, the definitions of "patriotism" and "American" have really been calls for white nationalism, maintaining white supremacy, and excluding Americans of color from helping create a multiracial democracy.

As a result, the greatest American patriots have often been the most substantive critics of the lack of democracy in America, doing all they could to prick the conscience of the country; to prod, cajole, confront, and shame ordinary citizens and those in power to create the "shining city on a hill" America claimed to be. People like formerly enslaved Reconstruction-era political leader James Greene; novelist, cultural critic, and public intellectual James Baldwin; civil rights activist-intellectual and political leader Fannie Lou Hamer; and civil rights activist-intellectual and educator Septima Clark were not often considered patriots or celebrated by the larger society in their lifetimes. But, if we are to have a better understanding of what has made (or makes) America important, redefine what love of country looks like, and create a genuine multiracial democracy, an understanding of the historical and contemporary Black freedom struggle is more necessary than ever. Looking at two watershed historical periods, the Reconstruction era and the Black freedom struggle of the mid-twentieth century, allows for the demonstration of how Black Americans have worked to create a genuine multiracial democracy throughout the country's history, provide opportunities for teachers and policymakers to connect the societal ills of the present day to historical antecedents, and give us concrete ideas about how to begin ameliorating the inequalities that still plague this American democracy.

Attempting to Create a Multiracial Democracy during Reconstruction

The ratification of the Thirteenth, Fourteenth, and Fifteenth Amendments to the Constitution between 1865 and 1870 allowed Black Americans, particularly men, to be defined as "American." Yet Black people have been only partial Americans, for all practical purposes. The activities of city, state, and federal governments and agencies demonstrated in stark relief just how partial Black citizenship was—and continues to be. During Reconstruction, "James Greene, a former slave who became a legislator in Alabama said, 'When I was a slave, I didn't know anything except to obey my master. But the tocsin of freedom sounded and I walked out like a man and shouldered my responsibilities." African Americans performed their patriotic duty to their country, which professed a foundational belief in human equality by helping govern it in the best interests of all who lived there. People such as James Greene in Alabama and nearly two thousand other African American men who held political office throughout the country during Reconstruction were patriots.[31] They labored to bring about a true democracy for the benefit of all Americans in the wake of the Civil War.

Yet Black politicians were vilified and ridiculed. Historian Eric Foner has written that the Democratic press during Reconstruction referred to southern legislatures as "menageries" and "monkey houses." Black lawmakers were monolithically portrayed as "ignorant, illiterate, propertyless, and . . . lack[ing] education," though untrue. In fact, after Reconstruction, Democrats in Georgia erased Black lawmakers from the biographical sketches that recorded service in the state legislature.[32] Black lawmakers were partial Americans at best, and white lawmakers asserted it was their prerogative to erase Black Americans' citizenship and service to the country entirely.

It is vital for all Americans to know that these Black men served in southern state legislatures alongside white Republicans during Reconstruction and that white Democratic lawmakers subsequently attempted to purge any memory of their service—not because it is some "cool" or "interesting" historical fact, but rather because it demonstrates that Black Americans contributed to the construction of democratic governance across the South during the 1870s, the decade when the first public school systems were being developed for all children, when there were attempts to create fairer tax codes to assess the values of former plantations, and when the resources of the federal and state governments were being marshaled to create social safety nets for those who had been disadvantaged under antebellum political and economic laws.[33]

Black Americans worked to shape the contours of American democracy in numerous ways during the Reconstruction era, and not only in terms of voting and holding political office. "Through speeches, pamphlets, conferences, direct lobbying, and newspaper editorials, Black Americans pushed an all-white Congress to enshrine equality into the Constitution, powerfully shaping what the country would be like in its second founding."[34] Black advocates, male and female, had been arguing since the 1830s that they were citizens of the United States from birth and therefore deserved all the rights of citizenship therein. Their efforts were largely responsible for eventually getting provisions for birthright citizenship included within the Fourteenth Amendment. After the ratification of the Fourteenth and Fifteenth Amendments, African Americans continued to push for the inclusion of all peoples living in the United States within the category of "citizen," including women and people of all racial backgrounds.[35] "Black people organized to fulfill freedom's promise." They came together to build institutions that they could control, such as churches, schools, businesses, and mutual aid societies. Black Americans rebuilt families torn apart during slavery, created new ones, and nurtured communities, participating in social gatherings and creating cultural works to celebrate their new lives in freedom.[36]

And Black people suffered for their efforts. Historian Vanessa Williamson shows that during Reconstruction, as Black and white Republicans came together in state legislatures across the South to raise the necessary revenue to create public infrastructure that could serve the entire population, wealthy white former Confederates mobilized under the banner of being "taxpayers" to foster resistance to higher taxation, the construction of public infrastructure, Black office holding, and democratic rule. As Williamson writes, "South Carolina's white elite developed a two-part strategy of opposition. First, they focused their critique of Reconstruction on rising government debt and excessive spending, painting government by black people and poor whites as intrinsically corrupt. Adopting a new identity as taxpayers helped bridge the divide with small white farmers, for whom new land taxes were heavy, while avoiding explicit opposition to black male suffrage, which might smack of treason to Northerners." The southern former Confederates worked to subvert democratic rule, not only in South Carolina but also in other southern states. Northern elites supported this ideology during the 1870s. They also questioned the wisdom of poor people, and particularly immigrants, engaging in governance.[37]

In the South, however, it would be Black local officials who bore the brunt of paramilitary resistance to taxpaying on the part of white southerners. In Vicksburg, Mississippi, in 1874 white members of the local "taxpayers' union" marched to the courthouse on Tax Day and demanded all Black officeholders resign, including the sheriff responsible for collecting taxes. After a weeklong standoff, the white members of the taxpayers' union opened fire on the Black militia, killing between seventy-five and three hundred people. According to economist Trevor Logan, "The chances of a local black politician being attacked increased three percentage points 'for each additional dollar of per capita tax revenue collected in 1870.' Where taxes increased more, the violence against black politicians was higher."[38] So, as Black Americans engaged in the necessary work of building democratic political and economic institutions, it was literally more dangerous for them than their white counterparts, in many cases, because of their race. Yet Black public servants did so anyway because it was necessary, and they wanted all to be freer.

Knowing about the efforts of white lawmakers to rewrite state history through omission of the violence perpetrated against Black politicians also illustrates the ways in which the deliberate creation of a false historical narrative imperils democracy. Not only were Black lawmakers completely purged from southern state legislatures by the turn of the twentieth century, but this paved the way for Black people to be largely denied the vote until the late 1960s. Generations of white and Black schoolchildren also learned a narrative of Reconstruction, popularized by William A. Dunning and his students in the early twentieth century, that characterized the period as one of corrupt politicians bankrupting southern states. The corruption necessitated the "redemption" of the region, and paramilitary domestic terrorists were made into the heroes of a national narrative about Reconstruction for decades to follow.[39] This narrative not only dominated white academic circles but was popularized by D. W. Griffith with his blockbuster film *Birth of a Nation* in 1915. Technologically advanced for the time, the film made the Ku Klux Klan the heroes of the South's "redemption," as they prevented crooked and lascivious African Americans from "ravaging" southern governments and white women.[40]

W.E.B. Du Bois attempted to refute these myths about Reconstruction during the 1930s, writing: "White historians have ascribed the faults and failures of Reconstruction to Negro ignorance and corruption. But the Negro insists that it was Negro loyalty and the Negro vote alone that restored the South to the Union; established the new democracy, both for white and black, and instituted the public schools." However, the white editor he submitted these words to refused to publish them.[41] It was extremely difficult to get more accurate analyses of the Reconstruction era into print. Although what Du Bois knew nearly a century ago has been proven true, generations of students could not read Du Bois's words as he originally wrote them. The concealment of analyses such as Du Bois's made it more difficult to counteract the white supremacist narratives that abounded from kindergarten through doctoral study. Could we be in a comparable danger today of a similar narrative being created in relation to the insurrection attempt at the U.S. Capitol on January 6, 2021? If reactionary conservative elements within society are allowed to suppress not only physical evidence from that day and the months leading to it but also knowledge of the histories of race, politics, and exclusion throughout U.S. history, then we are in danger of this happening.

The history of the Reconstruction era provides an example of how studying African American social movements can impart significant lessons about the origins of contemporary problems facing our democracy. These include what it means to govern in the interests of the collective and how those efforts were thwarted in an earlier period. The Reconstruction era also illustrates the role white supremacist activity in service of continued racial subordination and capitalist accumulation played in undermining Black Americans' efforts to create a nation in which all, regardless of race, could participate and benefit equally from government.[42] Finally, looking back to Reconstruction provides an opportunity to reexamine and redefine our popular notions of what and who is patriotic. It is possible to demonstrate that policies such as progressive taxation, funding for public infrastructure, and more inclusive voting laws move us toward a genuine multiracial democracy.

Attempting to Create a Multiracial Democracy in the Twentieth-Century Black Freedom Struggle

The same can be said of the Black freedom struggle of the mid-twentieth century. Just as during the Reconstruction era, Black activists struggled against the perpetual partiality of their American citizenship, pushing Black people to call systemic racial discrimination what it was: Jim Crow. This perpetual partiality compelled Black activists to patriotically take the nation to task for not living up to its ideals to treat all citizens equally as human beings with inalienable rights—to "criticize her perpetually," in the words of James Baldwin.[43]

In the pursuit of a genuine multiracial democracy, Black activists understood that racial equality was essential. They also demonstrated a willingness to call out political leaders, as well as the broader white public, for not living up to the nation's ideals; for valuing "order" over justice;[44] for writing a check to Black Americans with "insufficient funds";[45] for recognizing that if the egalitarian ideals expressed in the Declaration of Independence were worth pursuing, it would require dismantling white supremacist political, economic, and social structures that maintained the racial hierarchy and inhibited democracy. Whether it was James Baldwin demanding the "impossible" of white America,[46] Martin Luther King calling out the penchant of "white moderates" to ask Black Americans to quiet their demands for democratic participation and full citizenship so as not to be "disruptive,"[47] Fannie Lou Hamer articulating the difficulties of Black southerners to just register to vote, much less actually attempt to do it,[48] or Septima Clark running "citizenship schools" for Black people so they would have the intellectual and practical tools to exercise their citizenship rights, Black civil rights activists were acting in ways to create democracy in America. Their faith and belief in the liberatory potential of democratic action and participation make their examples all the more important for us in this moment when our democracy, to the extent it exists, is not only in jeopardy but is being ill defined and degraded.

Born into a sharecropping family in rural Mississippi in 1917, Fannie Lou Hamer had been a victim of economic and medical exploitation and sexual assault at the hands of Mississippi police after trying to register to vote and protest for voting rights in 1962 and 1963. Hamer did not even know it was possible for African Americans to vote before 1962. In that year she attended a mass meeting at a local church where representatives from the Student Nonviolent Coordinating Committee (SNCC) addressed her community about the importance of exercising their right to vote and helping others register. People in her Mississippi county were deliberately kept ignorant about the possibility of participating in politics, and physically and economically intimidated from ever trying to do so.[49] As a result, the words of these young SNCC activists were revelatory.

After the mass meeting, Hamer first tried to register to vote on August 31, 1962. The members of her eighteen-person delegation were only allowed to take the test to vote two at a time. None of them passed the literacy test, in which they were required to copy and interpret a section of the Mississippi state constitution. In the South, literacy tests were never about "literacy" but were always intended to disfranchise the largest swath of Black people possible. On their way back home, state police stopped their bus because it was "too yellow" and the driver was fined $100, although the fine was eventually reduced to $30. The money had to be raised on the spot to be released.[50] Although no one went to jail, this was just the beginning of the activism and harassment Fannie Lou Hamer experienced in becoming one of the most important democracy advocates of the Black freedom struggle.

As soon as Hamer reached her hometown of Ruleville, she was "greeted" by the white landowner for whom she and her husband had labored for more than twenty years between them. The white landowner, angry that Hamer dared step outside the rigid racial hierarchy of 1960s Mississippi and assert that she had claim to this American democracy, issued her an ultimatum. Either she withdraw her registration attempt or leave his land. Hamer said directly, "I didn't go down there to register for [you], I went down there to register for myself."[51] With that, she was forced to leave her husband and child that very night. Hamer was banished and her life threatened.[52] By trying to register to vote, she began a personal evolution that affected the struggle for an American democracy in substantial ways.

Hamer sacrificed a great deal personally in pursuit of the right to vote, for not only herself but also the members of her immediate community and all Black Americans. Hamer attempted to register a second time in December 1962 and this time was successful, as she had been better prepared than four months earlier. However, she still was unable to cast an actual ballot in an election for another two years because she had not paid two years' worth of poll taxes, another method of preventing poor and Black Americans from participating in the democracy. When Hamer finally voted, it would be for herself as she ran for Congress to represent her district in Mississippi.[53] This was no sudden decision. She began working with SNCC to register local community members soon after her first registration attempt. Hamer and the other volunteers faced harassment from police, local white politicians, and ordinary white residents. Death threats by phone and gunshots ringing into Black homes were commonplace. Hamer and other civil rights workers labored without any real protection from local or federal law enforcement. Nevertheless, Hamer and other SNCC workers established "freedom schools" that taught attendees, young and old, how to read, about the laws guaranteed under the state and federal constitutions, and more direct "citizenship education."[54] These were not just abstractions for Hamer and the SNCC volunteers. Rather, these were concrete lessons that showed students how and why participating in democratic processes at the local, state, and national levels was necessary for their survival and liberation.

Hamer is perhaps best known for helping found the Mississippi Freedom Democratic Party (FDP) to challenge the legitimacy of the all-white Mississippi Democratic Party delegation at the 1964 Democratic National Convention in Atlantic City, New Jersey. The all-white party prohibited Black Mississippians from being members and was unrepresentative of state demographics. African Americans were 42 percent of Mississippi's total population and were majorities in many of the state's rural counties in 1960 but only accounted for 6.7 percent of registered voters in 1964.[55] The FDP sought to unseat the Mississippi Democratic Party at the convention. Hamer's testimony at the convention about the lack of democracy for Black Mississippians was piercing in its indictment of segregation and voter suppression. She recounted the police harassment she and fellow Black Mississippians endured in their attempts to register to vote, her expulsion from her home of nearly twenty years, the attempts to shoot her and other activists in their homes, and the beatings she received from cops and Black inmates in a Mississippi jail that left her unconscious for a time and with permanent kidney damage. She ended with an appeal: "All of this on account of we want to register, to become first-class citizens. And if the Freedom Democratic Party is not seated now, I question America. Is this America, the land of the free and the home of the brave, where we have to sleep with our telephones off the hooks because our lives are threatened daily, because we want to live as decent human beings, in America?"[56] Hamer questioned whether real democracy existed in the United States, and whether it could if African Americans were intentionally excluded from helping build it. By helping build the FDP, Hamer was helping design the American democracy she wanted everyone to enjoy.

President Lyndon Johnson did not want to lose white southern Democratic voters in the upcoming election by allowing the FDP to gain too many seats at the convention. Johnson was so scared of Hamer's testimony, precisely because of its palpable honesty and alignment with the values the nation purported, that he made up a reason to hold a press conference to divert television cameras away from her live testimony. The move backfired, however, as news outlets across the country replayed her testimony in full for days afterward, perhaps allowing her words to be heard by more people than if there had been no intervention.[57] While the FDP's bid to unseat the all-white Mississippi delegation did not succeed in 1964, the uncompromising stance of Hamer and other FDP delegates on behalf of genuine multiracial democracy helped result in the ultimate passage of the 1965 Voting Rights Act, which opened up the ballot for millions of Americans across the country by enforcing the prohibition of poll taxes, literacy tests, and discriminatory state laws, and prompted the Democratic Party to reform the way it selected delegates. In 1968 Hamer became the first African American since Reconstruction to take a seat as an official delegate at a national party convention, as well as the first-ever woman from Mississippi.

The struggle for participation in creating a real democracy for all Americans did not end for Fannie Lou Hamer in 1968. Her analysis of how that democracy would be formed had continued to evolve since the establishment of the FDP as it melded racial, class, and moral analyses in attempts to bridge divides and include as many people as possible that were being disadvantaged by the current white supremacist, capitalist system in place.

She estimated that by the fall of 1965 the Freedom Democratic Party had about 78,000 members in Mississippi in a racially inclusive party that was "one way of bringing change, you know, for the poor people all across the country."[58] Hamer battled on, though the formation of the Loyalty Democrats, a Black party aligned with the Democratic Party establishment, before the 1968 Democratic convention undermined the FDP.[59] She even ran for the state senate in 1971. Hamer believed there had been malfeasance in the election. Nevertheless, it was necessary to keep fighting for racial and economic equality, despite the setbacks. For her, the fighting had moved from direct protest to politics.[60] Through voter registration, political campaigning, and cooperative economics Fannie Lou Hamer exemplified the work necessary in bringing about a genuine multiracial democracy.[61]

The "freedom schools" that Hamer participated in and helped establish as a field organizer and representative of SNCC in the mid-1960s were in large part the result of decades of work done by Septima Clark and other Black women activists as part of the Highlander Folk School and later the Southern Christian Leadership Conference. By the time Septima Clark first learned of the Highlander Folk School in Monteagle, Tennessee, in June 1954 and ultimately joined their staff about a year later, she had already been a teacher, activist, and educational and movement theorist for more than forty years in her native South Carolina. Clark began her teaching career in 1916 on Johns Island, South Carolina, in a one-room log cabin working with one other teacher and upward of 130 children.[62] Between her experiences growing up as a Black woman in South Carolina, experiencing the inadequate teaching conditions she had to labor in, and learning more about the social and economic conditions her students and their parents endured, Clark was inspired to increase her educational training whenever she could and become more politically active.

Septima Clark not only taught children but also began teaching adult literacy classes in Columbia, South Carolina, at the start of the Great Depression in 1929. The decision, although partly financial, ultimately allowed Clark to develop an educational and movement philosophy that rooted learning, leadership, citizenship, and democracy in the daily lives of Black students, unlocking the liberatory and revolutionary potential of literacy and citizenship education. By the time Clark attended workshops at Highlander Folk School she was intent on implementing her ideas on a larger scale. What Clark learned at Highlander confirmed what she already knew about effective teaching, yet still introduced her to new methods that enhanced what she would do (and teach many others to do). According to biographer Katherine Mellen Charron, "HFS pushed Clark to translate adult education theory into political and community action."[63]

Clark revolutionized Highlander's methods and focus as much as she learned from the school's philosophy of social action. Clark made her teaching about the people and the communities they came from, first and foremost, asking students what they wanted to learn and connecting basic literacy to their daily lives. She "recognized practical literacy as a key to political liberation for the black grassroots." Therefore, Clark took her lessons from the daily tasks that her adult students needed to conduct regularly, and then showed them how learning about local, state, and national political structures directly affected their daily lives. Clark and the Citizenship Education Program worked to increase literacy so that in the short term the participants would be able to register to vote, but it was as important, if not more so, to get pupils to be willing to advocate for themselves so their government worked on their behalf. Students progressed from tracing their names and learning arithmetic to soon discussing the meaning of the United Nations Declaration of Human Rights and South Carolina tax policy. "Participation in the Citizenship Schools profoundly affected daily life. Those who learned to read, write, and figure felt more self-sufficient and less vulnerable. More important, they had the means to preserve their independence." They could not be taken advantage of by unscrupulous white neighbors or officials as easily. Graduates of the schools could more ably handle their own affairs, and that included their political lives.[64]

Clark made sure that future citizenship teachers were cultivated from the communities whence they came. Previous teaching experience and high levels of formal education were not required. Trainees needed to know about the political and social conditions in their communities before arriving at Highlander, and this was because it was necessary to be of the community from which one came and show commitment to building democracy through education.[65] Citizenship schools spread all over the South from the 1950s into the 1970s as a result of Septima Clark and the efforts of many others who both took part in and furthered a Black women's educational and activist tradition that conceived of education and democracy broadly, as well as intimately linked. Clark was certainly a dreamer, designer, advocate, defender, and builder of U.S. democracy. And because of each of those positions in relation to an American democratic project, she was also a "perfecter" of U.S. democracy.

Black activist-intellectuals worked to "perfect the democracy" in various ways. They developed and refined community educational practice, made claims on the government to be as beholden to them as much as any other citizen, protested in the streets, and wrote and sang and created art that dramatized their efforts to create a genuine multiracial democracy. But as the Black freedom struggle facilitated a national conversation about structural inequality and the need for greater inclusivity across American society, oppositional forces criticized Black Americans for protesting inequality.

Conservative intellectual William F. Buckley, debating James Baldwin at Cambridge University in England in 1965, articulated a persistent yet ahistorical refrain that should sound familiar today. "What should James Baldwin be doing other than telling us to renounce our civilization? He should be addressing his own people and urging them to take advantage of those opportunities which do exist. And urging us to make those opportunities wider." Buckley continued, "Where Negroes are concerned, the danger, as far as I can see at this moment, is that they will seek to reach out for some sort of radical solution, on the basis of which the true problem is obscured. . . . They seem to be slipping into some sort of Procrustean formulation which ends up by urging the advancement of the Negro less than the regression of white people."[66] The irony and condescension of Buckley's argumentation blindly assumed three things: (1) that systemic racial discrimination perpetuated by whites against Blacks was Black people's problem to solve; (2) that improving American society was a zero-sum game in which one group had to lose in order for another to advance; and (3) that Buckley—as a white man—was entitled to diagnose the "true problem" Black people faced in America. Buckley implied it was Black Americans' own fault they were not advancing within society at the same rate as whites. Black people needed to just stop complaining and appreciate all that having been stolen to America had only partially afforded them.

Another blind spot in Buckley's argument against "radical solutions" to eradicate structural racial inequality is that democracy is itself a radical concept, and that of a multiracial democracy even more so. In fact, Buckley had argued explicitly against representative democracy less than a decade earlier, in 1957, when he wrote that the white community has the right to enforce its political and social prerogatives onto Black people even when in the demographic minority because "for the time being, it is the advanced race."[67] Black movement activists understood the radicalism of representative democracy and that demanding genuine democracy within a white supremacist society would appear "radical" to those for whom the society had been structured to benefit.

And so, Black activists have not listened to those voices constantly asking them to "go cautiously," in the words of Septima Clark, to placate an unjust society that would otherwise have no intention of extending equal rights to all its citizens—rights bestowed by virtue of birth. James Baldwin wrote in 1963, "I know what I'm asking is impossible [talking to white Americans]. But in our time, as in every time, the impossible is the least that one can demand—and one is, after all, emboldened by the spectacle of human history in general, and the American Negro history in particular, for it testifies to nothing less than the perpetual achievement of the impossible."[68] He pursued redemptive change, "not on the surface—change in the sense of renewal."[69] Renewal could only occur by going beyond what liberal whites and the broader white society were comfortable with or willing to give. There had to be the "tension" that Martin Luther King Jr. called for to usher forth "the presence of justice"[70]—the presence of democracy. The creation of that tension for the purpose of bringing about a more equal and just society is patriotic.

The Danger of Mythmaking to Creating a Genuine Multiracial Democracy

It is important that patriotism not be ritualistic and blind obedience to the American flag, military institutions, or the president.[71] Today, increasingly shrill calls for obedience as "patriotism" continue obscuring and ignoring fundamental problems facing the United States regarding racial, gender, economic, and sexual equality. In addition to the calls for "patriotic education" in 2021, just going back a few years, protests over police brutality toward African American men and women and obfuscation of those protests once again became part of our sporting culture in 2016 when Colin Kaepernick, then quarterback for the San Francisco 49ers National Football League (NFL) franchise, began refusing to stand—and eventually taking a knee—during the national anthem. The decision caused discussion in many mainstream political circles, not about eradicating police brutality against Black and Latino people or disparities within the criminal justice system, but rather about whether those who knelt were disrespecting the flag and unsupportive of American service members.[72] Then-President Trump told the country, via a tweet, that Kaepernick should "find a country that works better than him" if systemic discrimination against people of color did not work for him.[73] Trump's eliding the core issues of Kaepernick's protest allowed many commentators—particularly conservatives, but not exclusively—to disregard police brutality against communities of color and question whether protestors loved the United States or even deserved the rights of citizenship. Were, could, or should protesters be part of the democracy?

In telling Kaepernick to find another country, just as he later did in 2019 with congresswomen Ilhan Omar, Alexandria Ocasio-Cortez, Ayanna Pressley, and Rashida Tlaib, Donald Trump used a well-worn historical trope to define "Americans" as white, "patriotism" as silent acceptance of the status quo, and protest as "communist-inspired" and "anti-American."[74] Telling the four congresswomen to "go back [to the] places from which they came" excited Republican base supporters who shared his view that, for people of color, citizenship is contingent on their effusive gratitude for being here.[75]

George Floyd's murder in broad daylight at the hands of police officer Derek Chauvin in May 2020 catalyzed international demonstrations and mass mobilization on behalf of Black lives. The combination of the horrific brazenness of this murder caught on tape, the halted pace of life due to the COVID-19 pandemic, and the unceasing activism of Black people for years prior to Floyd's murder in organizations such as the Movement for Black Lives, Color of Change, and the Poor People's Campaign, among others, jolted the country and world into recognition that police brutality against Black people and people of color is still endemic in American society. Americans and others realized that to bring about real democracy, it will be necessary to "shift the moral narrative, impact policies and elections at every level of government, and build lasting power for poor and impacted people."[76]

Even more recently, in 2021, the insurrection of Donald Trump's Republican Party supporters at the U.S. Capitol to stop the democratic process of certifying electoral votes on January 6, as well as the efforts to push a largely incorrect and exclusionary narrative of U.S. history, are more dangerous examples of a right-wing effort to uphold a white nationalist interpretation of U.S. history. This right-wing movement seeks to eliminate discussions of white supremacy, misogyny, and structural discrimination from our educational and public discourses, topple the current version of democracy in America, and prevent the creation of a genuine multiracial democracy in the next several generations through structural means. As James Baldwin has written, "The American Negro has had the great advantage of having never believed that collection of myths to which white Americans cling: that their ancestors were all freedom-loving heroes, that they were born in the greatest country the world has ever seen, or that Americans are invincible in battle and wise in peace, that Americans have always dealt honorably with Mexicans and Indians and all other neighbors or inferiors, that American men are the world's most direct and virile, that American women are pure."[77] It is imperative that the rest of the nation also stop believing these myths—that we do not continue allowing these myths to be perpetuated uncritically. That advantage of which Baldwin spoke more than sixty years ago is a big part of the reason why Black Americans have been able to envision and work toward a genuine multiracial democracy in the United States.

Right-wing politicians, activists, and pundits are not patriots, nor do they seek a multiracial democracy. They cloak themselves in the American flag to stifle meaningful political discussion and legislative actions that could advance our society's realization of a genuine multiracial democracy and more equitable society. But this strategy is old, not new. Kaepernick, Omar, Ocasio-Cortez, Pressley, Tlaib, contemporary activist-intellectuals Tamika Mallory, Ayọ [formerly Opal] Tometi, Alicia Garza, Patrisse Cullors, Chris Smalls, and Rev. Dr. William Barber join the long line of real patriots that include James Greene, James Baldwin, Martin Luther King Jr., Fannie Lou Hamer, and Septima Clark, who loved their country enough to criticize it in the face of political and popular attacks.

If American democracy is to be "perfected," U.S. history will need to be reoriented in such ways as to cast Black movement leaders as the patriots in our national narrative, and then enact many of the policies they advocated during their lives. Actions, not objects, hold the potential for bringing about an enduring multiracial democracy. It will be to the detriment of our national historical memory, and ultimately the destruction of what exists of this democracy, if conservatives and mainstream political outlets continue to be allowed to stifle dissent, suppress our "hard history," and frame patriotism in such narrow, ahistorical terms.[78]

Notes

1 Portions of this chapter have been published previously at Public Seminar: "The Dilemma of Black Citizenship: Perpetual Partiality and Patriotism," August 23, 2019, https://publicseminar.org/?s=dilemma+of+black+citizenship, and "When It Comes to Racial Justice, Why Is It Wrong to Demand the 'Impossible'?," November 3, 2020,

https://publicseminar.org/essays/when-it-comes-to-racial-justice-why-is-it-wrong-to-demand-the-impossible/.

2 This argument builds on a rich literature about the patriotic ideals in African American protest, as well as social movement protest on the American Left, including but by no means limited to Nikole Hannah-Jones, ed., *The 1619 Project: A New Origin Story* (New York: One World, 2021); Simon Hall, *American Patriotism, American Protest: Social Movements since the Sixties* (Philadelphia: University of Pennsylvania Press, 2011); Michael Kazin, "A Patriotic Left," *Dissent*, October 1, 2002, 41–44.

3 W.E.B. Du Bois, "The Propaganda of History," in *Writings*, ed. Nathan Huggins (New York: Library of America, 1986), 1029.

4 Jacquelyn Dowd Hall, "The Long Civil Rights Movement and the Political Uses of the Past," *Journal of American History* 91, no. 4 (March 2005): 1262. In some cases, as in Florida public schools in 2023, African American history is framed as a Whiggish march toward racial equality that submerges structural barriers to racial and economic equality to such an extent that it practically forces African American history to end in the early 1970s because the "triumph" of the civil rights movement makes the succeeding sixty years inexplicable, other than to blame Black Americans themselves for whatever societal disparities still exist. "Florida's State Academic Standards—Social Studies, 2023," 3–21, https://www.fldoe.org/core/fileparse.php/20653/urlt/6-4.pdf.

5 Ana Rosado, Gideon Cohn-Postar, and Mimi Essen, "Erasing the Black Freedom Struggle: How State Standards Fail to Teach the Truth About Reconstruction," 27, Teach Reconstruction Report, https://www.teachreconstructionreport.org/coverage-feed/erasing-the-black-freedom-struggle-how-state-standards-fail-to-teach-the-truth-about-reconstruction, accessed February 13, 2022.

6 Ali Swenson, "Far-Right Group Moms for Liberty Poised to Clash with Teachers Unions over School Board Races Nationwide," *PBS News Hour*, July 2, 2023, https://www.pbs.org/newshour/education/moms-for-liberty-poised-to-clash-with-teachers-unions-over-school-board-races-nationwide.

7 Karen L. Cox, *Dixie's Daughters: The United Daughters of the Confederacy and the Preservation of Confederate Culture* (Gainesville: University Press of Florida, 2003).

8 Jack Brewster, "Trump Says Critical Race Theory Borders on 'Psychological Abuse,'" *Forbes*, June 18, 2021, https://www.forbes.com/sites/jackbrewster/2021/06/18/trump-says-critical-race-theory-borders-on-psychological-abuse/?sh=3cc736f8450e.

9 Carmen N. Decot, "Federal Court Issues Nationwide Order Enjoining Enforcement of Trump Executive Order on Diversity Training," *National Law Review* 11, no. 362 (December 28, 2020), https://www.natlawreview.com/article/federal-court-issues-nationwide-order-enjoining-enforcement-trump-executive-order.

10 Timothy Bella, "DeSantis Invokes MLK as He Proposes Stop Woke Act against Critical Race Theory," *Washington Post*, December 15, 2021, https://www.washingtonpost.com/politics/2021/12/15/desantis-stop-woke-act-mlk-crt/.

11 Justin Baragona, "Tucker Admits He's 'Never Figured Out What Critical Race

Theory Is,'" *Daily Beast*, November 3, 2021, https://www.thedailybeast.com/tucker-carlson-admits-hes-never-figured-out-what-critical-race-theory-is.

12 Adam Harris, "The GOP's 'Critical Race Theory' Obsession," *Atlantic*, May 7, 2021, https://www.theatlantic.com/politics/archive/2021/05/gops-critical-race-theory-fixation-explained/618828/.

13 Matthew Barakat and Sarah Rankin, "Youngkin Looks to Root Out Critical Race Theory in Virginia," AP News, February 15, 2022, https://apnews.com/article/education-richmond-race-and-ethnicity-racial-injustice-virginia-8ad5da65b9cb05265f2b8081c41827cd.

14 Hasan Kwame Jeffries, preface, "Teaching Hard History," Southern Poverty Law Center, January 31, 2018, https://www.splcenter.org/20180131/teaching-hard-history.

15 Harris, "GOP's 'Critical Race Theory' Obsession"; Hall, "Long Civil Rights Movement," 1237–38.

16 James Taranto, "America after Racism," *Wall Street Journal*, November 5, 2008, https://www.wsj.com/articles/SB122590798182101973; Wall Street Journal Editorial Board, "President-Elect Obama," *Wall Street Journal*, November 5, 2008, https://www.wsj.com/articles/SB122586244657800863; John McWhorter, "Racism in America Is Over," *Forbes*, December 30, 2008, https://www.forbes.com/2008/12/30/end-of-racism-oped-cx_jm_1230mcwhorter.html?sh=73eefd1c49f8.

17 "Florida's State Academic Standards—Social Studies, 2023," SS.68.AA.2.3, 6.

18 Cox, *Dixie's Daughters*, 3, 120–22, 124–27.

19 "Florida's State Academic Standards—Social Studies, 2023," SS.912.AA.3.6, SS.912.AA.3.9, SS.912.AA.3.13, 17–18.

20 Historians Jeanne Theoharis and Brian Purnell, among others, have critiqued the concept of a "culture of poverty" among Black Americans that had been crystallized by Senator Daniel Patrick Moynihan during the mid-1960s to shape federal policy toward Black and poor people. Brian Purnell, *Fighting Jim Crow in the County of Kings* (Lexington: University Press of Kentucky, 2013); Jeanne Theoharis, *A More Beautiful and Terrible History: The Uses and Misuses of Civil Rights History* (Boston: Beacon, 2018).

21 Theoharis, *More Beautiful and Terrible History*; Kimberlé Crenshaw, "King Was a Critical Race Theorist Before There Was a Name for It," *Los Angeles Times*, January 17, 2022, https://www.latimes.com/opinion/story/2022-01-17/critical-race-theory-martin-luther-king; Hall, "Long Civil Rights Movement," 1238.

22 Kristopher Bryan Burrell, "Black Women as Activist Intellectuals: Ella Baker and Mae Mallory Combat Northern Jim Crow in New York City's Public Schools during the 1950s," in *The Strange Careers of the Jim Crow North: Segregation and Struggle Outside of the South*, ed. Brian Purnell and Jeanne Theoharis, with Komozi Woodard (New York: New York University Press, 2019), 92.

23 Patricia Morgan, George Nardone, and Sherry Roberts, "RI H6070, Curriculum [See Title 16 1 Chapter 97—The Rhode Island Board of Education Act]," http://webserver.rilin.state.ri.us/BillText21/HouseText21/H6070.pdf.

24 "An Act: Enrolled House Bill No. 1775," Oklahoma State Legislature, https://legiscan.com/OK/text/HB1775/id/2387002; "An Act: House Bill No. 3979," Texas State Legislature, https://capitol.texas.gov/tlodocs/87R/billtext/pdf/HB03979F.pdf#navpanes=0; "House Bill 1255," New Hampshire State Legislature, https://legiscan.com/NH/text/HB1255/id/2461346; Elizabeth Elkind, "South Dakota Gov. Kristi Noem Announces Crackdown on 'Indoctrination' in Schools and Introduces Bill to Prevent a Political Ideology, Protests or Lobbying Being Forced on Students to Push Back against Critical Race Theory," *Daily Mail*, January 11, 2022, https://www.dailymail.co.uk/news/article-10390761/South-Dakota-Gov-Kristi-Noem-announces-crackdown-school-indoctrination-anti-protest-bill.html.
25 "Introduction," *Critical Race Theory: The Key Writings That Formed the Movement*, ed. Kimberlé Crenshaw, Neil Gotanda, Gary Peller, and Kendall Thomas (New York: New Press, 1995), xiii.
26 Benjamin Wallace Wells, "How a Conservative Activist Invented the Conflict over Critical Race Theory," *New Yorker*, June 18, 2021, https://www.newyorker.com/news/annals-of-inquiry/how-a-conservative-activist-invented-the-conflict-over-critical-race-theory.
27 "Map: Where Critical Race Theory Is Under Attack," *Education Week*, June 11, 2021, https://www.edweek.org/policy-politics/map-where-critical-race-theory-is-under-attack/2021/06.
28 There are so many examples of this in just the past few years, from former president Donald Trump insulting Colin Kaepernick during his protests against police brutality beginning in 2016, to his insulting four Congresswomen of color via tweet in 2019, to more recent attacks against Black Lives Matter protestors for also protesting police brutality and white supremacy in all areas of U.S. society. Sean Sullivan, "Trump Slams Colin Kaepernick: 'Maybe He Should Find a Country That Works Better for Him,'" *Washington Post*, August 29, 2016, https://www.washingtonpost.com/news/post-politics/wp/2016/08/29/trump-slams-colin-kaepernick-maybe-he-should-find-a-country-that-works-better-for-him/; Donald Trump, Twitter, July 14, 2019, https://twitter.com/realdonaldtrump/status/1150381395078000643.
29 Nikole Hannah-Jones, "Democracy," in Hannah-Jones, *1619 Project*, 10.
30 "Map: Where Critical Race Theory Is Under Attack."
31 Eric Foner, "South Carolina's Forgotten Black Political Revolution," Slate, January 31, 2018, https://slate.com/human-interest/2018/01/the-many-black-americans-who-held-public-office-during-reconstruction-in-southern-states-like-south-carolina.html.
32 Foner, "South Carolina's Forgotten Black Political Revolution."
33 Hannah-Jones, "Democracy," 27, 29; Vanessa Williamson, "The Austerity Politics of White Supremacy," *Dissent*, Winter 2021, https://www.dissentmagazine.org/article/the-austerity-politics-of-white-supremacy.
34 Hannah-Jones, "Democracy," 27.
35 Martha S. Jones, "Citizenship," in Hannah-Jones, *1619 Project*, 234–36.
36 Rosado et al., "Erasing the Black Freedom Struggle," 4.

37 Williamson, "Austerity Politics."
38 Trevor Logan quoted in Williamson, "Austerity Politics."
39 W. E. B. Du Bois, *Black Reconstruction in America, 1860–1880,* introduction by David Levering Lewis (1935; New York: Atheneum, 1992); Patricia Morton, *Disfigured Images: The Historical Assault on Afro-American Women* (Westport, CT: Praeger, 1991), 19; Foner, "South Carolina's Forgotten Black Political Revolution."
40 Rosado et al., "Erasing the Black Freedom Struggle," 7.
41 Du Bois, "Propaganda of History," 1029.
42 Rosado et al., "Erasing the Black Freedom Struggle," 3–4.
43 James Baldwin, *Notes from a Native Son* (Boston: Beacon, 1984), 9.
44 Martin Luther King Jr., "Letter from Birmingham Jail," April 16, 1963, 9–10, http://okra.stanford.edu/transcription/document_images/undecided/630416-019.pdf.
45 Martin Luther King, Jr., "I Have a Dream," August 28, 1963, https://www1.udel.edu/htr/Psc105/Texts/king.html, prepared by Gerald Murphy, National Public Telecomputing Network.
46 James Baldwin, *The Fire Next Time* (New York: Vintage International, 1962, 1993), 104.
47 Martin Luther King Jr., "Letter from Birmingham Jail," April 16, 1963, 9–10.
48 Fannie Lou Hamer, Testimony Before the Credentials Committee, Democratic National Convention, Atlantic City, New Jersey, August 22, 1964, https://americanradioworks.publicradio.org/features/sayitplain/flhamer.html.
49 Fannie Lou Hamer, "Interview of Fannie Lou Hamer by Neil McMillen, Part 1, April 14, 1972," in *An Oral History with Fannie Lou Hamer,* ed. Neil McMillen (Hattiesburg: University of Southern Mississippi, 2000), 3–4; Keisha N. Blain, *Until I Am Free: Fannie Lou Hamer's Enduring Message to America* (Boston: Beacon, 2021), x, 14.
50 Hamer, "Interview," 4–5; Blain, *Until I Am Free,* 28–29.
51 Hamer, "Interview," 7.
52 Blain, *Until I Am Free,* 30–31.
53 Hamer, "Interview," 8.
54 Hamer, "Interview," 8–12.
55 Campbell Gibson and Kay Jung, "Historical Census Statistics on Population Totals by Race, 1790 to 1990, and Hispanic Origin, 1970 to 1990 for the United States, Regions, Divisions, and States," Population Division, Working Paper no. 56, September 2002, 57, https://www.census.gov/content/dam/Census/library/working-papers/2002/demo/POP-twps0056.pdf; United States Commission on Civil Rights, *Racial and Ethnic Tensions in American Communities: Poverty, Inequality, and Discrimination,* vol. 7: *The Mississippi Delta Report,* chapter 3 (n14), https://www.usccr.gov/files/pubs/msdelta/ch3.htm, accessed February 14, 2022.
56 Hamer, "Testimony Before the Credentials Committee."
57 Janice D. Hamlet, "Fannie Lou Hamer: The Unquenchable Spirit of the Civil Rights Movement," *Journal of Black Studies* 26, no. 5 (May 1996): 571.
58 "Fannie Lou Hamer Interview," KPFA (Berkeley, California), September 24, 1965,

American Archive of Public Broadcasting, https://americanarchive.org/catalog/cpb-aacip_28-bg2h70895r.
59 Fannie Lou Hamer, "Interview of Fannie Lou Hamer by Neil McMillen, Part 2, January 25, 1973," in McMillen, *Oral History with Fannie Lou Hamer,* 19–20.
60 Hamer, "Interview, Part 2," 30.
61 Hamer, "Interview, Part 2," 25–27.
62 Katherine Mellen Charron, *Freedom's Teacher: The Life of Septima Clark* (Chapel Hill: University of North Carolina Press, 2009), 68.
63 Charron, *Freedom's Teacher,* 118–19, 217 (quotation).
64 Charron, 217, 248, 251–53, 259.
65 Charron, 255.
66 William F. Buckley, "The American Dream and the American Negro," *New York Times,* March 7, 1965, SM32.
67 William F. Buckley, "Why the South Must Win," *National Review,* August 24, 1957, https://adamgomez.files.wordpress.com/2012/03/whythesouthmustprevail-1957.pdf.
68 Baldwin, *Fire Next Time,* 104.
69 Baldwin, *Fire Next Time,* 92.
70 Martin Luther King Jr., "Letter from Birmingham City Jail," April 16, 1963, 10.
71 Charles M. Blow, "Who Loves America?" *New York Times,* February 23, 2015, https://www.nytimes.com/2015/02/23/opinion/charles-blow-who-loves-america.html.
72 Stacia L. Brown, "For Black America, Absolute Love of Country Is Impossible," *New Republic,* September 12, 2016, https://newrepublic.com/article/136694/black-america-absolute-love-country-impossible.
73 Sullivan, "Trump Slams Colin Kaepernick"; Matthew Yglesias, "Trump Versus the NFL, Explained," Vox, September 25, 2017, https://www.vox.com/policy-and-politics/2017/9/25/16360264/donald-trump-colin-kaepernick.
74 Trump, Twitter, July 14, 2019.
75 Lawrence O'Donnell, *The Last Word,* MSNBC, YouTube, July 18, 2019, www.youtube.com/watch?v=lT8QweuVdwc.
76 "About the Poor People's Campaign: A National Call for Moral Revival," Poor People's Campaign, https://www.poorpeoplescampaign.org/about/, accessed January 3, 2022.
77 Baldwin, *Fire Next Time,* 101.
78 Gloria Ladson-Billings, "Once upon a Time When Patriotism Was What You Did," *Phi Delta Kappan,* April 1, 2006, 585, https://journals.sagepub.com/doi/abs/10.1177/003172170608700809?journalCode=pdka&.

2

Black Women

The Backbone of Democracy

SHARLENE SINEGAL-DECUIR

> The most disrespected person in America is the black woman. The most unprotected person in America is the black woman. The most neglected person in America is the black woman.
> —Malcolm X

Nation of Islam leader Malcolm X uttered these words in 1962, a time of racial inequality, police brutality, and gender discrimination. In 2025, those words are still true for millions of women who are Black. And while Black women have made significant progress over the decades, their story is one of sheer struggle, determination, and perseverance. In the 2020 presidential election Americans made history by electing Joe Biden as president and Kamala Harris as vice president. Harris, the first woman ever elected to this position, is a woman of color. In her first speech addressing the nation, she stood proud and paid the ultimate tribute to the Black women who came before her—the women "who fought and sacrificed so much for equality and liberty and justice for all" so that she could be where she was in that moment. Black women, she said, are "too often overlooked, but so often prove that they are the backbone of our democracy."[1]

American democracy is based on the principle of political equality of all citizens, and yet, since its founding, American society has been plagued by racism and sexism. In the earliest decades of this nation's history, Black women were the torchbearers spreading the words that neither racism nor sexism had a place in our democracy. Through the major social movements in American history, Black women have demanded to be heard, leading when Black men were too afraid to do so, setting the bar for everyone around them and passing on the ideas of an inclusive democracy to generations of Black women after them.[2] The activism of these women dispels the traditional narrative of men alone pulling the nation closer to true democracy with women following suit. Instead, the stories of women like Sojourner Truth, Maria Stewart, Mary Ann Shadd Cary, Mary Church Terrell, Nannie Helen Burroughs, Sadie T. M. Alexander, Mary McLeod Bethune, Ella Baker, Dorothy I. Height, and many more allow us to see how democracy unfolded in the United States.

Bruised but not broken, the will of Black women to make something out of nothing has always been a steady force in America. That will, coupled with insurmountable strength, allowed Black women to survive in a "new world" that was not created for them. The world Black women entered as property and suffered in as forced laborers featured unimaginable horrors. Despite their plight, however, Black women's resiliency sanctioned their rise to leadership. When America counted Black women out, giving them two strikes, one for being a woman and the other for being Black, Black women stood up, not just for themselves but for the entire race. They refused to be silenced; they fought so that their voices would be heard, growing into their activism and creating a path for the next Black woman to follow.

Black Women's Suffrage Struggle

When Sojourner Truth asked "Ar'n't I a woman?" in 1851, her question sent shock waves through America. At the time, Black women were confined to roles as slaves or domestic workers. Yet, at a woman's rights convention in Akron, Ohio, Sojourner Truth, described as "a tall, gaunt black woman in a grey dress and white turban, surmounted by an uncouth sun-bonnet," marched into the meeting "with the air of a queen," walked "up the aisle," and took her seat. Sojourner was ready to speak her truth. "She spoke in deep tones, which, though not loud, reached every ear in the house." In her speech, Sojourner pointed out the clear differences between white and Black women in America. Discussing how white women were put on pedestals and helped across puddles, Sojourner pointed out that Black women were forced to toil, till the soil, and fend for themselves. She questioned it all with the simple statement, "Ar'n't I a woman?"[3]

Being a Black woman did not make Sojourner less of a woman, and if America was entertaining thoughts of women's rights, Sojourner wanted to make sure that Black women were included. Her speech answered several questions in the minds of white men who contemplated supporting women's rights. One of the most pressing questions was one of intelligence: could Black women truly understand the democratic process? To this Sojourner said, "What's dat got to do with woman's rights or nigger's rights? If my cup won't hold but a pint and yourn holds a quart, wouldn't ye be mean not to let me have my little half-measure full?" Sojourner was asking for an inch, not a foot. She clearly understood that asking for more at that time was not her mission. She was laying the groundwork for other Black women to continue asking for the inch until they got the foot.[4]

Prior to Sojourner Truth's appeal for Black women's rights to be intertwined in the fight for woman's rights, Maria Stewart, a free Black woman, spoke publicly and quite radically about the inclusivity of Black women to liberty and equality. In her 1831 speech in Boston, Stewart, the first American woman of any race to speak to an all-male audience, declared that prejudice, racism, and sexism had no place in America. While she understood her place as a Black woman, she asked, "Shall I, for fear of scoffs and frowns, refrain my tongue? Ah, no!" She refused to keep silent. "How long," she asked, "shall the fair daughters of Africa be compelled to bury their minds and talents beneath a load of iron pots and kettles?"[5] Stewart boldly called Black women to collectively fight in the struggle for equality and the democratic principles promised to all Americans under the Constitution. She challenged Black women to rise from the abyss and become leaders: "O you daughters of Africa, awake! awake! arise! no longer sleep nor slumber, but distinguish yourselves. Show forth to the world that ye are endowed with noble and exalted faculties. O you daughters of Africa! what have you done to immortalize your names beyond the grave? What examples have you set before the rising generation? What foundation have you laid for generations yet un-born?"[6] Stewart firmly planted the seed that would sprout Black women activists well into the twenty-first century. She inspired Black women to create seats at the table of democracy, and when there were no seats, her words inspired Black women to create their own tables.

In 1853, with the publication of the *Provincial Freeman* newspaper, Mary Ann Shadd Cary created her own table, becoming the first Black woman in North America to own and edit a newspaper. Cary grew up a free person of color in Delaware; her father owned a shoemaking store, and the family actively participated in the Underground Railroad. In 1851, she moved to Canada, shortly after the passage of the Fugitive Slave Act of 1850. It was there that she developed strong opinions relating to equality and integration, believing that society should be fully integrated and that Blacks should have full equality under the law. Her radical views caused several people in both the Black and white abolitionist communities to write her off, thus provoking her to create her own platform so that her voice would not be silenced. Her iconoclastic views about equality and democracy led her to become, with her graduation from Howard University Law School in 1870, the first Black woman to earn a law degree in the United States, which is a testament to the resilience of Black women. She used her law degree to help the Black community fight for equal rights and their right to vote.[7]

Black women understood early on that in order to fully engage in the democratic process, the right to vote was imperative. Legal suffrage rights for Black men were achieved in 1870 with the passage of the Fifteenth Amendment to the Constitution, although Black men were effectively disfranchised through the 1900s due to poll taxes, literacy tests, property requirements, and grandfather clauses. The struggle for suffrage rights was an uphill battle for both Black and white women but a steeper climb for Black women. Suffrage rights for Black women were questioned not only by Black and white men but by white women as well. It is fair to say, not all women were created equal in American history, as was explained in Sojourner Truth's, "Ar'n't I a Woman?" speech. In the beginning of the suffrage movement, Black women were relegated to either exclusion or holding supporting or marginal roles behind white women.

Black women fought hard to combat the duality of sexism and racism. They were forced to fight against racism before confronting sexism. Their right to vote did not align with the racial superiority of white women. White suffragist Alice Paul argued that "the disenfranchisement of black women was a race, not a sex, matter."[8] She supported women but did not want to engage in the issues of race that plagued American society; therefore, her support of Black (race) women (gender) was not central to her suffragist movement. Still, Black women stood their ground and continued to fight for full inclusion in the democratic process, marching for both their race and gender.

Mary Church Terrell did not allow the objections of white suffragists to hinder her goal of securing the vote. If she was told to march at the back of the suffragists' parade in accordance with the racial climate, then that is what she did. But she was there, sending the clear message that Black women would not be excluded. Terrell, the daughter of former slaves, became a significant activist in the struggle for racial equality and women's suffrage. Terrell's mother and father prospered after the Civil War, affording her the privilege of obtaining an education, eventually graduating from Oberlin College, where she earned both bachelor's and master's degrees. She was part of the socially conscious rising Black middle and upper class.[9]

Terrell's activism, education, and resources led her to become "friendly" with Susan B. Anthony, one of the founders of the National Women Suffrage Association (NWSA). Despite their rapport, NWSA refused to grant Terrell and other Black suffragists permission to create their own chapter within the organization. Taking a page out of Mary Ann Shadd Cary's book, Terrell created her own table. She understood and accepted the fact that she and other Black women were handicapped in the struggle for democracy. Terrell explained, "A white woman has only one handicap to overcome, that of sex. I have two, both sex and race. . . . Colored men have only one, that of race. Colored women are the only group in this country who have two heavy handicaps to overcome."[10]

In 1896, Terrell founded the National Association of Colored Women (NACW), dedicated to fighting for both gender and racial equality. Terrell served as the first president of NACW from 1896 to 1901, working tirelessly for equality and democracy for her race and gender. She created its powerful motto, "Lifting as We Climb . . . Seeking no favors because of our color nor patronage because of our needs, we knock at the bar of justice and ask for an equal chance."[11] Terrell firmly believed in Black self-determination and ideas similar to W.E.B. Du Bois's concept of the Talented Tenth. If one Black person succeeded, the whole race benefited, but it was the duty of the race to reach back and help the next Black person become successful. In 1909, she became a charter member of the National Association for the Advancement of Colored People (NAACP). The NAACP continued the fight for equality and the right to vote through the civil rights movement until the passage of the Voting Rights Act of 1965.

Well before her national activism, Terrell practiced her "Lifting as We Climb" motto, becoming a mentor to a young student named Nannie Helen Burroughs, whom she met while teaching at M Street High School in Washington, D.C. Burroughs, born to formerly enslaved parents, excelled at M Street School, graduating with honors in 1896. After graduation she joined NACW, and by 1900 she was addressing the National Baptist Convention advocating for the inclusion of a woman's auxiliary group to contribute to the mission of the church. Burroughs became the first secretary of the Women's Convention (WC), auxiliary to the National Baptist Convention. The WC created a platform for Black women that allowed them to become leaders and advocates for women's rights in the democratic process. In 1909, through donations from the Black women of the WC, Burroughs founded the National Training School for Women and Girls in Washington, D.C.

The school taught both industrial and liberal arts education to Black girls, in addition to Black history.

Through her involvement with NACW, the WC, and later the NAACP, Burroughs became a huge supporter of women's and civil rights. She believed that Black women deserved the right to vote as much as anyone in America. In 1915, she wrote an article for the NAACP monthly magazine, *Crisis*, expressing her views. The article titled "Black Women and Reform" began with Burroughs answering a question of a white suffragist, "What can the Negro woman do with the ballot?" To this, Burroughs answered, "What can she do without it?" Burroughs argued that Black women needed the right to vote to "ransom [their] race," noting "that in every reform in which the Negro woman has taken part, during the past fifty years, she has been as aggressive, progressive and dependable as those who inspired the reform or led it."[12] Burroughs fought tirelessly until her death in 1961 for gender and racial equality, proving to America that Black women belonged in the arena of democracy and could most definitely handle the responsibility of voting.

Civil Rights and Black Women

After the 1920 ratification of the Nineteenth Amendment—which said that the right to vote could not be abridged because of sex—the struggle for inclusion now focused on the battle for civil rights, and Black women were not afraid to wage a war. Black women used the platforms they created years prior to collectively chip away at the cemented barriers of democracy, sexism, and civil rights.

In 1946, when Harry S. Truman created the President's Committee on Civil Rights, charged with examining the conditions of civil rights in the United States, he chose two women out of a total of fourteen committee members. One of the two women, Sadie T. M. Alexander, was the first Black person to receive a PhD in economics and the first woman to receive a law degree from the University of Pennsylvania Law School. Alexander, like Burroughs and Terrell, had a connection to M Street School in Washington, D.C.; while Terrell taught there in the late 1800s, both Burroughs and Alexander were graduates, in 1896 and 1915, respectively. Alexander and the committee were instrumental in creating a 178-page report titled *To Secure These Rights: The Report of the President's Committee on Civil Rights*. The report proposed the establishment of a Civil Rights Commission, a Joint Congressional Committee on Civil Rights, and a Civil Rights Division in the Department of Justice. These new government agencies would work to eradicate racial injustices including lynching, segregation, unfair voting practices, and employment discrimination.[13]

On November 6, 1947, just ten days after the report was published, the National Council of Negro Women (NCNW) held their twelfth annual convention. The NCNW was founded by Mary McLeod Bethune in 1935 as an umbrella group for twenty-nine Black women's groups. Bethune, born to formerly enslaved parents in 1875, was a staunch advocate for racial and gender equality. She understood that although women had received the right to vote in 1920, the battle had now turned to civil rights because as long as there was voter suppression based on race, Black women would never be able to fully engage in the democratic process. In 1936, Bethune was named director of Negro affairs for the National Youth Administration, making her the highest-ranking Black woman in government, a position she held until 1944. She was also a leader in President Franklin D. Roosevelt's unofficial "black cabinet." Her voice was the voice of Black women, and she used it wisely. As president of the NCNW, Bethune declared that the President's Committee on Civil Rights Report had "stimulated black women all over the country to take an increased interest in present-day issues."[14] At the NCNW convention, over six hundred delegates endorsed a "Ten-Point Program," similar to points made in the President's Committee report. Black women were more determined than ever to fight for equality, civil rights, and democracy, yet inclusion in the arena of the modern civil rights movement was no easy task for Black women.

Black women served as the beating heart of the modern civil rights movement. They organized, strategized, and fundraised, yet their leadership was deemphasized by Black men because they were women. These women, who were reliable, faithful, and devoted to the struggle for civil rights and democracy, continued their fight on two fronts, race and gender. The leadership of the modern civil rights movement was a Black male club filled with sexist ideas of a woman's place and role in the movement. Women like Ella Baker, Dorothy Height, and others struggled to have their voices heard as leaders in the movement.

Ella Baker, born in 1903 in Norfolk, Virginia, began her career with the NAACP in New York in the late 1930s as assistant field secretary and later as director of branches. In these positions Baker traveled throughout the Deep South encouraging Blacks to join the NAACP. During her travels she met Black folks from all walks of life. It was at this time she realized that the civil rights movement would only be successful if it had the full participation of Blacks at the grassroots level. Baker tried in 1946 to get the NAACP to understand that its middle-class branch leadership was not inclusive of all Blacks. The same year she ended her NAACP membership because the organization was unwilling to change its tactics in fighting for civil rights by not being open to a grassroots approach nor democratic decision-making within its ranks. In 1952, she rejoined the NAACP as the president of the New York branch, hopeful that the NAACP would one day see the advantages of a grassroots approach to civil rights.[15]

One month after the start of the Montgomery bus boycott in 1955, Baker partnered with Stanley Levison and Bayard Rustin to cofound In Friendship, an organization created to provide aid to local movements like that of Montgomery. In Friendship donated thousands of dollars to the Montgomery Improvement Association, which Martin Luther King Jr. presided over. Her collaborations with King through In Friendship along with her knowledge of King's ability to mobilize Blacks from all walks of life led her to help King organize the Southern Christian Leadership Conference (SCLC), serving as the organization's first staff person and later the interim executive director in Atlanta.[16]

While working for SCLC Baker grew disillusioned with the sexist authoritarian leadership styles of King and other male leaders of SCLC. After the success of the 1960s sit-ins, both the NAACP and SCLC put more energies into their youth-affiliated organizations. Prior to this, Baker organized a conference at Shaw University to encourage college and high school student activists to form their own organization. Baker advocated decentralized leadership, more local participation by Blacks in their communities, and student control of the new organization. At the conference Baker's speech titled "Bigger Than a Hamburger" challenged the younger generation to find larger targets for the movement: "something bigger than a hamburger or even a giant-sized Coke."[17] Baker challenged the students to fight for voting rights, housing, jobs, and health care. At the close of the conference, the participants formed the Student Nonviolent Coordinating Committee (SNCC). Baker was instrumental in fighting within the several civil rights organizations so that the democratic process that applied to Black men would be true for Black women. She was not a woman who blindly followed male leadership. Her ideals of shared cooperative leadership allowed SNCC to flourish in the civil rights movement as SNCC made decisions based on the collective majority. The voices of women and leadership in the organization were welcomed as seen through the strong leadership of Diane Nash during the 1961 Freedom Rides; still, all SNCC chairs were men, which caused the females in the organization to question the sexist nature of SNCC.[18]

Dorothy I. Height was just as vocal as Baker about the suppression of women's voices in the movement. Height, born in Richmond, Virginia, in 1912, was a graduate of New York University, where in 1930 she earned a bachelor's degree in education and later a master's degree in psychology. After working for a short time as a social worker in New York, Height began working at the Harlem Young Women's Christian Association (YWCA). The Harlem YWCA was the unofficial meeting place of several like-minded Black women who believed women had every right to be heard, especially in organizations that fought for civil rights. It was there that Height met Terrell, Burroughs, Baker, and Bethune, all strong women with a clear voice for democratic principles and women's rights. Height eventually became the fourth president of the National Council of Negro Women. As president of such a large organization of potential voters, her position commanded a seat at the table of democracy and civil rights. She became one of the most powerful Black women of the time, often offering advice on civil rights to Presidents Eisenhower and Johnson.[19]

In 1963, Height collaborated with the male leadership of the "Big Six" civil rights organizations to form the Council of United Civil Rights Leadership (CUCRL). CUCRL worked as an umbrella civil rights organization instrumental in connecting white donors and philanthropic organizations to the civil rights movement. It was in this organization that Height voiced her loudest concerns about the male civil rights leaders' attempt to silence the voices of women in leadership, relegating them to a second-class status. In her essay "We Want the Voice of Black Women to Be Heard," written years after the march, Height discussed her dismay with the planning of the 1963 March on Washington. When she asked Bayard Rustin about women's representation as speakers for the march, she was met with the response, "Women are included." Rustin stated that women were members of several organizations and as such they were included.[20]

The men who organized the march wanted to control the speaker platform to ensure that the march focused on racism and not sexism. In Height's opinion the march was about racism and sexism because women experienced both. Still, she did not understand why a woman could not address the march strictly about issues surrounding civil rights, like jobs, discrimination, and lynching. Height argued that "most of the Civil Rights Movement audiences were largely comprised of women, children, and youth," yet "whenever there was a civil rights rally, the platform was filled predominately by males," with women and youth often left out.[21]

The only woman who officially spoke at the march was Daisy Bates, former president of the Arkansas branch of the NAACP, who earned fame for her leadership in integrating Little Rock Central High School. Bates was a substitute speaker for Myrlie Evers, who was supposed to give a speech on behalf of several female civil rights leaders. Bates spoke for one minute; her speech pledged the continued support of women in the fight for civil rights. Bates's speech was safe and did not go against the male power structure of the movement, but the next scheduled female leader was a wild card. Gloria Richardson, cofounder of the Cambridge Nonviolent Action Committee in Maryland, was scheduled to speak for two minutes at the march. As soon as she reached the podium, her microphone was taken away and she was only able to say hello. Richardson's reputation as a strong and powerful Black female voice who fought racism and sexism threatened male leadership in the civil rights movement, and that was unacceptable, especially in such a public arena as the march. In the end, Black women were not given the platform to speak about their contributions or ideas for advancing the cause of civil rights; instead, they were relegated to sitting quietly on the platform as men spoke. According to Height this was "disappointing, because actually women were an active part of the whole effort. . . . Women were the backbone of the movement."[22]

In response to not having Black women speakers at the march, Height held an NCNW meeting called "After the March" to discuss what Black women should do so that their voices would be heard: "We began to realize that if we did not address issues such as this, if we did not demand our rights, we were not going to get them." The women at the meeting decided that they "needed to be much more aggressive in dealing with male leadership in the movement."[23] Despite her frustration with the sexist nature of the movement, Height continued to work for racial equality because she understood that racial equality was ultimately tied to democracy. She, like all the Black women trailblazers before her, was fighting an uphill battle against racism and sexism for inclusion in the democratic process.

After the passage of the Voting Rights Act of 1965, the voices of Black women could no longer be contained. Black women could now vote, and they did so in significant numbers, taking every opportunity to show America that democracy was in capable hands. In 1968, Shirley Chisholm became the first Black woman elected to Congress, beginning a wave of Black women leadership at some of the highest levels in government that ultimately led to the election of Kamala Harris, a woman of color, as the first female vice president of the United States. Harris's powerful acceptance speech to the office of vice president was one that legitimized and gave voice to the Black women who came before her.

The legacy of strong Black female voices in the democratic process is just as powerful today as it was in the past. Black female voices like Alicia Garza, Patrisse Cullors, and Ayọ [formerly Opal] Tometi, founders of the Black Lives Matter movement, continue to echo the strength and passion of numerous past sheroes. They and other Black female voices unapologetically make the United States live up to its principles of democracy for all. As Cullors stated in a BBC interview, "What I'm excited about is that my child gets to say that his mom, alongside other fierce black women, did everything that she could to make this place better for us. I'm excited about that history being told."[24] The history is being told, and the rightful place of Black female voices as the backbone of democracy is unquestionable.

Notes

1 Joe Biden and Kamala Harris Election Acceptance and Victory Speech Transcripts, November 7, 2020, https://www.rev.com/blog/transcripts/joe-biden-kamala-harris-address-nation-after-victory-speech-transcript-november-7.

2 Diana Ramey Berry and Kali Nicole Gross, *A Black Woman's History of the United States* (Boston: Beacon, 2020). This book provides several stories of women throughout history who led when Black men were unable to, particularly during enslavement and in telling the story of Isabel de Olvera, a free woman of African descent who fought for justice.

3 On April 23, 1863, Frances Gage reprinted Sojourner Truth's "Woman's Rights Convention" speech in the *New York Independent*. Scholars including Nell Painter question whether Truth actually spoke the specific words "Ar'n't I a woman" or if they were attributed to her by Frances Gage. The slogan, regardless of whether it was said by Truth herself, captures the gist of her presentation.

4 Nell Irvin Painter, *Sojourner Truth: A Life, a Symbol* (New York: Norton, 1996), 166–67.

5 Marilyn Richardson, ed., *Maria Stewart, America's First Black Political Writer: Essays and Speeches* (Bloomington: Indiana University Press, 1987), 38.

6 Maria Stewart, "Religion and the Pure Principles of Morality: The Sure Foundation on Which We Must Build" (October 1831), Teaching American History, https://teachingamericanhistory.org/document/religion-and-the-pure-principles-of-morality-the-sure-foundation-on-which-we-must-build.

7 Jane Rhodes, *Mary Ann Shadd Cary: The Black Press and Protest in the Nineteenth Century* (Bloomington: Indiana University Press, 1999).

8. Ellen Carol DuBois, *Suffrage: Women's Long Battle for the Vote* (New York: Simon & Schuster, 2020), 289.
9. Alison Parker, *Unceasing Militant: The Life of Mary Church Terrell* (Chapel Hill: University of North Carolina Press, 2020).
10. Mary Church Terrell, *A Colored Woman in a White World, Selection 1* (1940), Papers of Mary Church Terrell, container 35, folder 4, Library of Congress.
11. Mary Church Terrell et al., *The Progress of Colored Women* (Washington, D.C.: Smith Brothers, 1898), Library of Congress, www.loc.gov/item/90898298/.
12. Nannie Helen Burroughs, "Black Women and Reform," *Crisis,* August 1915, 187.
13. Charles Erwin Wilson, *To Secure These Rights: The Reports of the President's Committee on Civil Rights* (President's Committee on Civil Rights, 1947).
14. Bettye Collier-Thomas and V. P. Franklin, eds., *Sisters in the Struggle: African American Women in the Civil Rights–Black Power Movement* (New York: New York University Press, 2001), 34.
15. Barbara Ransby, *Ella Baker and the Black Freedom Movement: A Radical Democratic Vision* (Chapel Hill: University of North Carolina Press, 2005), 105–48.
16. Ransby, *Ella Baker,* 170–209.
17. Ella Baker, "Bigger Than a Hamburger," *Southern Patriot,* May 1960, https://www.crmvet.org/docs/sncc2.htm.
18. Dennis J. Urban, "The Women of SNCC: Struggle, Sexism, and the Emergence of Feminist Consciousness, 1960–66," *International Social Science Review* 77, nos. 3/4 (2002): 185–90.
19. Dorothy Height, *Open Wide the Freedom Gates: A Memoir* (New York: Public Affairs, 2003).
20. Dorothy Height, "'We Wanted the Voice of a Woman to Be Heard': Black Women and the 1963 March on Washington," in Collier-Thomas and Franklin, *Sisters in the Struggle,* 86–88.
21. Height, "We Wanted the Voice," 86.
22. Height, 87.
23. Height, 89.
24. "Black Lives Matter Founders: We Fought to Change History and We Won," BBC News, November 20, 2020, https://www.bbc.com/news/world-us-canada-55106268.

3

Constructing a Way Forward

Civil Rights and the National Council of Negro Women

CASSANDRA NEWBY-ALEXANDER

On a windy October evening in 1940, Vivian Carter Mason, a prominent member and future president of the National Council of Negro Women (NCNW), read the organization's seven-point program that was adopted during their three-day conference. In the adopted plan, the NCNW proclaimed that people of color in America must integrate at every level and capacity in society if they were to survive and thrive. Mason announced that the NCNW condemned segregation, discrimination, and inequity in every manifestation from the federal, state, or local governments or other source. She concluded by arguing that people of color have the "right to live under this form of government and equally so we shall defend our right to be free men and free women and to continue to contribute to America and the world the rich heritage of the years."[1]

This seven-point plan was the first national salvo cast by an African American organization demanding equal rights for both men and women. Calling on President Franklin Roosevelt, Mason wanted him to issue an executive order allowing Blacks to be admitted as equals in America's armed forces and condemning segregation at every level in American society. Although presented by Mason, it was the vision of Mary McLeod Bethune, president of the NCNW, that the voices and activities of women would be interwoven into the civil rights movement. Using the NCNW and its partner organizations, which included the National Association for the Advancement of Colored People (NAACP), the League of Women Voters, and the Young Women's Christian Association (YWCA), Bethune fashioned the fight for equality with intentionality and a more global perspective that transcended race, class, gender, and nationality.² Indeed, Bethune wrote about her unwavering commitment to this cause in a June 1941 article titled "Faith That Moved a Dump Heap," in which she said, "I am my mother's daughter, and the drums of Africa still beat in my heart. They will not let me rest while there is a single Negro boy or girl without a chance to prove his worth."³ Even after her death in 1955, Bethune's vision and her role as what Sharlene Sinegal-DeCuir described in the previous chapter as a torchbearer for American democracy continued as new generations of African American women stood on the proverbial shoulders of their ancestors forging a pathway that promoted an image of agency and power.

Despite the work of these women's groups, female activists were left unrecognized, marginalized, and discriminated against within these civil rights organizations. This was especially true for southern Black women, whose leadership was seldom recognized even though they were the ones who initiated the protests. Documenting their invisibility, Bernice McNair Barnett argued that these women's activities were previously erased because of their gender, race, and class. Nevertheless, Black women were the bridge leaders whose intricate network of supporters enabled the civil rights efforts to succeed. Jo Ann Gibson Robinson, a professor at Alabama State College, is an example of a leader who tapped into the women's organizations to create synergy and mobilization for civil rights activities. Writing her memoir, *The Montgomery Bus Boycott and the Women Who Started It* (1987), Robinson highlighted how she and other women were the actual organizers and implementers of the Montgomery bus boycott. She attempted to correct the false narrative of an all-male leadership of the boycott, detailing how her organization, the Women's Political Council (formed in 1949), actually planned and sustained the boycott through regular meetings and a support network. Robinson's activities exemplified those of bridge leaders. She, like many other bridge leaders, tapped into Black women's shared experiences, identities, and organizations to cross the boundaries of public and private life to create a mobilizing network during the fight for civil rights.⁴ And while Black men were important partners in this effort, such as the leadership of E. D. Nixon and Rufus Lewis, the work of women's groups was critical in the fight for civil rights. The patriarchal nature of leadership in American society, and particularly among African Americans, meant that African American women's leadership was excluded in favor of "'the great man' leadership" model.⁵ Nevertheless, women were the bridge leaders whose intricate network of supporters enabled the civil rights efforts to succeed.

Despite the lack of recognition, Black women set aside these indignities in favor of supporting the advancement of their race as a whole because of the nonnegotiable and intertwined nature of race and gender for them. While countless historians have addressed the marginalization of female activists, the overall discussions about civil rights, especially with regard to voting rights, have continued the male-centric trope that highlights their work exclusively. This chapter, however, repositions the narrative to focus on the work of the NCNW as illustrating the grassroots work of African American women who were the bridge leaders and builders. The NCNW, in particular, was a national organization that crowdsourced all the women's organizations so that they spoke with a single national voice. As such, the organization was instrumental in framing the goals and methodologies of the modern civil rights movement by using its comprehensive network of clubs to initiate and coordinate grassroots efforts that resulted in removing many of the legal vestiges of institutionalized racism. It was Black women who navigated the challenges posed between voicing their concerns about gender discrimination within organizations such as the SCLC, the NAACP, SNCC, and the Black Panthers with maintaining the outward veneer of a united front.

Bethune said that Black women, by "the very force of circumstances," had been expected to play a "subtle and indirect" role in the larger civil rights movement. The Black female activist had not, Bethune insisted, "always been permitted a place in the front ranks where she could show her face and make her voice heard with effect." She had, however, "been quick to seize every opportunity which presented itself to come more and more into the open and strive directly for the uplift of the race and nation."[6] Bethune had an unapologetic vision for how African American women could claim the full scope of their freedom and civil rights; that vision differed fundamentally from that of the lens through which society defined leadership in the civil rights movement. For Bethune, whose agency represented countless generations of African American women, civil rights was not just about freedom from racial limitations. Rather, it included the removal of gender and national boundaries. Since its formation by Bethune in 1935, for example, the NCNW sponsored international discourse and activities with women because they understood that when it came to human rights and social justice, nation-states were dominated by white males and therefore did not address issues involving women specifically, people of color, or colonialism. As such, Bethune reshaped the voice of African American women through the NCNW, which created a platform to address what the

NCNW saw as the triple threat (race, class, gender) facing Black women. Their purpose was "to advocate and facilitate African American women's political connections with the federal government" with the idea that this would enable them to transform their nation and the world.[7] They were unconcerned, however, with getting individual credit for their efforts.

The posture taken by twentieth-century Black women leaders germinated in the post–Civil War period with the emergence of strong self-help organizations led by African American women. Initially, these organizations were formed in each community's social center: the church. Bereft of public services such as orphanages, retirement homes, nursery schools, kindergartens, and libraries, women pooled their resources for the moral, financial, and material advancement of the Black community. The impulse for organizing these clubs arose whenever and wherever there was an urgent social and civic need. The virtual absence of social welfare institutions in many southern communities that assisted Blacks, and the frequent exclusion of Blacks from citywide cultural engagement and activities, led Black women to create opportunities for themselves and their communities. Indeed, when African American men cast their ballots prior to passage of the Nineteenth Amendment, women were determined to participate, even if it was only ceremonial. In Norfolk, Virginia, for example, women organized parades and ceremonies at local churches that highlighted the importance of voting. After the church programs, the women marched side by side with their husbands to the polling places as the men cast their votes in each election. In Louisiana, a similar women-based voting initiative occurred and eventually resulted in the 1878 publication of a pamphlet demanding their voting rights.[8]

Black women likewise led one of the most important efforts to achieve racial equality: the campaign for educational advancement. This cadre of African American women leaders benefited from an educational system created in the post–Civil War years that formed a gateway to middle-class professional life. They came of age at this critical juncture in American history as racism, segregation, and discrimination continued and were seemingly incompatible cohorts with society's emphasis on social advancement and progressive thought. This group of educated middle-class women set the nation on fire with their enthusiasm, organizational skills, determination, and vision for themselves and the African American community, often defying conventional expectations of gender and race. They were nascent "race women" who used the language of protest to advocate for the advancement of their community. The appearance of this new elite galvanized the community's economy and educational structure and transformed the expectations of its members. Emphasizing education and social justice, these leaders operated both in the public sector as professionals and within the social sector as economic, religious, fraternal, social, and civic organizers.[9]

By the end of the nineteenth century, Freedom's First Generation emerged to take a leadership role on the regional, national, and world stages through various organizations that had their roots in the antebellum world. This generation moved away from the individualized approach to a collaborative organization of women's clubs that promoted "social interaction and self-education." These clubs were reform-oriented, organized, and willing to combat racism by fostering a clear self-identity and solidarity as Black women.[10] The foundational institutions formed by free Blacks during the antebellum years were an important starting point as this new generation expanded their agency through economic, educational, fraternal, and religious pathways. And while most historical interpretations have focused on African American male agency, the backbone undergirding all of these organizations was African American women whose efforts resulted in their emergence as pioneers in health care, childcare, education, civil rights, employment, and neighborhood growth and development. Leaders quickly emerged who championed these areas, developing strategies to remedy the most egregious human rights violations.

Navigating societal pressures for those who assumed leadership positions in women's organizations in the century that brokered advancement in gender rights and roles was challenging, and their achievements were both extraordinary and uneven. Initially, Black women worked closely within their communities, supporting the leadership of African American men because they "realize[d] that to get ahead they [had] to work with the black man because he [had] been so beaten down it would be a form of self-destruction to do otherwise."[11] Women understood that society had so devalued Black men that Black women lessened their visible ambitions to ensure that Black men could emerge as leaders.

Yet Black women fighters were always a part of the American landscape. Indeed, they were the major strategists, organizers, and ground troops for civil rights efforts, although their activities and leadership roles were often ignored in part because they chose to operate within their networks of kinship, church membership, and communities. For example, when Elizabeth Cady Stanton and Susan B. Anthony severed ties with the American Civil Rights Association and formed the National Woman Suffrage Association over the idea that white women should receive the right to vote prior to

Black men, African American women, such as Anna Julia Cooper, countered this indignity, cofounding the Colored Women's League as their national voice.[12]

Black women, according to Rosalee Clawson and John Clark in their 2003 article, "The Attitudinal Structure of African American Women Party Activists" cut their proverbial teeth through their activism that included "organizing, mobilizing, and fundraising" in "women's clubs and the black church."[13] Despite their successes with grassroots organizing, educational advancement in the community, and leadership in the Progressive movement, however, Black women were not recognized by their male counterparts as spokespersons or leaders. Instead, they were expected to support the largely patriarchal society that focused on race, with the expectation that gender would be a side note. For example, while Ida B. Wells and Mary Church Terrell were among the founders of the NAACP, not until 1979 did Margaret Wilson become the first Black woman to head the NAACP. Her four-year tenure was controversial, however, and ended when she attempted to fire the organization's executive director, Benjamin Hooks. Wilson's dismissal left the embittered former president claiming that discrimination and male chauvinism were the cause. Another progressive civil rights organization, the National Urban League, has never seen a woman serve as president. Yet, for Black women, race and gender were and are inseparable. And it is this position that has given Black women a unique perspective of public policy and the remedies needed for society's challenges.[14]

It is therefore not surprising that one of the first national organizations that emerged carrying this banner for Black women was the National Association of Colored Women (NACW), founded by Mary Church Terrell. Terrell was one of the nation's most committed advocates for racial and gender equality. The organization's motto, "Lifting as We Climb," symbolized the efforts of women activists of this and later generations who understood that the eventual fate of African Americans was in the group's rise to power and gaining civil rights not limited to simply the rights of individuals. The history of discrimination and slavery singularly focused on those of African descent with the laws and practices limiting anyone to that designation, regardless of individual accomplishment, financial circumstances, or status. The NACW chose not to enter into the political fray to fight discrimination and inequality directly, although some of their most prominent members did so as individuals. Instead, the NACW sought to strengthen the African American community by building a coalition from within. Because of Terrell, the pathway she navigated did not aim to change the social position of women. Rather, it was to improve the status of all African Americans. In fact, an early priority was the establishment of pre-K and early childhood educational institutions and day care nurseries.[15] This more moderate approach did not bode well for Blacks by the end of World War I as white racism and violence reemerged in an unprecedented way.

Consequently, the NACW shifted away from the more conciliatory position favored by sympathetic white liberals by the 1920s. As Black men were pushed out of politics in public life, Black women through organizations like the NACW affirmed their position at the center of Black culture. This shift was bolstered by Black business success, which created a powerful economic foundation for the Black community, especially the middle classes, causing some to sink into what many regarded as complacency with regard to racial advancement. Moving away from individualized attacks, which sought to remove racially restrictive laws and practices, a new guard of Black leaders adopted a more collective organizational strategy. This new approach meant that some Black organizations found themselves pitted against the NAACP during these years, which appeared to be more focused on white philanthropic support that favored working within the Jim Crow system rather than forcing real change in America. Marcus Garvey's Universal Negro Improvement Association and the Brotherhood of Sleeping Car Porters and Maids were two national organizations that opposed the more moderate positions of the NAACP. Instead, these two groups wanted to see economic independence, thereby removing pressure to satisfy moderate white philanthropists.[16]

Pressures from increased discrimination, especially under Woodrow Wilson's presidency, resulted in an alliance beginning in the 1930s between some of these organizations and the NAACP, despite their concerns over losing financial support. The Legal Defense Fund of the NAACP, headed by Charles Hamilton Houston, launched a legal offense challenging unequal opportunities in a college education and unequal pay for teachers. Yet the NAACP did not embrace challenging Jim Crow directly until Houston's legal strategy gained headway.[17]

The NAACP's position refusing to directly confront Jim Crow quickly hit a wall once it collided with the goals of Black women's organizations and leadership. This was especially an issue since the leadership of many of the branches of the NAACP featured women whose stance often differed from those of the national leadership. A. Clement MacNeal, for example, served as an executive committee member of the Chicago NAACP. Her savvy leadership was on display when NAACP executive secretary Walter White and assistant secretary Roy Wilkins instructed the Chicago branch to ignore discriminatory practices at the Sears store in Chicago because protests might anger William Rosenwald, who had taken over as chair of the Sears and Roebuck board after his father Julius Rosenwald's death in 1932, and who was not as committed to helping African Americans as his father had been. Therefore, the fears of the NAACP leadership that William Rosenwald could withdraw financial and political support from the NAACP had some credibility. MacNeal, however, was livid, especially because this discrimination directly affected some of Chicago's most prominent Black women. Prior to Rosenwald's intervention in the Chicago branch's "Don't Buy Where You Can't Work" boycott in 1933, White and Wilkins were in support. Once the boycott began cutting into Sears's profits, however, the NAACP's national leadership was contacted by Rosenwald. Forced to suppress the boycott, the NACW instead took up the effort during its July 1933 conference in Chicago, putting pressure on the NAACP's new position.[18]

Clearly, this coordinated runaround between the NACW and the Chicago NAACP branch highlighted how Black women would not allow Black men to impede their efforts, especially when women were harmed. Adding to the pressure was the appearance of Daisy Lampkin, regional field secretary for the NAACP, at the NACW conference. Lampkin was one of the main organizers of the NACW and a member of numerous other Black women's clubs. When she refused to visit the Chicago branch office, this allowed MacNeal to complain to Wilkins and White that the reputation of the NAACP's Chicago branch was on the line, signaling to the NAACP that women could make or break the organization if they disagreed with the leadership. The 1930s were a turning point not only for the NAACP, whose "defensive posture and tactics" were incompatible with the efforts of the day, but for African American women. The Great Depression severely limited the NAACP's funding patterns with two primary groups (Rosenwald and Peabody funds) providing the outside funding while the branches were the primary sources of internal funding. Feeling more empowered because the primary funding sources were branch-based, this new guard of women wanted the NAACP to divest itself of its dependence on white patronage by focusing instead on economic, social, and legal discrimination. Afterward, lip service was paid to restructuring the NAACP by allowing branches to be "centers of economic and political education and agitation." Eventually, the more conservative voices prevailed, pigeonholing the changes demanded as too radical. Ironically, while the NAACP got behind an anti-lynching agenda as well as equalization in higher education and teacher salary equity, these were seen as less controversial and did not threaten the NAACP's structural foundations, and they were already being championed by African American women.[19]

As African Americans migrated to urban locales, in both the North and South, the vast support network created by Black clubwomen became even more essential. This network conveyed information, protest strategies, and political tactics and agendas. For example, as influential as the NAACP in Chicago was, its reach was limited because of the competition with other Black organizations that looked out for the interests of African Americans. The result was that when the Brotherhood of Sleeping Car Porters and Maids (BSCP) mobilized, it was initially met with a tirade of negativity and pushback from the established Black middle class, which included clergymen, the press, and politicians. Nevertheless, the BSCP created a network to educate the community about this labor union that included influential women in the NAACP such as Ida B. Wells-Barnett, newspaperwoman and anti-lynching advocate. Moreover, the South Parkway branch of Chicago's YWCA invested time and resources into championing the interests of Black female industrial workers, hiring Thelma McWorter in the 1930s to teach and train female workers about labor laws, labor unions, and coping with industrial work.[20]

Many of the women in the NACW were progressives and, as such, sought to confront the challenges posed by a burgeoning urban society that directly impacted the married and single African American women who made up the majority of the Black workforce. Working collaboratively with other women's organizations, Mary Church Terrell sought to focus the NACW's attention toward the social welfare aspect of progressivism, which was solution oriented. The Federation of Colored Women's Clubs in Illinois took up the challenge, becoming the first to open the Phyllis Wheatley House for Girls in 1896, whose namesake was the famous enslaved poetess of the eighteenth century. Following a mission similar to that of other settlement houses springing up in the nation, Black women sought to provide those migrating into urban areas with accommodations, career education, and civic engagement that organizations such as the YWCA denied to them because of racism. The NACW supported the Phyllis Wheatley clubs and their agendas.[21]

During these early years, the emergence of the Phyllis Wheatley YWCA was critical because it provided a space where civil rights discussions and efforts were debated, cultivated, and acted on. Throughout the nation, YWCAs served as settlement houses, vocational training facilities, employment agencies, and gathering spaces for those who found themselves in unfamiliar cities and towns and with no support systems. African American women, in particular, created the Phyllis Wheatley branches because the national YWCAs restricted access to whites only or segregated Black women into the "Negro" Ys that later became known as the Phyllis Wheatley Ys. Most importantly, the Phyllis Wheatley YWCAs taught their guests life skills, academic information, and lessons in civil rights and civil liberties, including voting rights. And the women who worked within these organizations were social workers, educators, attorneys, and professionals whose efforts were intentional in building a community of advocates and active participants.[22] It was in these organizations and settlement houses that "Black women maneuvered this intersectionality [the voting rights debate between white women and Black men] addressing their specific needs as to both women's rights and 'improving the lives of African Americans.'"[23]

By 1935, Mary McLeod Bethune emerged as an important voice that articulated this intersectionality. Indeed, as Martha Jones opined in *Vanguard*, Bethune worked at the "political crossroads" both in bridging the late nineteenth-century woman's era with the modern women's movement and in negotiating disparate approaches to working within Jim Crow America. As the founder of the NCNW, Bethune believed that Black women needed a national political voice and platform, and she envisioned that the organization would bring leaders from various women's organizations together, liaising with other groups such as the NAACP, the Urban League, the YWCA, and the League of Women Voters to combat racism, discrimination, and segregation at the state and national levels. The goal was to plan and direct Black women to galvanize their collective power politically, economically, socially, educationally, and culturally at every level to effect change. By building bridges and collaborations with every Black organization, especially those that included women, the collective power would unite women toward a common goal and foster leadership that would effect change. As a result, she successfully initiated one of the most important vehicles for African American women to speak with one harmonious voice about the importance of civil rights. She was a practical and aspirational leader, incorporating the philosophies of both W.E.B. Du Bois and Booker T. Washington into her philosophy and outlook. She avoided challenging Washington's exclusive support of vocational education while spearheading a curriculum that trained professionals. She formed a close alliance with Washington's wife, Margaret, once she became president of the NACW, to better navigate her relationship with Booker T. Bethune also accessed Du Bois's network to her advantage; she cultivated alternative northern supporters to achieve her goals, such as creating a Talented Tenth leadership group of African American women while also working within the system. Bethune first gained notice as the founder of the Daytona Normal and Industrial School (later Institute) for Negro Girls in Daytona Beach, Florida, in 1904. By 1912, with the help of white philanthropist James Gamble, the school expanded and, in 1923, merged with Cookman Institute, creating the Bethune-Cookman College with one thousand students. So successful was her influence on the planning and management of the college that it became the first institution of higher education for Blacks in Florida that promoted both the liberal arts and vocational preparation within the Bethune-Cookman College curriculum. And like most Black women presidents of colleges, Bethune saw her leadership style as a consensus-building process for decision-making. Combined with the purposeful objectives of a transformational leader, her governance was also reflective of the early twentieth century's racial uplift paradigm.[24]

Bethune's leadership of Bethune-Cookman College situated her to serve on numerous national commissions and organizations, including the National Commission for Child Welfare under Presidents Calvin Coolidge and Herbert Hoover, president of the Florida State Federation of Colored Women's Clubs, and the National Association of Colored Women's Clubs. It was through the NACW (when she served as president in 1927) that she first met Eleanor Roosevelt. This growing friendship continued, especially after Bethune's formation of the National Council of Negro Women. Eventually, her close friendship with Eleanor, which continued until Bethune's death in 1955, led to her appointment as director of the Division of Negro Affairs (originally the Office of Minority Affairs) in the National Youth Administration. This appointment was the first time a federal office was created for a Black woman.[25]

Some historians speculate that Bethune's friendship with Eleanor Roosevelt, who openly opposed racism and discrimination, helped her shift Black votes from the Republican to the Democratic Party, using voting rights as the backdrop to reviewing issues of sexism, racism, lynchings, and intimidation.[26] For Bethune, "self-help Christian Morality, and the embodiment of the National Association of Colored Women's motto of 'Lifting as We Climb' were all central to Black women's clubs during the Jim Crow Era."[27] As such, Bethune's position as the first Black female advisor in 1936 to President Franklin D. Roosevelt and later to President Harry S. Truman opened educational and economic opportunities for Blacks and generated optimism that change was on the horizon.[28]

Bethune's influence led her to an appointment on President Franklin Roosevelt's "Black Cabinet," formally known as the Federal Council on Negro Affairs, beginning in 1936. As the only woman and educator on the council, her efforts were critical for both women and children. While the council focused primarily on encouraging a broader inclusion of Blacks in New Deal programs, the group also advised New Deal officials about the civil rights needs of African Americans. President Truman appointed Bethune to his Civil Rights Commission and as a consultant on the San Francisco Conference that wrote the charter for the United Nations.[29]

Like most Black women who engaged in transformative community action, Bethune knew that women had a central role in the struggle for civil rights. Playing up the tenets of sisterhood, Bethune called for unity and public action, arguing that women could no longer afford to limit their activities to "church, home, and family." Rather, they must work for systematic change that required active participation as leaders in mainstream politics. Thus, she advised women to take a holistic approach that would include political and civic rights, educational opportunities, housing needs, and public support to counter the challenges created by institutionalized racism and discrimination. As the director of Negro affairs, Bethune helped boost college enrollment for Blacks and spearheaded the creation of a special grant fund for those pursuing graduate degrees. She also supported labor unionization and advocated for working class women's rights, particularly expanding public housing, social welfare support, and social security to include coverage for domestic workers.[30]

Clearly, the 1930s were a turning point for the NCNW, whose activist posture and tactics were incompatible with the more moderate civil rights efforts of the day. Representing a new guard of "bridge leaders," the organization led the way for women to become more radicalized by believing they must be on the vanguard of change. Other NCNW leaders also echoed Bethune's position, including the third president of the NCNW, Vivian Carter Mason. As early as 1940, Mason addressed her sorority sisters, the Alpha Kappa Alphas or AKAs, during their luncheon at the New York World's Fair. In what many described as a fiery speech, Mason drew on her experience under Mayor Fiorello Henry La Guardia during the 1930s as director of the Division of Social Services in New York City's Department of Welfare, arguing that women needed to awaken to how the columns of economic and social discrimination, widespread unemployment, armament buildup, and the denial of civil liberties in the courts were still a threat that must be defeated.[31] She reminded the gathering that "'things worth working for may be some day worth dying for.'"[32]

By the 1940s, the NCNW claimed to have had a membership of five hundred thousand women, many of whom were accomplished civic activists and professionals. World War II instigated a slightly different tactic of transformation for many African American women. Adopting a three-point program that involved equality in military service and preparation for African Americans, the program also called for integration in the military. Determined to push for change, Black women also made efforts to reinitiate partnerships with whites to advocate for equality and desegregation. As early as 1919, efforts were made through groups such as the Commission on Interracial Cooperation (CIC) that opposed lynching, mob violence, and racial bias in education and society in general. Although the CIC was based in Atlanta, it spearheaded local committees throughout the nation. A women's committee was created by 1921 that focused specifically on matters critical to women. In the 1930s, the CIC had over eight hundred committees, and Will W. Alexander, an administrator with President Roosevelt's Resettlement Administration and the Farm Security Administration, served as its executive director with a board that included the president of Morehouse College, John Hope, and his wife, Lugenia Burns Hope, who headed the Women's Committee. By the next decade, the Women's Council for Interracial Cooperation (WCIC) emerged as a powerful organization with hundreds of branches. Vivian Carter Mason understood its potential, encouraging the NCNW membership to form branches in their local communities. Mason even led the creation of one in her hometown of Norfolk, Virginia, in 1942.[33]

Determined to eradicate the more egregious segregation issues in Norfolk, Mason called together a group of influential women who were interested in making a difference. Many of the white women were unaware of the extent to which segregation and discrimination sustained impoverished communities who lived in primitive apartments, some without flooring. By 1945, eight African American and eleven white women initially agreed to form the local chapter of the WCIC. Within a year, this number quickly increased to eighty-six women who wrote and submitted countless reports on the horrific conditions in Norfolk because of racism. Nevertheless, change was slow, even though pressure was mounting because some of the women were the wives of city council members and prominent business leaders.

The primary advancement accomplished by the WCIC was their influence in the newly created Norfolk Housing and Redevelopment Administration (NHRA), which created better housing for poorer Blacks and made slight improvements in some of the African American schools. Despite her best efforts, Mason was unable to move Norfolk's white leadership away from racial management to real racial progress.[34] Resistance was deeply engrained in the fabric of many communities, especially in the South. Mason understood all too well that African American women had to explore other avenues to accomplish their goals.

In 1953, Mason became the third president of the NCNW, which allowed her to directly push her agenda to internationalize issues that involved all women of color and to specifically push for complete civil rights for African Americans in the United States. She believed that international pressure might succeed where interracial cooperation did not. A year later, the nation was rocked by news that the U.S. Supreme Court had ruled that racial segregation in public schools was inherently unequal in *Brown v. Board of Education of Topeka, Kansas*. The NCNW positioned itself to be at the table with Mason leading the charge. The NCNW worked closely with organizations throughout the country as part of the vast network created by Bethune, such as the NAACP, who heralded the announcement of the decision as an important step forward for the nation. For Mason, the NCNW would use this opportunity to eliminate all barriers for African Americans. As a member of the NAACP board of directors, Mason was involved in devising strategies to implement this ruling across the board. Ever the collaborator, Mason continued partnering with the NAACP, the YWCA, the AKAs, and other organizations in an effort to eliminate barriers to civil rights, especially as opposition mounted in many quarters throughout America but especially among white southerners.[35]

Although the civil rights movement in the 1950s and 1960s was carried out primarily by women, most were ignored in favor of Black males in leadership roles. Consider the cases of *Brown v. Board of Education*, the Montgomery bus boycott, Emmett Till, and the Student Nonviolent Coordinating Committee activities. Most of the attention was given to the men who led the efforts rather than the women who either brought the cases forward or ensured that these activities were organized and implemented. Even the majority of Black Panthers were women, although few photographs and articles included so much as a mention of the women leaders of these chapters.[36]

Expectantly, African American women throughout the nation, independently and as part of their network of organizations, rallied to support efforts to desegregate. And for most, the objective was not integration so much as equalization. As long as schools remained segregated, African American children would receive resources and accommodations that were less than those provided to white children. In multiple cities and counties, Black women supported community challenges to enforce the *Brown* decision that included housing and providing sanctuary to legal representatives challenging noncompliance, galvanizing community support, backing lawsuits, signing petitions, and educating the children when white officials closed schools. These activities often led to a concerted effort to increase civic advocacy and voter registration, and supporting African American political candidates.[37]

National women's organizations understood that it was through grassroots organizations that they could empower the Black community and help breach the barriers of prejudice and segregation. As now, these earlier groups were unwilling to be inhibited by gender roles only. They struggled with both the milieu of the "feminine mystique" and their advocacy for civil rights. Until the latter part of the twentieth century, America continued to constrain women to concentrate on educational pursuits that enhanced the community rather than on careers that allowed for "self-expression and personal enrichment." Concerning themselves with issues of importance to the Black community, the Black women's club movement effectively harnessed the collective power of women professionals to have an impact on the community. Some of the notables included Fannie Lou Hamer, Josephine St. Pierre Ruffin, Jo Ann Gibson Robinson, Rosa Parks, Ella Jo Baker, Evelyn Butts, and Pauli Murray, advocates for civil rights, voting rights, and social justice.

Jo Ann Gibson Robinson was a local activist in Montgomery, Alabama, whose singular focus on eliminating all forms of discrimination and violence against Black women and African Americans in general resulted in change. Indeed, Robinson was one of the primary planners of the Montgomery bus boycott. Her efforts through the Women's Political Council (WPC) also helped sustain their efforts, especially since most of the bus riders were women. She led efforts to plan, initiate, and sustain the bus boycott. As a member of the WPC in Montgomery that was dedicated to increasing voter registration, civic engagement, and aiding women who were victimized by sexual and physical violence, the organization responded quickly once Rosa Parks was arrested in 1955 for refusing to comply with the racist bus policies in the city. Robinson spearheaded this effort, calling for a one-day boycott through a circular that convinced the ministers to support their efforts fearing they would alienate their predominantly female congregants. This clarion call to action eventually led to a sustained 381-day campaign that eliminated all discriminatory transportation policies in the city of Montgomery. She also helped establish the Montgomery Improvement Association (MIA), which selected Dr. Martin Luther King Jr. as its president, in part because unlike Robinson, who was an English professor and state employee at Alabama State College, King was independently employed and beyond the direct reach of the white establishment. Working quietly in the background allowed Robinson to continue her teaching at Alabama State. However, when determined to support the student sit-ins, Robinson resigned her teaching position rather than comply with the political pressure from the state.[38]

Black women always occupied the intersectionality between race and gender, but by the 1960s, their voice emerged as a publicly powerful influence that reimagined the Democratic Party as a liberal political force representing progressive ideals and diverse voices. Paradoxically, despite their grassroots efforts, Black women were relegated to support roles rather than leadership positions, even in organizations they founded. However, it was Black women who forced a shift within the political parties, with white supporters of segregation moving into the Republican Party while everyone else entered the larger tent of the Democratic Party. This did not mean that the Democratic Party embraced inclusivity. Rather, it was the party more willing to support liberal ideas that benefited African Americans. Using their power as bridge leaders who connected the local community activism with political activism, Black women were at the forefront of all the civil rights efforts. Ella Jo Baker, for example, was the founder of the Student Nonviolent Coordinating Committee (SNCC). Yet she was never selected to be the president of that organization even though her leadership skills placed her as a highly respected community organizer. Other notable women such as Rosa Parks and Fannie Lou Hamer were similarly respected but marginalized as community advocates rather than leaders.[39]

Baker framed the intellectual and programmatic foundations for SNCC. She rejected the artificial divisions between the educated middle classes and the undereducated working classes as problematic for the civil rights movement that needed all voices, ideas, and experiences to defeat racism and inequality. Perhaps it was her willingness to work at every level, not just as part of the leadership, that resulted in her marginalization as simply one of the members.[40] The involvement of Black women in SNCC, more than any other organization, was the catalyst that transformed their consciousness about their power and womanhood and ignited a feminist response. Although Ella Jo Baker was the founder of SNCC and its ranks were filled with African American women, the operations of the organization still expected women to be on the front lines and serving in traditional female roles at their headquarters: cooking, cleaning, and doing office work.[41]

Similarly, narratives that canonized Rosa Parks "as an older woman who defied segregation laws in Montgomery, Alabama in 1955 by refusing to give up her seat on a bus because she was too tired to move" refuse to see her as a savvy and "'militant race woman.'"[42] By her own confession, Rosa Parks was feisty, most notably when confronting white men who were racists. Danielle McGuire detailed Parks's experiences growing up in Montgomery, Alabama. She was especially disappointed by many of the Black men who feared, despite owning guns, that they would be injured if they stood up to white society's racism and injustices in her area. At the time she was arrested for refusing to comply with the racialized bus policies in Montgomery, forty-two-year-old Parks was an activist who had joined the NAACP as early as 1943, later serving as the local advisor to its Youth Council. Parks had also organized protests against segregation and was finally registered to vote after two rejections. She also attended training at Tennessee's Highlander Folk School for nonviolent resistance especially following the *Brown* decision.[43]

Jeanne Theoharis's *The Rebellious Life of Mrs. Rosa Parks* (2013) drove home the legacy of Parks as more than the Montgomery bus boycott, despite the determination of previous writers who depicted her as an "accidental midwife" devoid of a larger political agenda. Parks was an activist with a fully developed plan to destroy racial injustice rather than a fabled woman who was too tired to move out of her seat on a bus. Parks understood that fighting for civil rights was not over, especially considering ongoing efforts to prevent or reverse racial equity. She was particularly outspoken in the 1980s and 1990s as federal and state agencies and courts retreated from the civil rights gains, stressing the need to cultivate youth as the next generation of civil rights activists. Soledad O'Brien's *The Rebellious Life of Mrs. Rosa Parks* ably translated Theoharis's biography into an award-winning documentary, illustrating the real Rosa Parks with film clips, interviews, and a narrative that highlighted the story of a woman who asserted that "'freedom fighters never retire.'"[44]

Despite accounts that focus on the role of Martin Luther King Jr. in the Montgomery bus boycott, it was Black women in Montgomery who constantly brought attention to the disrespectful and brutal treatment of Blacks by white male bus drivers. Women were particularly hard hit because as domestics and cooks, many rode the buses as they traveled to work. Not surprisingly, women banded together as clubwomen to provide mutual support and comfort in the face of this horrendous treatment, which sometimes included threats and racial epithets hurled at them, as well as outright violence. Perhaps it was this reality that resulted in the quick and ongoing support of the boycott. Indeed, Black women formed the WPC in the fall of 1946 to collect stories of police and bus driver abuses, develop leverage with city officials, establish a national network sharing similar accounts with others, and strategize how they could apply pressure to achieve their goals through voting and boycotts. Jo Ann Robinson, an English professor at Alabama State College and a member of the WPC, spoke out passionately about the ill treatment at the hands of these men.[45]

Parks and Robinson, like all the women involved with the movement, were clubwomen and members of the National Council of Negro Women. This enabled the organization to leverage its deep reach into the Black community with effective results. When Dorothy Height became the fourth NCNW president in 1958, she was able to coordinate civil rights activities and initiatives across many different organizations throughout the 1960s until the 1980s. Her deep roots in other numerous organizations, such as the YWCA and the NAACP, meant that men regarded her as a formidable ally. Perhaps this was why she was the only woman invited to be a member of the Taconic Foundation, a philanthropic organization founded by Stephen Currier, a proponent of civil and human rights. Others invited included Whitney Young (National Urban League), A. Philip Randolph (Brotherhood of Sleeping Car Porters), Jack Greenberg (NAACP Legal Defense Fund), James Farmer (Congress on Racial Equality), C. Eric Lincoln (Black Muslims), and Martin Luther King Jr. (Southern Christian Leadership Conference). Later, James Foreman and John Lewis were invited into the group because of their leadership of SNCC. The group examined specific areas, producing a study as a way to solicit donations, including a focus on housing, criminal justice, employment, social agencies, health services, business, and education. For Height, these issues were an important and direct reflection of the NCNW's agenda. Consequently, she insisted that they include the related areas of hunger, children, and social welfare among these agenda items.[46]

Another occasion for Height to push the NCNW to the forefront was following the March on Washington. While transformative for the nation, Bayard Rustin, the primary organizer of the march, refused to include women's voices on the platform. Nevertheless, the day after the march, Height helped assemble women at the NCNW offices with the theme "After the March—What?" This was part of Height's agenda to steer national conversation to focus on a broader range of issues rather than simply discrimination against Blacks. She wanted those issues highlighted by the Taconic Foundation because they were critical to the success of all African Americans. Indeed, Height believed that Black women were the "shock absorbers" of discrimination against Blacks in America and understood that if issues critical to them were ignored during this transformative period, it would be a long time before another opportunity presented itself for those issues to be addressed.[47]

As women ventured into public spaces to participate in civil rights marches and protests, they became more vulnerable to physical and sexual violence from counterprotesters and police. Fannie Lou Hamer spoke about her horrific experiences while in police custody in Greenwood, Mississippi, in June 1963. Dorothy Height went on New York's most popular radio station, WNEW, to discuss the brutalization that Black women experienced in police custody and particularly in southern prisons. She also noted that twenty-four women's groups had gathered firsthand accounts of incidences of brutality and sexual abuse faced by Black women during the civil rights efforts. Unfortunately, these calls for attention were ignored. Undeterred, the following year Height convened a meeting of leaders from the YWCA, the National Council of Catholic Women, the NWNC, the Church Women United, and the National Council of Jewish Women so that they could hear about and discuss the sexual and physical violence directed against Black women. The women formed the group Wednesdays in Mississippi to bring outside resources and institutional attention to these issues. Despite the documentation, most of the white women chose to focus on typical clubwomen's work, such as helping the poor, rather than addressing the sexualized and physical violence against Black women. It is unclear why those issues did not bubble to the surface in the same way as the broader civil rights issues unless one considers the societal misogynist perspective that dominated during that period.[48]

In the aftermath of the civil rights battles that were won with the 1964 Civil Rights Act and the 1965 Voting Rights Act, the journey toward eliminating all barriers to civil rights and liberties was a divided effort. Other organizations, such as the Black Panthers, were vilified by the press and within the larger African American community because of their militancy and the visual attacks against the stereotypes of Blacks as passive and nonviolent. Instead, the Panthers flaunted their Second Amendment rights to brandish guns and engage in vitriolic rhetoric that labeled them in a negative way. Yet the majority of the Panthers were actually women whose work focused on feeding and educating children and building a positive image of Blacks within each community.[49]

Height, like Bethune and many others, believed that "women were the key" to changing the world. By 1966, the NCNW was aware that Black women were frustrated that civil rights initiatives were not yielding the results expected. Calling their new initiative Project Womanpower, the NCNW sought to recruit six thousand Black women into volunteer community service believing that if they were successful in mobilizing, they could correct the injustices in their communities.[50]

The NCNW found its success in bringing together sixty-four national organizations and over two thousand people for the national Convocation on Hunger in 1972. Publicized as the first Black woman's institute, this initiative set in motion an annual conference. These grassroots efforts to provide health care, education, job training, and civic advocacy meant that its reach would go to the heart of the community because it directly engaged women.[51]

Black women demonstrated "a strong and persistent commitment to promote civil rights and equal opportunities for themselves, their families, and their race." They petitioned courts, formed self-help and civil rights groups, published newspapers, books, poems, stories, and music, fought lynchings, and forged the modern civil rights movement.[52] Despite the dilemma of gender and racial prejudice, many African American women worked diligently to deconstruct the culture of prejudice and discrimination that destroyed the lives and opportunities of Blacks. By the latter half of the twentieth century, Black women's rights advocates pierced through the veil that constrained America's long-standing images and expectations.

Middle-class, working-class, rural, urban, professional, domestic, skilled, unskilled, educated, and uneducated Black women played a critical role in the civil rights movement, sharing "their resources, talents, and faith." In the South, Black women were the "backbone of the movement" with many drawing their strength from the church and the support systems they created. However, regardless of the region, the majority of the women were members of the NAACP, the Phyllis Wheatley YWCA, the Citizenship/Freedom Schools, the Highlander Folk School, the NCNW, or the Urban League. The only exception to this illustrious group of supporters were schoolteachers whose support for these civil rights efforts had to be covert because of political pressure that could result in the loss of their jobs.[53]

In the 1980s, these alliances continued with the announcement by the Reverend Benjamin Hooks, executive director of the NAACP, about the importance of coalition building in confronting future civil rights challenges. National women's organizations joined with the NAACP and other civil rights groups to fight against President Ronald Reagan's administration and agenda in creating a more conservative Supreme Court—against what they referred to as the excessively conservative judiciary that demonstrated hostility toward "victims of discrimination." Specifically, these efforts were singularly directed against the confirmation of William H. Rehnquist as chief justice of the U.S. Supreme Court.[54] Even though they eventually lost this battle, this enabled the groups to restart their activities away from the acquisition of civil rights to the maintenance and expansion of those rights and the fight against institutionalized racism. By the 1990s, the recognition that new community organizations must unite with the established ones to create new strategies to build Black unity as the larger community faced challenges of drug abuse and family disassociation.[55]

Yet the ongoing battles of the late twentieth and early twenty-first centuries have raised issues among many Black women who have broken with the traditional lines of power, leadership, church affiliation, or male dominance. Instead, the significant rise of college-educated Black women who have pursued careers in law, public service, and the academy especially has resulted in the emergence of a different pathway in which women are no longer yielding to men as the spokespersons for Black America. Instead, women have come out of the shadows and are taking their agency to the gateways of power, challenging any who question them and demanding change. The women leaders of today are rebuilding the community and focusing on these and other threats, such as the effort to undermine civil rights advancements and voting rights. *And so the battle continues.*

Notes

1 "Women Want Equality in Armed Forces; Condemn Segregation," *Journal and Guide*, November 9, 1940, 4.
2 Helen Rappaport, "Mary McLeod Bethune," *Encyclopedia of Women Social Reformers*, vol. 1 (Santa Barbara, CA: ABC-CLIO, 2001), 75–76.

3 "Women Want Equality in Armed Forces," 4.
4 Belinda Robnett, "African American Women in the Civil Rights Movement, 1954–1965: Gender, Leadership, and Micromobilization," *American Journal of Sociology* 101 (May 1996): 1663–64; Jo Ann Gibson Robinson, *The Montgomery Bus Boycott* (Knoxville: University of Tennessee Press, 1987), x, 20, 26–29.
5 Judy Alston and Patrice McClellan, *Herstories: Leading with the Lessons of the Lives of Black Women Activists* (New York: Peter Lang, 2011), 54.
6 LaVerne Gyant, "Passing the Torch: African American Women in the Civil Rights Movement," *Journal of Black Studies* 26 (May 1996): 629.
7 Alexandria Russell, "Sites Seen and Unseen: Mapping African American Women's Public Memorialization" (Ph.D. diss., University of South Carolina, 2018), 85.
8 Jewel Prestage, "In Quest of African American Political Woman," *Annals of the American Academy of Political and Social Science* 515 (May 1991): 91–92; Cassandra Newby-Alexander, "Norfolk, Virginia: Civic, Literary, and Mutual Aid Associations," in *Organizing Black America: An Encyclopedia of African American Associations*, ed. Nina Mjagkij (New York: Garland, 2001), 525–27.
9 Beverly M. Jones, "Mary Church Terrell and the National Association of Colored Women, 1896 to 1901," *Journal of Negro History* 67 (Spring 1982): 20.
10 Beverly Jones, 20.
11 *Virginian-Pilot*, August 28, 1974.
12 Joyce Hanson, *Mary McLeod Bethune and Black Women's Political Activism* (Columbia: University of Missouri Press, 2003), 2; Teresa Nance, "Hearing the Missing Voice," *Journal of Black Studies* 26 (May 1996): 547.
13 Rosalee Clawson and John Clark, "The Attitudinal Structure of African American Women Party Activists," *Political Research Quarterly* 56 (June 2003): 213.
14 Clawson and Clark, "Attitudinal Structure"; Douglas Martin, "Margaret Wilson, First Black Woman to Head NAACP Board, Dies at 90," *New York Times*, August 13, 2009, https://www.nytimes.com/2009/08/14/us/14wilson.html.
15 Beverly Jones, "Mary Church Terrell," 21, 24, 27–29.
16 Beth Tompkins Bates, "A New Crowd Challenges the Agenda of the Old Guard in the NAACP, 1933–41," *American Historical Review* 102 (April 1997): 340, 343–44; Martha Jones, *Vanguard: How Black Women Broke Barriers, Won the Vote, and Insisted on Equality for All* (New York: Basic Books, 2020, 2021), 152, 176–77, 200.
17 Martha Jones, *Vanguard*, 177.
18 Bates, "New Crowd," 341, 347–50.
19 Bates, 350–51, 357.
20 Bates, 347.
21 Beverly Jones, "Mary Church Terrell," 29.
22 Katherine Corbett, *In Her Place: A Guide to St. Louis Women's History* (Chicago: University of Chicago Press, 2000), 187.
23 Eboni Njoku, "Review of *Lifting as We Climb: Black Women's Battle for the Ballot Box*," *Book Reviews*, September 16, 2020, 176.
24 Bethune navigated the various positions of Booker T. Washington and W. E. B. Du

Bois by taking elements from both while working independently to create her own financial supporters. See Martha Jones, *Vanguard*, 219; Timeka Rashid, "Leading by Example: An Examination of Mary McLeod Bethune's Leadership as a College President" (Ph.D. diss., Ohio University, 2009), 15–16, 34–35; Hanson, *Mary McLeod Bethune*, 4, 61, 64–69; Lorraine Williams, "The Interracial Conference of the National Council of Negro Women," *Journal of Negro Education* 26 (Spring 1957): 204–6.

25 Hanson, *Mary McLeod Bethune*, 4, 8; Williams, "Interracial Conference," 204–6.
26 Hanson, *Mary McLeod Bethune*, 131–32.
27 Rashid, "Leading by Example," 69.
28 Hanson, *Mary McLeod Bethune*, 4–5.
29 Hanson, 4–5.
30 Hanson, 8, 137–38, 143, 146, 199.
31 *New York Amsterdam News*, July 6, 1940, 11; Cassandra L. Newby-Alexander, "Vivian Carter Mason: Community Feminist," in *Virginia Women: Their Lives and Times*, vol. 2, ed. Cynthia Kierner and Sandra Treadway (Athens: University of Georgia Press, 2016), 229–30.
32 *New York Amsterdam News*, July 6, 1940, 11.
33 Diane Kiesel, *She Can Bring Us Home: Dr. Dorothy Boulding Ferebee, Civil Rights Pioneer* (Lincoln: Potomac Books / University of Nebraska Press, 2015), 105; Ann Pullen, "Commission on Interracial Cooperation," *New Georgia Encyclopedia*, last modified April 5, 2021, https://www.georgiaencyclopedia.org/articles/history-archaeology/commission-on-interracial-cooperation/.
34 Newby-Alexander, "Vivian Carter Mason," 232–33; Jeffrey Littlejohn and Charles Ford, *Elusive Equality: Desegregation and Resegregation in Norfolk's Public Schools* (Charlottesville: University of Virginia Press, 2012), 40.
35 Newby-Alexander, "Vivian Carter Mason," 235–37; *Journal and Guide*, July 10, 1954, C12.
36 Gyant, "Passing the Torch," 630–33.
37 Amy Tillerson-Brown, "Black Women in Prince Edward County: Grassroots Education and the Fight for Public Schools, 1959–1964," in Kierner and Treadway, *Virginia Women*, 2:294–95.
38 "Our American Story: Jo Ann Robinson: A Heroine of the Montgomery Bus Boycott," National Museum of African American History and Culture, https://nmaahc.si.edu/explore/stories/jo-ann-robinson-heroine-montgomery-bus-boycott, accessed August 6, 2022; Nance, "Hearing the Missing Voice," 547.
39 Clawson and Clark, "Attitudinal Structure," 211–12.
40 Ransby, *Ella Baker*, 271.
41 Sara Evans, "Catalyst for Feminism," in *Half Sister of History: Southern Women and the American Past*, ed. Catherine Clinton (Durham, NC: Duke University Press, 1994), 224–25, 237–38.
42 Tondra Loder-Jackson, Louis McFadye Christensen, and Hilton Kelly, "Unearthing and Bequeathing Black Feminist Legacies of *Brown* to a New Generation of Women and Girls," *Journal of Negro Education* 85 (Summer 2016): 201.

43 "Parks, Rosa," Martin Luther King, Jr. Research and Education Institute, Stanford University, https://kinginstitute.stanford.edu/encyclopedia/parks-rosa; Danielle McGuire, *At the Dark End of the Street: Black Women, Rape, and Resistance—A New History of the Civil Rights Movement from Rosa Parks to the Rise of Black Power* (New York: Vintage, 2010), 11, 13.
44 Jeanne Theoharis, *The Rebellious Life of Mrs. Rosa Parks* (Boston: Beacon, 2013), xxv (quotation), 234–35, 242.
45 McGuire, *At the Dark End,* 72, 75–76, 78–79, 98.
46 Height, *Open Wide the Freedom Gates,* 138–39, 141–42.
47 Height, 145–46, 155.
48 McGuire, *At the Dark End,* 192–95, 201.
49 Gyant, "Passing the Torch," 633.
50 Height, *Open Wide the Freedom Gates,* 84, 157, 201.
51 "First Black Women's Institute 1972 Hunger Convocation Program," April 21, 1972, National Council of Negro Women, African American Museum and Library, Oakland, California; Height, *Open Wide the Freedom Gates,* 204.
52 Gyant, "Passing the Torch," 630.
53 Gyant, 633–35, 637.
54 Rhonda McKinney, "Organizations Ban Together to Oppose Rehnquist Nomination," *New Journal and Guide,* August 6, 1986, 9.
55 Ron Daniels, "Summits Build Black Unity," *New Journal and Guide,* August 3, 1994, 2.

4

"I Don't Believe This Has Anything to Do with the Alleviation of Poverty"

Voting Rights, Economic Justice, and the Struggle for Democracy in Houston

Wesley G. Phelps

From his new office in Washington, D.C., Houston's recently elected Republican congressman and future U.S. president George H. W. Bush took note of a development in his home city in January 1967 that alarmed him. For several months, activists affiliated with the federal War on Poverty had been conducting voter registration drives in the city's segregated Black neighborhoods, helping residents capitalize on the promises of the Voting Rights Act of 1965 and the recent elimination of the state poll tax requirement. Bush, a central figure in the Republican effort to break the hold of the Democratic Party in Texas and across the South, recognized the potential consequences of a mobilized African American electorate. Registering more Black voters in Houston "would not bode well for yours truly at the polls," he wrote to a business acquaintance on learning of the registration effort. "But, more importantly, I don't believe this has anything to do with the alleviation of poverty." While Bush had been reluctantly tolerant of the implementation of President Lyndon Johnson's War on Poverty in Houston since its launch in 1964, the prospect of thousands of newly empowered Black voters turned the freshman congressman into a vocal opponent of the federal antipoverty effort and ignited fierce debates about the relationship between voting rights and economic inequality.[1]

Black Americans had been struggling for the right to vote since the previous century. In Texas, local activists successfully agitated against the all-white Democratic Party primary system in 1944 and the state poll tax in

1966, which had effectively curtailed African American political participation for most of the twentieth century. When these achievements combined with the protections Congress offered with the passage of the Voting Rights Act in 1965, African Americans in Texas encountered new political opportunities not seen since Reconstruction. These civil rights victories, however, did not represent a victorious end of the movement for equality. The passage of the Voting Rights Act and the demise of other barriers to the franchise were instead catalysts for change, as grassroots activists recognized that to make democracy meaningful in the lives of most Americans, access to the ballot would need to be paired with efforts to advance economic justice. For many activists, the federal War on Poverty presented an opportunity to expand the meaning of democracy and to ensure that the gains of the civil rights movement would translate into lasting political and economic change. In Houston, African American activists and their anti-poverty allies used the War on Poverty to strengthen democracy by linking voting rights with economic justice. They also faced a tremendous amount of resistance to their efforts from public officials like Bush and other defenders of the status quo, who attempted to separate demands for economic justice from the expansion of the franchise. Despite an increase in voting rights, a more limited version of democracy ultimately prevailed in Houston and across the nation.

Efforts to strip Black Texans of their constitutional right to vote began during the late nineteenth century and continued into the twentieth. Unlike most southern states that relied on literacy tests and grandfather clauses, officials in Texas achieved disfranchisement by combining a state poll tax, which affected a wide swath of working-class and poor residents, with a whites-only Democratic Party primary election system, which explicitly excluded African American voters. In 1902, state legislators approved a new constitutional amendment authorizing a poll tax, and the following year they passed a revised election law that empowered county election judges to deny African Americans the ballot in state primary elections. In 1921, the executive committee of Houston's Democratic Party resolved to exclude Blacks from its primary election, and two years later the legislature followed their lead and approved a more far-reaching statute that explicitly required election judges to throw out any ballot submitted by a Black voter. These measures were effective; Black participation in Texas elections declined from about 100,000 in the 1890s to fewer than 5,000 by the 1920s.[2]

Black Texans mounted fierce resistance to these disfranchisement measures. In 1924, Lawrence A. Nixon, a Black El Paso physician, filed a lawsuit in federal district court claiming the state directive to disallow African Americans from voting violated the Fifteenth Amendment. When the case reached the U.S. Supreme Court, the justices ruled in Nixon's favor but based their decision on narrower grounds. While the Constitution barred the state of Texas from prohibiting Black Texans from voting in primary elections, the high court reasoned, the Democratic Party, as a private organization, was free to restrict participation in its primaries to white voters only. Democratic Party officials wasted no time in approving a statewide resolution disallowing African Americans from voting in primary elections, and federal courts repeatedly upheld the constitutionality of a whites-only Democratic Party primary when challenged by Black voters. In 1935, the U.S. Supreme Court clarified that since the Democratic Party was a voluntary organization made up of private citizens, it had a right to hold members-only primary elections and to place limitations on membership in whatever manner its leaders saw fit.[3]

Since Texas was a one-party state with Democrats in firm control of the levers of power, the Democratic Party primary functioned as the only competitive election of consequence in state politics. A Democratic candidate who succeeded in a primary election was almost certain to emerge victorious against any competitor in the general election. Many Black Texans recognized that their exclusion from Democratic Party primary elections shut them out of any meaningful election in the state, and a few challenged the white primary on those grounds. In 1940, Harris County Democratic Party officials refused to allow Lonnie Smith, a Black dentist from Houston, to vote in the party's primary election. Represented by attorney Thurgood Marshall of the NAACP, Smith filed a federal lawsuit challenging the legality of the party's policy of racial exclusion. In 1944, the U.S. Supreme Court reversed course. In *Smith v. Allwright*, the justices ruled that whites-only primaries violated the Constitution and ordered the state Democratic Party to allow African American voters to participate in its primary elections. The elimination of the white primary in Texas gradually changed electoral politics in the state. Approximately 75,000 Black Texans voted in the 1946 Democratic Party primary, but that number still only represented 14 percent of eligible African American voters. By the next decade, the percentage had grown to nearly 40 percent but still lagged behind white voter participation. Many white candidates nevertheless recognized the increasing political power of African Americans and sought their votes.[4]

The state poll tax continued to limit Black political participation in Texas, although there were few direct legal challenges to its legitimacy compared to the decades of activism against the white primary. In 1964, a sufficient number of states ratified the Twenty-Fourth Amendment, which outlawed the poll tax in federal elections, but the state of Texas continued to require the payment of a poll tax to vote in state and local elections. After Congress passed the Voting Rights Act the following year, Black Texans and the state NAACP launched widespread voter registration and poll tax drives across the state, which drove up African American registration to nearly 60 percent. The following year, the U.S. Supreme Court finally drove the last nail in the coffin of state poll taxes, ruling in *Harper v. Virginia Board of Elections* that requiring the payment of a poll tax to vote in a state or local election violated the equal protection clause of the Fourteenth Amendment. By 1966, many of the legal barriers to Black voting in Texas had been removed, and within two years the percentage of registered African American voters rose to 83 percent.[5]

President Lyndon Johnson launched the federal War on Poverty in the midst of these multifaceted struggles to guarantee equality for African Americans. In August 1964, at the president's request, Congress created the Office of Economic Opportunity (OEO), funded it with nearly one billion dollars, and charged it with the ambitious goal of eradicating poverty from American society. The centerpiece of the new federal anti-poverty initiative was the Community Action Program (CAP), an elaborate and potentially explosive plan to coordinate the resources of local communities and marshal them to meet the needs of the poor. CAP called for the creation of local community action agencies all over the country responsible for not only bringing together social service providers and improving their assistance efforts but also effecting institutional change by organizing and empowering the poor to make demands on local power structures. This last goal was to be accomplished through the "maximum feasible participation" of the poor, an OEO directive mandating that community action agencies include poor residents on their boards, hire them to work in their outreach programs, and even employ community organizers to help them assert their needs to local public officials and institutions. It was this language contained in the War on Poverty guidelines that many poor Houstonians, particularly Black residents of the city, capitalized on in their quest to use the federal program as a vehicle for social change.[6]

From the beginning, the implementation of the War on Poverty touched off a variety of power struggles in Houston. Mayor Louie Welch and other elected officials attempted to use CAP funds for infrastructure projects and other municipal services that would earn them political rewards. Some local anti-poverty activists, however, together with federal War on Poverty administrators, pushed for a more robust community action agency in Houston that would take the "maximum feasible participation" requirement seriously. For the first year of the War on Poverty, Welch and other public officials won these battles, and Houston's first iteration of a community action agency was governed by a cautious board unwilling to consider empowering the poor or even including them in their decisions. Beginning in 1966, however, the composition of the board changed dramatically, as many members completed their one-year terms and turned over their seats to new leaders. Many of these new board members brought with them a different vision for CAP that included organizing and empowering the city's poor residents of color to begin making demands on local officials and institutions, and their efforts produced a few quick and impressive results. Within a few months, poor residents had organized to demand increased city services in their neighborhoods, the establishment of free neighborhood health clinics, an end to police intimidation and brutality, and closer regulation of the local housing industry. By the end of the year, local activists and poor Houstonians had successfully used the War on Poverty to demand a participatory role in the decisions that affected their everyday lives.[7]

In early 1967, many civil rights and anti-poverty activists in Houston decided that the War on Poverty could also be employed to empower previously disfranchised voters in the city. One such activist was Earl Allen, an African American Methodist minister and native Houstonian with a long history in the Black freedom struggle. In March 1960, while a student at Texas Southern University (TSU), Houston's Historically Black University, he participated in Houston's sit-in movement and helped force local elected officials to respond to student demands for desegregation of the city's lunch counters. During the next few years, when Allen was a theology graduate student at Southern Methodist University in Dallas, he served as a regional representative of the Congress of Racial Equality and helped lead sit-in demonstrations, pickets, and boycotts targeting downtown businesses that refused to desegregate. When Allen returned to Houston in 1965 to accept a position as a chaplain at TSU, he had five years' worth of experience with grassroots organizing and had learned how to use it to win concessions from members of the local power structure.[8]

It was Allen's aggressive philosophy that prompted leaders of Houston's new community action agency to bring him into the administration of the War on Poverty. "I wanted to change the status quo," Allen later remembered, "so I was abrasive and not afraid of confrontation." Neither was William Ballew, a white attorney and new director of the city's anti-poverty agency. Convinced that the only way to help improve the lives of poor Houston residents in any lasting or meaningful way was to upset the city's traditional balance of power, Ballew hired Allen in 1966 to oversee his agency's efforts to organize the poor to make demands on the local power structure. Allen promptly began training a 140-member army of community organizers in methods to empower the poor. According to Allen, he wanted to find what was "both a relevant and a realistic approach to achieving the maximum feasible participation of the poor in the total decision-making process in Houston." Allen and his staff initially focused their efforts in a predominantly African American neighborhood in northeast Houston known as Settegast, an area of the city that suffered from an appalling lack of basic municipal services like clean drinking water, adequate sanitation, and access to health care facilities. With assistance from Allen's community organization team, Settegast residents began showing up in large groups at meetings of the Houston city council and the county public hospital board demanding improvements in their neighborhood. This impressive display of determination and solidarity produced results; Mayor Welch and members of the city council immediately authorized the extension of city water services to Settegast to replace the mostly contaminated backyard wells that currently provided water in the neighborhood. The Harris County Hospital District followed by opening a satellite clinic in Settegast, and over the next few years they constructed similar clinics in poor neighborhoods across the city of Houston. Impressed by the effectiveness of Allen's community organizing strategy, a *Houston Post* reporter noted in the aftermath of these victories that the "dawn of a quiet revolution may have broken over Houston" when an empowered group of Settegast residents demanded their voices be heard.[9]

After securing these achievements, Allen and his staff turned their attention to registering new voters as a way to continue empowering poor and Black Houstonians. In January 1967, Houston's community action agency launched Project Freedom with the goal of registering every nonregistered resident currently living in the agency's target neighborhoods, which they estimated to be between 100,000 and 200,000 people. Giving the new project top priority for the month, agency officials reassigned Allen and his entire community organization staff to Project Freedom. "The name Freedom has a particular significance this year in Texas," CAP field director Jack Matthews stated in a memorandum launching the initiative, "as 1967 is the first year in which a citizen may register to vote free, that is, without the payment of a poll tax." Matthews stressed the importance of the right to vote for individuals living in poverty, particularly since the poll tax had disfranchised many of them for decades, and he emphasized that Project Freedom would require a tremendous amount of labor. "This goal can be accomplished through the use of our staff and volunteers . . . working together in a . . . door to door, block by block, neighborhood by neighborhood, canvass of every eligible registrant to get them to register."[10]

During Project Freedom's first week, Allen and his staff enlisted nearly a thousand volunteers to fan out across the city of Houston registering new voters in the city's poor and mostly African American neighborhoods. Since volunteers were not deputized registrars, Allen and other community action agency leaders submitted detailed plans for preapproval to the Harris County Tax Assessor-Collector, who had the responsibility of collecting completed voter registration forms in the county. According to the agreed-upon arrangement, Allen's organizers and volunteers would knock on doors, provide unregistered residents with new voter applications and instructions for filling them out, and offer to deliver completed applications to the tax assessor's office by the January 31 deadline to vote in that year's elections. Allen also insisted that the registration drives be conducted in a strictly nonpartisan manner. As participants in a federally funded program, Allen's staff members and volunteers were required to abide by the Hatch Act, a law passed by Congress in 1939 prohibiting employees associated with programs funded by the federal government from promoting the interests of a particular political party. In November 1966, federal OEO officials stressed that everyone working in the poverty program, including all local community action agency employees, was covered by the Hatch Act, but nonpartisan voter registration and education campaigns were allowed. That month, Ballew relayed this information to the executive committee of Houston's community action agency, and all members agreed that Project Freedom complied with the Hatch Act. By the end of the month, Allen's staff members and Project Freedom volunteers had collected and submitted almost sixty thousand new voter registration forms.[11]

Project Freedom drew immediate responses from elected officials and members of the public. A few, such as county judge Bill Elliott, wrote to Ballew to congratulate him on the agency's "tremendous job done in Voter Registration in Harris County." Many more individuals, however, expressed their opposition to Project Freedom through both words and deeds. On January 16, an arsonist set fire to a community action agency service center in Settegast, causing $4,000 in damages and destroying approximately two thousand completed voter registration applications that had not yet been submitted to the tax assessor's office. While police and fire investigators never determined a motive, leaders of Houston's community action agency were convinced that the completed applications were the intended target and called for a full investigation by the Federal Bureau of Investigation (FBI). The FBI declined the request. After newspapers reported on the fire and the destroyed voter applications, some local public officials, rather than expressing outrage at the destruction of property, began voicing their concern about the potential consequences of Project Freedom. Mayor Welch, while not openly criticizing Project Freedom, nevertheless wrote to Ballew suggesting that the two men convene periodically so the mayor could stay informed about all of the community action agency's planned activities in the city. Harris County Republican Party chair Jim Mayor was more vociferous; he charged the city's community action agency with violating the state's election laws through its "mass handling of voter registration forms." Congressman Bush expressed similar concern and vowed to investigate federal policies governing the activities of anti-poverty workers. He was mainly concerned about the political reverberations associated with adding thousands of new Black voters to the electorate. The new congressman contacted Franklin Moffitt, a federal attorney responsible for advising local community action agencies, and claimed that even if the voter registration drives were legal under current election laws, they still violated federal policies governing the poverty program. Moffitt assured Bush that since Project Freedom was conducted in a nonpartisan manner, the voter registration drives were indeed legal and fell within the parameters of allowable community action agency activities. The congressman received a similar response when he complained to the Texas attorney general, who notified Bush that Project Freedom did not violate any state laws.[12]

Ballew, Allen, and agency board members were determined to continue using their staff and volunteers to register new voters despite these criticisms. They reiterated that Allen and his staff were simply distributing and collecting the same voter registration applications that were printed daily in the city's newspapers, a plan that had been approved by Houston's election officials. Allen admitted, however, that the registration drives were bound to upset some members of the local power structure, and he viewed their opposition as evidence of the effectiveness of their work. "The problem is that the present structure isn't adequate for changing the situation" for those living in poverty, Allen told a reporter from the *Houston Chronicle*.

"People in these communities are apathetic, not because they don't want to change their situation, but because they're hopeless, deprived of dignity and frustrated from years of methods which don't work." Allen recognized that helping poor Houston residents gain access to the ballot and empowering them to demand economic justice had the potential to restore their hope and motivate them to voice their needs to those in power. Ballew agreed and announced that his agency would continue to combine its twin emphases on political and economic rights by expanding Project Freedom to additional neighborhoods across the city of Houston.[13]

Unable to halt the voter registration drives, Bush enlisted Mayor Welch as an ally in an attempt to limit the full range of the agency's activities. The mayor had supported Houston's community action agency as long as he enjoyed some control over the allocation of federal money and the design of local programs. When Ballew became director of Houston's poverty program in late 1966, however, he intentionally weakened the mayor's power over the agency by coordinating his efforts directly with federal OEO officials, effectively going around Welch in the process. As a result, Ballew was able to guide the organization in a more activist and confrontational direction. When Settegast residents staged protests at city hall demanding improved water and sanitation services and access to adequate health care, they caught Welch off guard and alerted him to the potential consequences of empowering a large group of poor and mostly Black Houstonians. If allowed to continue, these types of demonstrations might force Welch and other elected officials to cede more power to this previously disfranchised group of residents. On the other hand, Welch was not particularly concerned about the voter registration drives, perhaps because he had historically enjoyed the support of a majority of the city's African American voters. Yet the mayor found common cause with Bush when the congressman condemned the confrontational tactics of Ballew and Allen more broadly and sought to curtail a wide range of the community action agency's activities in Houston.[14]

Welch and Bush saw their opportunity at the height of Project Freedom in late January 1967. Following the arson that burned down a community action agency office in Settegast and destroyed a collection of voter registration applications, Allen's staff helped plan a demonstration in downtown Houston protesting a recent incident in which a group of deputy officers from the county constable's office brutalized Settegast resident Betty Gentry during an eviction. When the officers arrived on her doorstep to evict her from her home, Gentry, who was seven months pregnant, began attempting to reach her landlord on the telephone. "When I was on the phone," Gentry remembered, "one of the men pushed me. . . . I hit him with the phone to defend myself; he threw me by the hair into the bedroom and handcuffed me and threw me across the bed." After officers had removed her belongings from her home, they arrested and charged Gentry with assault. Word of the incident spread around the Settegast neighborhood as the day wore on, and the next day more than two thousand residents met with a handful of Allen's community organizers to plan a protest of Gentry's treatment. A few days later, about eighty Settegast residents traveled by bus to downtown Houston to stage the demonstration. Welch and Bush seized the moment to voice their displeasure at the involvement of community organizers affiliated with the War on Poverty in a protest march, and after a bit of superficial research the two public officials discovered a way to rally supporters behind their attacks. Settegast residents had paid for the buses to transport them downtown on the day of the demonstration, but because of a clerical error the bus company accidentally sent the bill to the city's community action agency. Although the error was remedied immediately and no agency funds were used, Bush and Welch nevertheless filed a complaint with federal officials claiming a misappropriation of funds.[15]

The following month, Welch used growing tensions on the TSU campus to attack the city's community action agency further. TSU students began a series of protests on campus that semester focused on a variety of complaints ranging from poor food quality in the dining halls to administrators' refusal to recognize a campus chapter of the Student Nonviolent Coordinating Committee (SNCC). When the mayor discovered that a handful of community organizers employed by the city's community action agency had taken part in some of the TSU demonstrations, he began providing a local radio station with this information. Welch even gave radio producers the full police records for some of the individuals, and news anchors shared much of this information with their audiences during the weeks that followed. In March, President Lyndon Johnson appointed Welch to the National Advisory Council of the Office of Economic Opportunity, and from that position the mayor continued his assault on Houston's community action agency. Later that month when he traveled to Washington, D.C., to bring his accusations directly to federal officials, he met with Bush, who eagerly accepted Welch's information and added it to his own list of accusations against the poverty program in Houston.[16]

Welch and Bush soon agreed that the most effective approach to taming Houston's community action agency would be to present to federal OEO officials what they viewed as the flawed philosophy of Ballew, Allen, and their community organization staff. The day after his strategy conference with Welch, Bush met with several OEO representatives and passed along the mayor's information regarding the arrest records of several anti-poverty activists in Houston. He criticized the focus on community organizing that seemed to dominate the city's community action agency and questioned the wisdom of trying to empower poor and mostly Black Houstonians, arguing instead that the War on Poverty should be delivering social services to poor neighborhoods. Bush also continued to repeat the fallacious charge that Allen's staff had used federal funds to rent buses for the Gentry protest and suggested that Houston's community action agency had been infiltrated by radical extremists and convicted criminals. After the meeting, one OEO official concluded that Bush's "approach is basically that of a well-intentioned conservative, who believes that a CAP program should consist of . . . service-oriented activities . . . and who is fearful of the consequences of a program of community organization under any circumstances." As evidenced by his correspondence with a business acquaintance and elections officials in Houston, Ballew and Allen's voter registration drives had sparked Bush's fear of the potential consequences of organizing and empowering Black Houstonians.[17]

Although OEO officials tried to reassure Bush and Welch that their office was in the process of backing off from their support for activist community action agencies, they were nevertheless reluctant to interfere directly with how Ballew and Allen administered their agency. In response, Welch and Bush discovered more indirect ways of influencing the activities of the city's community action agency. Using their contacts in Houston's philanthropic world, they convinced a majority of the agency's board of directors that they could either rein in Ballew and Allen or face continued assaults on their operations. Already facing diminishing support from federal officials for their confrontational approach, the board chose the first option, convening a special meeting in late March to approve a new mission statement and organizational plan without input from Ballew or Allen. These new guidelines repudiated the agency's previous emphasis on community organization and empowerment and instead called for placing professional social workers in poor neighborhoods to direct residents to existing social service agencies. Sensing his waning authority over the poverty program in Houston, Ballew stepped down as board chair the following month. The board quickly appointed a new chair who made it clear that confrontational politics and community empowerment no longer had any place in Houston's War on

Poverty. Allen held on to his position for a short while longer, but he faced almost constant harassment by the organization's new leadership and the city's public officials, including the reassignment of much of his staff elsewhere in the city and police surveillance of his activities. Hamstrung in his efforts to empower Houston's poor and Black citizens and convinced that his efforts could be put to better use elsewhere, Allen resigned in August.[18]

As the agency's board of directors scaled back their efforts under pressure from Welch and Bush, a group of residents and community organizers from a mostly Black and Latino/a neighborhood on the east side of Houston appeared at a board meeting to advocate for continuing their work, including their voter registration drives, uninhibited by the external criticism. Resident and organizer Mario Gallegos began the presentation by describing the vision that guided their efforts. "America is, has been, and will be, as strong as the individuals residing here," Gallegos told board members. "We have learned that we grow in our ability to be better individuals and citizens through exercising our right and responsibility to think, plan, work, for our good and that of our neighborhoods and our country." He argued that the residents of his multiracial and multiethnic neighborhood had been able to work together effectively because the War on Poverty gave them opportunities to exercise their democratic rights and responsibilities. Wilbert Williams, another neighborhood resident and organizer, pleaded with the board to allow them to continue focusing on grassroots empowerment. Williams told board members, "Our success . . . came through hard work and the dedication of grass-roots people in our area. Most of all we are proud of the hundreds of thousands of grass-roots people who have become involved and the spirit by which they move and dedicate themselves." He joined Gallegos in urging the board to continue supporting their efforts to empower the poor even in the face of increasing criticism.[19]

Residents were particularly proud of their success in helping so many of their neighbors register to vote. According to Mrs. Joel Hinojosa, she and a team of more than four hundred residents had coordinated the work of nineteen organizations to launch a voter registration drive and had fanned out across the area knocking on doors and helping residents complete applications. Within a few months, this team had registered more than 6,500 new voters. She and other organizers noticed that the registration drives inspired residents to find additional ways to improve their community and exercise their rights. Hinojosa reminded board members that organizers like her were "telling them and showing them how—how to become a part of 'Community Action.'" She asked the board to remain firm in its commitment to empower the poor and to retain voter registration drives as vital tools for making democracy meaningful in the lives of poor Houstonians. These pleas fell on deaf ears; board members continued with their plan to sideline advocates of empowering the poor and adopt a less confrontational philosophy that emphasized delivering social services to the poor.[20]

By the summer of 1967, Bush and Welch had won their battle against the activist elements in Houston's community action agency. Faced with a barrage of criticism, behind-the-scenes lobbying, and sometimes false accusations, the agency's board members tamed their own organization to make it more palatable to public officials and members of the city's power structure. In the process, they undermined the successes Ballew, Allen, and the community organization staff had achieved during the previous year, including their impressive voter registration drives.

Allen, who resigned from his position as the community action agency's director of community organization in August 1967, remained committed to empowering poor and Black Houstonians. A few weeks later he created a new anti-poverty and civil rights organization dedicated to continuing the work he had begun with the War on Poverty. During an interview with the *Houston Chronicle,* Allen stated that his resignation represented "the admission of a militant Negro professional that he cannot work in the politically charged atmosphere of the antipoverty program," a reference to the way politicians like Welch and Bush had gained undue influence over the city's community action agency. His new organization, he said, would continue to use confrontational tactics to empower Houston's marginalized populations, and he included helping them register to vote as part of those efforts. As Allen explained it, organizing Houston's poor and Black residents to put pressure on pillars of local power and to vote in meaningful ways was the only way to effect change. "Numbers are usually the only strength poor people have," he said. "It's a very honorable technique in the whole scheme of things for creating a bargaining atmosphere and it should not be denied the folk who have no alternative." Allen committed his new organization to the task of empowering poor and Black Houstonians and making sure they enjoyed all of the rights they deserved, including the right to vote.[21]

That fall, Allen unveiled his new organization, which he called Human Organizational, Political, and Economic Development, Incorporated (HOPE), and announced that he would continue what he had started with Houston's community action agency. According to Allen, HOPE was "committed to the task of transforming the theory of mass-based community development, working through the democratic process, into a functioning and realistic instrument for effective social change." The problem with the city's anti-poverty efforts, Allen argued, was that they had abandoned community organizing as a tactic to empower the poor. The War on Poverty, in particular, had become nothing more than a "political football," he said, and was "rapidly becoming a disheartening repetition of old and proven failures." For Allen, power should be at the center of any analysis of poverty. "Power means nothing more or less than an ability to make your voice heard and interests known in the decisions that govern your life." The mission of HOPE was to organize poor Houstonians into powerful groups capable of taking control of their own lives.[22]

Allen also revealed a detailed plan to empower Houston's poor and mostly Black neighborhoods. "We of HOPE Development Inc.," Allen stated, "are not so naive as to believe that we have exclusive remedies for the evils of poverty; but we do have . . . both a conceptual and a practical approach." A significant component of that approach was political empowerment through voter registration, education, and engagement. "One of the major underlying causes for the perpetuation of poverty," Allen argued, "is to be found in the fact that the poor have thus far been politically powerless." Historically denied access to the ballot, poor and Black Houstonians, according to Allen, had allowed outside forces to control their destinies. These outside forces "base their decisions on what is best for their own self-interests and not on what is necessarily best for the poor." The effects on this situation were far-reaching. "Streets in slum areas go unpaved, schools remain inferior, transportation is inadequate, housing codes are not enforced and there is a high degree of unemployment." Allen proposed to remedy this political powerlessness by implementing voter registration and education drives and encouraging political candidates and public officials to visit Houston's poor neighborhoods. Once residents were registered, Allen wanted to form powerful organizations to put pressure on elected officials. "Political unions will be formed," Allen promised. "The function of these unions will be that of involving the poor in the investigation of the qualifications and platforms of political candidates and in recommending to the community those candidates who propose to do the most to improve the conditions" of their neighborhoods. "Lasting social change," Allen concluded, "is going to require the diligent efforts of all segments of our society, working in concert toward the realization of the democratic ideal."[23]

As evidenced by these calls for continued voter registration and mobilization campaigns, community organizers and poor residents in Houston recognized the importance of the ballot in their efforts to eradicate poverty.

When leaders of the city's community action agency scaled back their efforts, shifted their focus from community organizing to service delivery, and eliminated programs to register new voters, activists like Gallegos, Williams, Hinojosa, and Allen continued to advocate for a poverty program that included political empowerment. As they saw it, poverty was not only a problem of material goods; it was also closely related to powerlessness. They urged Houstonians to think about political and economic rights as two sides of the same coin, and the solutions they offered sought to unite the two into a comprehensive attack on poverty and discrimination in Houston.

Before public officials successfully tamed Houston's community action agency and curtailed its efforts to empower the poor, organizers had been able to help register tens of thousands of new voters across the city, the majority of whom were African Americans. For a brief period of time, anti-poverty and civil rights activists offered an expansive vision of grassroots democracy by linking voting rights with economic justice. Despite being a short-lived experiment, these efforts changed the face of electoral politics in the city. Black voter participation increased, more Black candidates won elections, and more public officials had to pay attention to the concerns of Black Houstonians. Unfortunately for many grassroots activists and poor Houston residents, however, the city's official community action agency, whose leaders had backed off from their commitment to organize the poor and register new voters, continued to receive the most financial support and therefore remained the dominant anti-poverty organization in Houston. In 1968, members of the agency's board diverted funds away from the east side neighborhood whose residents had requested a commitment to the empowerment of the poor, and HOPE struggled to compete for funding to carry out its mission. As confrontational tactics and political empowerment disappeared from the city's poverty program, Houston's community action agency became little more than a bureaucratic charity organization responsible for coordinating the city's paltry social services.

By 1968, the pressure from elected officials like Louie Welch and George Bush had separated political rights from economic justice. When Bush expressed to an acquaintance the previous year his discomfort with the voter registration drives that War on Poverty organizers were conducting in Houston, he baldly stated that adding thousands of new Black voters would not improve his chances of reelection. Yet the most troubling part of the registration drives, according to Bush, was that they were being conducted as part of a purported campaign to end poverty. Over the subsequent two years, Bush was able to convince other public officials in Houston, particularly Mayor Welch, that they should keep a more watchful eye over the city's poverty program and work together to curtail any activities they found objectionable. These pillars of the local power structure transformed the congressman's criticism of the voter registration drives into a more general attack on the anti-poverty philosophy that guided Houston's community action agency. Other grassroots organizations in Houston picked up the mantle of voter registration, but by 1968 the dominant discourse on political rights had become detached from ideas about economic justice. Bush, Welch, and their allies in Houston had made sure of that.

Ultimately, as in other major U.S. cities, Houston's elected officials preserved a more limited version of democracy in the city by defeating local activists' attempts to turn the federal War on Poverty into a vehicle for meaningful social change. While neither Bush nor Welch had the power to stop all African Americans from exercising their right to the franchise, now more effectively protected by the Voting Rights Act of 1965, they could help ensure that increased access to the ballot would not be accompanied by demands for a more ethical economy. This narrower interpretation of democracy, with its emphasis on individual rights and representative democracy, largely failed to address the needs and desires of a large class of Houston's—and the nation's—poor and working-class citizens. While increased Black voting and officeholding were certainly tremendous achievements of the civil rights movement, many activists like Earl Allen and William Ballew tried to point out that the struggle for equality and justice must also encompass demands to build an economic system that treats everyone with dignity and humanity. Without attention to economic justice, political rights alone tend to benefit those individuals who possess the material resources to organize and mobilize their communities around particular candidates or political issues. Such inequality and outright exclusion of the poor are indicative of how much work remains to make sure everyone is able to participate in our experiment in democracy.

Notes

1 George Bush to Frank Harmon, January 25, 1967, box 1, folder Correspondence January–February 1967, William V. Ballew Jr. Papers, 1965–1968, MS 254, Woodson Research Center, Fondren Library, Rice University, Houston, Texas (hereafter cited as Ballew Papers).

2 Randolph B. Campbell, *Gone to Texas: A History of the Lone Star State* (New York: Oxford University Press, 2012), 330–31; Robert V. Haynes, "Black Houstonians and

the White Democratic Primary, 1920–1945," in *Black Dixie: Afro-Texan History and Culture in Houston,* ed. Howard Beeth and Cary D. Wintz (College Station: Texas A&M University Press, 1992), 194; Alwyn Barr, *Black Texans: A History of African Americans in Texas, 1528–1995* (Norman: University of Oklahoma Press, 1996), 79–80; Brian D. Behnken, *Fighting Their Own Battles: Mexican Americans, African Americans, and the Struggle for Civil Rights in Texas* (Chapel Hill: University of North Carolina Press, 2011), 5. See also Mark Stanley, "Populism and the Poll Tax in Cooke County, Texas," in *This Corner of Canaan: Essays on Texas in Honor of Randolph B. Campbell,* ed. Richard B. McCaslin, Donald E. Chipman, and Andrew J. Torget (Denton: University of North Texas Press, 2013), 293–308.

3 Campbell, *Gone to Texas,* 366; Haynes, "Black Houstonians," 195–96; Behnken, *Fighting Their Own Battles,* 19–20.

4 *Smith v. Allwright,* 321 U.S. 649 (1944); Campbell, *Gone to Texas,* 404; Haynes, "Black Houstonians," 204–7; Barr, *Black Texans,* 174–77; Behnken, *Fighting Their Own Battles,* 21.

5 Barr, *Black Texans,* 178–79; "24th Amendment, Banning Poll Tax, Has Been Ratified," *New York Times,* January 24, 1964, 1; *Harper v. Virginia Board of Elections,* 383 U.S. 663 (1966). See also *United States v. Texas,* 252 F. Supp. 234 (1966).

6 Allen J. Matusow, *The Unraveling of America: A History of Liberalism in the 1960s* (Athens: University of Georgia Press, 2009), 243–46; Wesley G. Phelps, *A People's War on Poverty: Urban Politics and Grassroots Activists in Houston* (Athens: University of Georgia Press, 2014), 9–10. See also Office of Economic Opportunity, Community Action Program, *Community Action Program Guide* (Washington, D.C., February 1965); Office of Economic Opportunity, Community Action Program, *Community Action Program Workbook* (Washington, D.C., March 1965).

7 Phelps, *People's War on Poverty,* 13–37, 60–88.

8 Behnken, *Fighting Their Own Battles,* 74–81; "E. E. Allen Named to EOO Post," *Houston Post,* November 20, 1966; Earl Allen, interview by the author, December 11, 2008.

9 "E. E. Allen Named to EOO Post"; Earl Allen, interview by the author, December 11, 2008 (first quotation); Earl E. Allen to All Community Organization Staff, memorandum, December 9, 1966, box 59, folder Houston Texas CAA 1968, OEO CAP Records of the Director, Subject Files, 1965–1969, record group 381, National Archives and Records Administration, College Park, Maryland (hereafter cited as NARA) (second quotation); Office of Economic Opportunity, Office of Inspection, "Houston-Harris County Economic Opportunity Organization," February 1967, box 10, folder Contracts, Office of Economic Opportunity, Southwest Region, Community Action Programs, District Supervisors, Records Relating to City Economic Opportunity Boards, 1965–1968, record group 381 (hereafter cited as OEO Contracts), National Archives and Records Administration, Southwest Region, Fort Worth, Texas (hereafter NARASW); Earl E. Allen to All H-HCEOO Personnel, memorandum, December 21, 1966, box 59, Folder Houston Texas CAA 1968, OEO CAP Records of the Director, Subject Files, 1965–1969, record group 381, NARA (hereafter Director's Records); Sarelee Tiede, "Settegast—a Powderkeg or a

Community on the Move?," *Houston Chronicle,* January 22, 1967; Houston-Harris County Economic Opportunity Organization, "The Settegast Report: A Program for Community Development," August 31, 1966, Director's Records; Blair Justice to Louie Welch, memorandum, September 6, 1966, box 33, Louie Welch Papers, Houston Metropolitan Research Center, Houston Public Library, Houston, Texas (hereafter cited as Welch Papers); Harold Scarlett, "Poverty's Captives: Planners Finally Get Some Action," *Houston Post,* November 10, 1966 (third quotation); Office of Economic Opportunity, Office of Inspection, "Houston CAP," February 1967, OEO Contracts; H-HCEOO, "Announcement of Grand Opening of Settegast Clinic," January 28, 1967, box 1, folder Correspondence January–February 1967, Ballew Papers.

10 Jack Matthews to All Area Coordinators, memorandum, January 4, 1967, box 1, folder 3, Ballew Papers (quotations); Minutes of the Houston-Harris County Economic Opportunity Organization Board of Directors, January 11, 1967, box 1, folder 9, Ballew Papers.

11 James M. Simons to Edgar May, memorandum, January 26, 1967, box 73, folder 1, OEO Inspection Division, Inspection Reports, 1964–67, record group 381, NARA (hereafter OEO Inspection Reports); Minutes of H-HCEOO Executive Committee, November 28, 1966, box 73, folder 3, OEO Inspection Reports; "Operation Freedom—Recap on Area Totals," memorandum, February 3, 1967, box 1, folder 4, Ballew Papers; Earl Allen to Community Organization Committee, memorandum, February 8, 1967, box 1, folder 4, Ballew Papers; OEO Office of Inspection, "Houston CAP," February 1967, box 10, folder 4, OEO, Southwest Region, Community Action Programs, District Supervisors, Records Relating to City Economic Opportunity Boards, 1965–1968, Houston, NARASW (hereafter cited as Opportunity Boards Records).

12 Bill Elliott to Bill Ballew, February 8, 1967, box 1, folder 4, Ballew Papers (first quotation); Simons to May, January 26, 1967; Louie Welch to W. V. Ballew, February 16, 1967, box 1, folder 4, Ballew Papers; James M. Simons to Edgar May, memorandum, February 23, 1967, box 73, folder 1, OEO Inspection Reports (second quotation); "Prober Says EOO Fire Arson," *Houston Post,* January 18, 1967, 13; George Bush to Frank Harmon, January 25, 1967, box 1, folder 4, Ballew Papers.

13 Simons to May, February 23, 1967; OEO Office of Inspection, "Houston CAP," February 1967; Tiede, "Settegast" (quotations).

14 Peter Spruance to Edgar May, memorandum, March 20, 1967, box 59, folder 3, Director's Records.

15 "Beating Pregnant Woman Arouses Resentment," *Houston Informer,* January 14, 1967 (quotations); Ed Terrones to Edgar May, memorandum, March 15, 1967, and Charles Kelly to Ed Terrones, March 17, 1967, box 73, folder CAP, Houston, Harris County, Texas, January–March 1967, OEO Inspection Reports; Minutes of Houston-Harris County Economic Opportunity Organization Board of Directors, January 11, 1967, box 1, folder Minutes January–April 1967, Ballew Papers; Tiede, "Settegast."

16 Ray Reusche to Edgar May, memorandum, May 26, 1967; KTRH Radio, "Allegations Made Pertaining to EOO Workers," April 7, 1967; Peter Spruance to Edgar May, memorandum, April 10, 1967; James M. Simons to Edgar May, memorandum, April 10, 1967, all in box 73, folder CAP, Houston, Harris County, Texas, April–June 1967, OEO Inspection Reports; Minutes of Houston-Harris County Economic Opportunity Organization Executive Committee, April 17, 1967, box 73, folder CAP, Houston, Harris County, Texas, July–September 1967, OEO Inspection Reports. For more on the troubled spring 1967 semester at Texas Southern University, see Behnken, *Fighting Their Own Battles,* 156–62; William S. Clayson, "The War on Poverty and the Fear of Urban Violence in Houston, 1965–1968," *Gulf South Historical Review* 18 (2003): 38–59; Bill Helmer, "Nightmare in Houston," *Texas Observer,* June 9–23, 1967; David Ponton, "Criminalizing Space: Ideological and Institutional Productions of Race, Gender, and State-Sanctioned Violence in Houston, 1948–1967" (PhD diss., Rice University, 2017), 363–456; Dwight Watson, *Race and the Houston Police Department, 1930–1990: A Change Did Come* (College Station: Texas A&M University Press, 2005), 77–86.

17 Peter Spruance to Edgar May, memorandum, March 20, 1967, box 59, folder 3, Director's Records.

18 Minutes of Houston-Harris County Economic Opportunity Organization Executive Committee, March 27, 1967, box 1, folder Minutes 1967, Ballew Papers; Spruance to May, April 10, 1967; James M. Simons to Edgar May, memorandum, April 12, 1967, and Fred Baldwin to Francis Williams, April 14, 1967, both in box 73, folder CAP, Houston, Harris County, Texas, April–June 1967, OEO Inspection Reports; Saralee Tiede, "New EOO Head Has Red-Hot Job, but Cool Judgment to Work It," *Houston Chronicle,* April 16, 1967; Ben Haney to Jack Tinkle, memorandum, August 17, 1967, box 10B, folder Inspection and Evaluation Reports, Opportunity Boards Records; Blair Justice to Louie Welch, memoranda, June 5 and 27, 1967, box 33, Welch Papers; Saralee Tiede, "Beliefs of the Civil Rights Leader Who Quit HCCAA," *Houston Chronicle,* August 13, 1967.

19 Mario Gallegos, "EOO Area 9—Our Goal and Our History," March 15, 1967, and Wilbert Williams, "EOO Area 9—Support Needed," March 15, 1967, box 1, folder 9, Ballew Papers.

20 Mrs. Joel Hinojosa, "EOO Area 9—What Is Happening in Our Program," March 15, 1967, box 1, folder 9, Ballew Papers.

21 Tiede, "Beliefs of the Civil Rights Leader Who Quit HCCAA."

22 "Hope Development Inc.: A Proposal for Community Development," n.d., box 1, folder 14, Ballew Papers.

23 "Hope Development Inc."

5

Overcoming the American Lie

HBCUs' Role in Advancing Democracy

REGINALD K. ELLIS

> We can build the sort of Negro university which will emancipate not simply the black folk of the United States, but those white folk who in their effort to suppress Negroes have killed their own culture.
> W.E.B. Du Bois, "The Negro College," in *The Crisis*, 1933

Many Americans were preparing themselves for the unofficial beginning of summer—but this Memorial Day weekend of 2020 was different. Since mid-March, much of the United States had been shut down, forcing citizens to stay home, become reacquainted with their families, and possibly catch up on shows they DVR'ed over the past year. Already frustrated by forced home confinement and perhaps the lack of a severe pandemic response, tensions were slowly rising. At the same time, some decided to take the risk of welcoming summer similarly to how they would under normal circumstances—going to the beach, hosting backyard barbecues, traveling for family reunions; others decided to adhere to the Centers for Disease Control's recommendations of staying away from large crowds, practicing physical distancing, and wearing masks. Memorial Day 2020 is now a watershed moment in American history—but not due to the different responses to celebrating a solemn holiday. That Memorial Day will be remembered for the eight minutes and forty-six seconds in which Derek Chauvin lynched George Floyd for the world to see. This moment—no matter how brief—caused Americans to deal with what James Baldwin referred to as "the Lie."[1] Specifically, the novelist/activist argued that at the foundation of America, leaders of this nation dehumanized Black folk and claimed that their origins were subhuman—thus justifying their enslavement and continued mistreatment.

Since before 1619, individuals of the African diaspora have lived, labored, and loved on the land that is now the United States of America. Throughout that time, foreigners of this area desired to exert their liberty from an oppressive rule. Thus, in 1776 in Philadelphia, several influential members of early American society decided to draft a document that would bind the thirteen colonies not to British rule, but to a new national ideal with its cornerstones of life, liberty, and the pursuit of happiness. In the very midst of these intense dialogues, these founders intentionally accepted "America's Lie."

As Jefferson, Adams, Franklin, and Madison supported the ideals of what is now America, millions of Black folk were legally enslaved. Although the first American to shed blood during the Revolutionary era against the mother country was an African- and Indigenous-born man, the founders still embraced the lie. This lie remains in America's physics nearly 250 years later. The lie that was created at the very foundation of this nation is the lie that empowered a no-knock warrant to be executed in Louisville, Kentucky, in which Breonna Taylor was lynched by the same first-line responders she served with. This lie gave George Zimmerman the authority to follow, question, and execute an unarmed Black teenager—simply because he decided to walk in the rain. This lie was on full display on May 25, 2020, when Derek Chauvin placed his knee firmly on the neck of George Floyd, despite the pleas of bystanders begging the officer to let Mr. Floyd up—and despite the cries of Mr. Floyd himself, calling out to his mother, whom he surely saw as he was transitioning to the realm of the ancestors. Derek Chauvin, George Zimmerman, and the thousands of Americans who have openly lynched Black people have often been shielded from prosecution[2] and moral reflection due to America's Lie.

With the founding of America coinciding with the development of the Lie, Black folk, since their arrival on the shores of colonial America, fought to overcome the Lie. Fighting to prove their humanity by becoming active participants in the American experiment via military involvement, joining the paid labor force, and participating in national celebrations—many Black folk, while always understanding the bridge and connection to the continent of Africa, became true believers in the idea of the American dream. Thus, at the close of the institution of slavery, Black folk fought for and achieved access to two institutions that laid the foundations for their multigenerational fight to advance American democracy: the Black church and Black education. Thus, this chapter will examine the role that Black colleges and universities had in defending and promulgating the ideals of

American democracy and the continued battle waged against the sustained success of Black educational institutions. Special attention will be given to two founding presidents of Black colleges established in the late nineteenth and early twentieth centuries. This study aims to reveal the advocacy of democratic values and the early development of Black college campuses.

In the spring of 1854, with the founding of the Ashmun Institute (present-day Lincoln University),[3] the first degree-granting Black college in the United States, the Black college movement began. These colleges and universities served as what historian Jelani Favors refers to as communitas of Black political and social development. The Black college movement, unknowingly to benefactors of these early institutions, created a crusade that attacked the concepts of the Lie. These institutions developed leaders—religious, educational, and political leaders who forced America to deal with the Lie it created. From Fisk University came alumni W.E.B. Du Bois and John Hope Franklin—scholars who informed the world of the history of Africans in America—their civilizations and their culture. The Morehouse Man, Martin Luther King Jr., forced America to revisit the Declaration of Independence and challenged her to live up to what she said she was on paper. Lincoln University's own Thurgood Marshall, the civil rights icon, changed the law to include Black people in all aspects of the judiciary. Black colleges, from my assessment, since the mid-1800s have created a firewall around the ideals of American Democracy—and citizens of the United States of America owe these institutions and their alumni a great deal of gratitude for that.

Specifically, during the nation's infancy, there was a chief struggle over actual concepts of what a liberal democracy was—who "the people" were as related to the U.S. Constitution. Keenly, Black folks, as early as the 1830s, through the creation of Black higher educational institutions, systematically challenged the framers of America for inclusion. Via the establishment of Black higher education, first in Cheney, Pennsylvania, then in Lincoln, Pennsylvania, advocates of Black higher education desired to educate a race of people with the ultimate desire to gain full citizenship. This point is best highlighted by Charles Whiteside when his former "master" informed him that he had no freedom because he had no education, and education is what made a man free. Notably, according to Carter G. Woodson, this line of thinking was promoted by the abolitionist William Lloyd Garrison during an address to the Black professional class in Philadelphia when he argued that "knowledge was power" and that to break the chains of slavery, the Black community must have access to higher forms of education.[4]

Through the struggle to establish Black higher education, Black folk and their advocates were also pushing the nation to consider the concepts of liberal democracy. Due to the generational fight that Black folk waged to secure access to higher education and the barriers erected to ensure that access would not come quickly, the United States of America moved closer to the ideals of a liberal democracy by the mid-twentieth century. However, the headwinds erected remained prevalent throughout.

This chapter will therefore profile two of the early southern-based Black colleges, their development, and the challenges of white supremacy they fought to overcome to ensure the survival of their institutions. Also, this study will provide a present-day analysis of the fight Black colleges still face in the twenty-first century in relation to the historic underfunding models that several Black colleges are legally challenging. My chief argument in this study is that since their inception, Black colleges have imbued a deep appreciation of the ideals of American democracy—despite the barriers established to ensure their downfall. Principally, if not for Black colleges and their graduates, the idea of American democracy would have been on life support over a century ago.

To frame this discussion, this study opens by profiling two founding Black college presidents: one of a publicly funded institution and one of a private institution that was eventually absorbed by the state. Thomas DeSaille Tucker of the Florida State Normal and Industrial School for Colored Students, predecessor to Florida Agricultural and Mechanical University, is the first leader under consideration. Acting through his institution, Tucker played a crucial role in American history as he created a Black state-supported college with a liberal arts curriculum in the era of Booker T. Washington.

Thomas Tucker was born at Victoria, in Sherbro, Sierra Leone, on July 21, 1844. His mother was the hereditary princess of Sherbro, which made him an African prince. The name Tucker came from an Englishman on his paternal side. At the age of twelve, Tucker traveled to the United States to complete his education, which led the young scholar to Ohio's Oberlin College, first as a student in the preparatory school and then as an undergraduate.[5]

After graduating from Oberlin in 1865, Tucker moved to Louisiana, earning a law degree from Straight College (present-day Dillard University) before moving to Pensacola, Florida, to open a practice with his law partner, J. D. Thompson. Tucker's move to Florida coincided with the Black middle class of that state asserting themselves as leaders of their race. For example, over two hundred prominent Black leaders met in Gainesville, Florida, for the State Conference of the Colored Men of Florida. This meeting was scheduled to create a plan for African Americans in Florida a few years removed from the false promises of Reconstruction. Well aware of the political unrest within Florida and on the national level, this meeting addressed local and federal civil rights issues.[6]

During this convening, Black journalist and political spokesman John Willis Menard sparked the idea of a state-supported institution for advanced education for African Americans. But it was Menard's son-in-law, Thomas Van Renssalaer Gibbs, who enacted the necessary legislation and financial support for the school as a delegate to the 1885 Florida Constitutional Convention and as a state representative. The institution would open in 1887 under the name Florida State Normal and Industrial School for Coloreds, or FSNIS.[7]

While many Floridians assumed that Thomas Gibbs would step into the presidency of the new school, white political leaders desired someone else, a fact that would carry significant implications for the institution's future administrators. This situation came about because former Confederate general Edward A. Perry of Pensacola had assumed the governor's chair in 1885. Perry generally acted to reverse the gains achieved through Reconstruction-era trends and policies. It appears likely that Perry and his advisers mistrusted Gibbs, whose connections in Black social and political circles ran to the highest levels.[8]

In these circumstances, Perry surprisingly turned to a fellow Pensacola resident to take FSNIS's helm, and he likely did so based on advice from unexpected sources. The turn of events reflected relationships tested over decades. First, Perry's immediate predecessor as governor, William D. Bloxham, had assumed office as secretary of state and, as such, sat on the board of education. Bloxham meanwhile enjoyed an extremely close association with Leon County's state senator, John Wallace. In turn, Wallace had kept close ties with his fellow Black Civil War veteran and one-time congressman Josiah T. Walls.

Interestingly, at the time of FSNIS's founding, Wallace and Walls had been well acquainted with Pensacola attorney Thomas Tucker for almost a quarter of a century. The friendships trace back to the Civil War when the lawyer likely taught the two public officials at the army's Mary S. Peak School in Hampton, Virginia. At the school, Tucker and other instructors combined basic academic exercises with liberal doses of religious training. Whether Wallace and Walls retained the former cannot be ascertained, but they did not forget Tucker. Although spotty, evidence suggests that they recommended Tucker to Bloxham, who, in turn, pressed his name on the governor as the proper man to head the state regular school.

On September 24, 1887, Tucker was selected as the first president of FSNIS, located in Florida's capital city, Tallahassee. Reluctant to take this position miles from his Pensacola home, Tucker nevertheless submitted to his call to duty and arrived in the Florida capital a few days before the first classes. During his initial year at the new school, his wife, Charity, remained in Pensacola to hone her teaching skills.

On October 3, 1887, the Florida State Normal and Industrial School for Colored Students opened its doors to fifteen students. Initially, admittance into this school proved difficult. Historian Leedell Neyland said admission was restricted to persons sixteen and over. Facing the challenge of educating individuals who were only twenty-two years removed from slavery, the forty-three-year-old Tucker and his new partner in education, Thomas Gibbs, "deemed it necessary to examine all newcomers and place them in categories based on the scores received." Therefore, the courses of study were divided into preparatory and regular school. Surprisingly, for an upstart Black college during the late 1880s, the normal department courses consisted of Latin, higher mathematics, physiology, astronomy, general history, rhetoric, pedagogics, and natural, mental, and moral philosophy.[9] Given the era's emphasis on industrial and vocational training, Tucker's curriculum at FSNIS was totally out of step with other Black educational institutions, especially those in the South.[10]

A deeper assessment of the curriculum of FSNIS speaks to the desire of not only the administrators but of the students as well. This group aspired to broaden the critical thinking ability of their community with a deep appreciation and understanding that knowledge was power. Also, they recognized the relationship between education and freedom. Essentially, these freedmen and their partners viewed a liberal arts education as a direct path to the American dream.

With one year under his belt, Tucker began to assert himself in Tallahassee as the preeminent educational leader for Blacks in Florida. The president gained approval from the state legislature to hire another instructor at the institution. Tucker appointed Laura Clark, a graduate of Wilberforce College, the first woman instructor at the school. Clark lightened Tucker's teaching load by instructing English and literature courses in the preparatory department. The three instructors were surprisingly paid on par with white regular schools of the state, with Tucker's annual salary equaling

$1,100, Gibbs $1,000, and the newly hired Clark's $700.[11] This sign of confidence from state officials launched the Tucker administration into full gear as his vision for the institution grew.[12]

Building on this momentum, Black leaders in the state created a chapter of the Colored State Teachers Association, electing Tucker as the organization's first president on July 11, 1889. Thomas Gibbs also joined the new teachers' association, which supported FSNIS and other Black educational institutions throughout the state. Although a full-time college president, Tucker understood the importance of providing this type of leadership for Black educators in Florida. With his proximity to the state's capitol and his relationship with Black and white politicians, Tucker had the opportunity to flex his political muscle to benefit Black education—which, from their perspective, supports the establishment of a Black middle class less than forty years removed from the institution of slavery.

While serving the entire Black population in Florida as their educational leader, Tucker's focus remained on the progress of FSNIS. In September 1889, the staff of the young institution released its course catalog, a neatly printed pamphlet of sixteen pages. This catalog revealed the number of students at the school and the course offerings. Moreover, the pamphlet assured Florida citizens that their tax dollars were not being spent in vain. For example, the catalog expressed that "their annual expense account can easily be kept under $100."[13]

Tucker's influence over the curriculum of FSNIS began to dwindle as Booker T. Washington's reputation grew. Nonetheless, Tucker's ideas of creating a prominent Black middle class never faltered. This can be best observed in his address to the graduates of 1895, the same year that Booker T. Washington gained national acclaim for his famous Atlanta Cotton State Exposition address. While Washington argued for Blacks in the South to remain on the land that they knew and to master skills they had learned during slavery, Tucker encouraged his graduates to carry themselves respectably while creating a positive image that would elevate the race. Washington argued that the Black population would become economically independent and self-reliant if they followed his plan. Meanwhile, Tucker emphasized the importance of duty. In his 1895 address, the president informed the graduates, "To the one who desires to serve his fellow man, duty is easily perceived and the discharge of its attended with pleasure."[14] Tucker went on to charge the young graduates with continuing to work professionally while understanding their new societal roles.

For eight years, the FSNIS president served as the educational voice for African Americans in Florida. Available evidence shows that white state politicians supported Tucker before Washington's speech in 1895, as his approach was the only one openly embraced in Florida.[15] The goal of white conservatives was being achieved at FSNIS, as the institution was creating a better, more industrious Negro. On the other hand, this radical form of education prepared Black students to think critically about their situation. Also, it gave them the analytical ability to devise a plan that would rescue their race from the shackles of white supremacy.

With the Washington model of Black higher education taking form, private Black colleges faced similar curriculum challenges—with a bit more nuance. Thus, the second individual profiled in this study is James Edward Shepard. Shepard's role as founding president of the present-day North Carolina Central University provides a unique interpretation of the role of a Black college president during the Jim Crow era. Specifically, in 1909, Shepard established a private liberal arts educational institution. Initially created to train Black ministers, it was absorbed by the state of North Carolina nearly fifteen years later, thus making the North Carolina College for Negroes the first state-supported Black college with a liberal arts curriculum in the South.

Scholars of the Jim Crow era have grappled with how Shepard maintained a liberal arts agenda in the South during this era while also benefiting from the support of both Washington and W.E.B. Du Bois. This question is best answered by providing insight into Shepard's upbringing. The privilege of being born into a leading southern Black family offered the young man many advantages. For example, Shepard was able to enroll in the model department of Shaw University in Raleigh, North Carolina, at the age of eight due to his father's status as a prominent minister.[16] Shortly after that, he completed his primary training under the tutelage of his uncle at the Shiloh Institute in Warrenton, North Carolina, then he enrolled in the pharmaceutical department of Shaw University, where he graduated in 1894 at the age of nineteen. Equipped with this degree, Shepard became one of the first African American druggists in the state of North Carolina, a profession he excelled in for three years before changing career paths.

In 1897, he was appointed as the chief clerk in the Recorder of Deeds office in Washington, D.C. A year later, he became deputy collector of internal revenue back in Raleigh, where he was able to strengthen his connections with influential whites throughout North Carolina. After several years of governmental service, Shepard's religious calling led him to accept the position as the field superintendent for the International Sunday School Association. This was his first opportunity to advance the Black race through education. His job was to "improve Sunday Schools in management, methods, and equipment; and to endeavor to bring the denominations into . . . closer . . . cooperation to uplift the race."[17] In this position, Shepard saw the need to properly educate African American ministers, many of whom he found ill equipped for their positions and largely illiterate even at the turn of the twentieth century. With the help of Durham's Black and white communities, he opened the National Religious Training Institute and Chautauqua (NRTIC) in 1910, the predecessor of North Carolina Central University, to elevate Blacks both morally and educationally.

The concept of enhancing the morality of the Black community via education was not unique to Shepard. Leaders of the Black upper class during the age of accommodation presumed that the best way to defeat white supremacy was to prove that African Americans were socially, politically, and educationally equal to their white counterparts. Therefore, these leaders desired to not only drive illiteracy out of the Black community but also exile common behaviors and conditions that were deemed immoral such as vagrancy, failing to attend church, and unemployment.

Black leaders preferred to take the lead in tackling these problems during a time when Rudyard Kipling's 1899 poem "The White Man's Burden" was enormously popular. White businessmen, along with leading politicians like South Carolina senator Ben Tillman and future president Theodore Roosevelt, regarded Kipling's poem as an appeal not only in support of America's imperialistic aims but also of their desire to "civilize" nonwhites in America. In response, Black leaders at the turn of the twentieth century argued that they were best suited to "ease the white man's burden" by taking the lead in advancing their race. By doing this, these leaders assumed their guidance would prove that Black Americans were civilized and equal to white Americans.

By the summer of 1910, the NRTIC was moving full steam ahead. The school quickly reached numbers nearing a hundred, made up primarily of teachers, preachers, and "others from varied walks of life among the Negroes." The course of study was described as "normal and primary methods, history, geography, grammar, pedagogy, domestic science, dressmaking and millinery, basketry and vocal music."[18] This curriculum reveals Shepard's desire to incorporate both the classical and vocational forms of higher education.

During the school's first summer, Shepard invited a series of lecturers, including Rev. Jesse Hurburt of Newark, New Jersey, who lectured the students on Bible instruction. Although Bible instruction was an essential factor in the NRTIC's curriculum, other forms of classical education were also promoted during the opening weeks of "Shepard's School." For example, Miss Grace Hemmingway, "the well-known child storyteller," instructed the students on storytelling. From all accounts, the first six-week summer session of the NRTIC was successful, as the number of students had doubled by the fall term. About the good deeds of Dr. Shepard and his school, Bishop Robert Strange of the Episcopal Diocese of East Carolina stated: "I think highly of Dr. Shepard, and I believe this institution will be a real help to the Negro."[19]

During the infancy of the NRTIC, President Shepard continued to display his ability to connect with the most prominent citizens of both races of the South. Shepard also created a number of intellectual partnerships that benefited the NRTIC while helping "uplift the race" by incorporating Washington's philosophy of "placing black progress on display."

For the first two decades of the NRTIC, renamed the National Training School in 1915, Shepard and his supporters faced several challenges. No challenge weighed more than that of finances. Specifically, America's involvement in World War I was a chief contributor to the diminished donations coming into the school by 1919. According to North Carolina Central historians, from 1919 to 1923 the school virtually operated in the red while continuing "its policy of open door[s] as it aided indigent students."[20] With Shepard's primary focus on the institution's overall fiscal operation and the school's debt growing larger by the year, the board began to consider changing the environment in which the institution operated. While the school's objective of training ministers was a significant selling point to the Black and white community, the trustees grappled over whether one of the religious denominations should take control of the school. There were already Black colleges in North Carolina that were controlled by Black churches, such as Johnson C. Smith University in Charlotte, which fell under the auspices of the Presbyterian Church, and James Shepard's alma mater, Shaw University in Raleigh, which was affiliated with the Baptist Church. It is not clear why Shepard and his board decided against affiliating with one of the many denominations, but one major issue was surely the fact that the Black church itself was a not-for-profit entity, and therefore, denominational control could have led to the same financial perils that Shepard's school was already experiencing.

The second option eventually became the one that Shepard and his trustees chose, allowing the state of North Carolina to gain control of his institution. That decision was also risky, as there were already state-supported Black colleges in North Carolina, including North Carolina A&M College in Greensboro, led by one of Shepard's advisors, James B. Dudley. This risk was magnified by Shepard's mission of "changing the man" through moral uplift, which primarily focused on a sound knowledge of liberal arts instruction. Therefore, if the state of North Carolina agreed to purchase the school and keep its mission, the National Training School would become the first state-supported liberal arts Black college in the state of North Carolina and arguably in the South. On the other hand, Dudley's school focused on agricultural and mechanical training for African Americans, thus advancing a nonthreatening mission that appeased many conservative whites during the early twentieth century.

Shepard's school had no such disclaimer. Nevertheless, in 1923, North Carolina agreed to purchase the National Training School, changing its name to the Durham State Normal School. While no longer a private entity, neither the mission nor the school's leader changed, as government officials agreed to keep James Shepard as the president of their new institution of higher education. This is an important note as it reveals state officials' respect for Shepard in developing a curriculum and employing appropriate faculty to help advance his race. By relieving Shepard of the task of securing funds for the school's operation, he would have the ability to broaden the overall scope of the institution with the backing of the Republican legislators and higher educational leaders in the state of North Carolina.

Shepard's ability to stay at the helm of his institution was largely due to the partnerships he had created. His savvy gained him the support he needed to remain the head of the newest public Black college in North Carolina. True, the challenge of "walking the tightrope" would become more difficult for Shepard in the years that followed, as individuals from both the white and Black communities began to demand the president's accurate positions on the issue of race relations. But notwithstanding these difficulties, the partnerships that Shepard created with philanthropists, educators, and clergy throughout the United States placed him and his institution on a solid foundation. Therefore, the institution that would eventually become North Carolina Central University has continued to influence the development of Black life in the city of Durham and the state of North Carolina right up to the present day—due in large part to the groundwork that Shepard and his partners laid during the formative years of the NRTIC.

In an in-depth analysis of Black college presidents during the Jim Crow era, Tucker and Shepard are perhaps not as well known as some of their counterparts, such as John Hope of Atlanta University, Benjamin E. Mays of Morehouse College, or Mordecai Johnson at Howard University. All of the aforementioned presidents led institutions in the South, relying heavily on financial support from southern white men. Instead, Tucker and Shepard led institutions that depended on funds derived from state allocations or private donations.

With Shepard's and Tucker's presidencies serving as a backdrop, Black colleges have played a significant role in developing the Black middle and professional class in America—despite the challenges of overcoming white supremacy. Since the summer of 2020, Black colleges have faced a push-pull factor they may have never faced before. Now, with a heightened profile, the need for a serious national conversation about the importance of Black colleges can no longer be overlooked. Perhaps the most essential part of that conversation is fairness in funding. As high-profile scholars, students, and even coaches choose Black colleges, the historic funding disparities are now being magnified. And the need to address and overcome past disparities is now more pressing than ever.

Since the early 2000s, several research-intensive Black colleges, for example, have operated without receiving the total amount of dollars they were entitled to under federal law. One study published by the Association of Public and Land-Grant Universities found that, between 2010 and 2012, more than half of the nation's Black colleges failed to receive their total funding. And the history runs much deeper than the three years covered by that study.[21] Here is how the model has failed Black colleges. As reported by CBS, publicly funded Black colleges are awarded funds by both their state and the federal government, and each state is required to match the funds provided by the federal government. For example, if Tennessee State University is awarded $40 million in federal aid, the state of Tennessee must match that funding with $40 million, for a total of $80 million to TSU.

Yet the one-to-one match has very rarely occurred. To stick with the example of TSU, a legislative investigation in 2020 found that the state of Tennessee had underfunded the school to the tune of $544 million, with the shortfall stretching back to the 1950s. And TSU isn't alone. In 2021, Maryland agreed to a $577 million settlement to resolve a lawsuit alleging the state had underfunded its four HBCUs.

This long history of underfunding has been devastating. Because of this, simple projects like building maintenance were placed on hold. And, of course, when maintenance of facilities is not addressed in a timely manner, the proverbial leak becomes a flood. For example, an assessment from 2021 concluded that Tennessee State University's maintenance needs alone totaled more than $337 million. At HBCUs across the country, historic dorms and classrooms have fallen into disrepair, and now black college administrators are facing the question of either repairing these spaces that provide a sense of place for alumni who wandered these cherished halls decades earlier or demolishing these relics and replacing them with new facilities altogether. Going with the latter option will perhaps make these spaces more user-friendly for the present age, but the price tag can be astronomical. It's an example of past injustice creating an intractable dilemma for the administrators, faculty, and students at Black colleges today.

The issue, from my perspective, has never been about "the mismanagement" of funds by Black college administrators. The problem is the lack of funds they have received, which has always placed administrators in a posture of "having to rob Peter to pay Paul." They have faced critical questions of making payroll, paying student scholarships, and maintaining facilities with less financial resources than they were legally owed.

Ironically, in several southern states, where most Black colleges are located, the budgets of flagship and even second-tier PWIs have increased over the past two decades to ensure that their physical and human resources are prepared for the twenty-first-century marketplace. And yet, even while carrying the brunt of a funding shortfall, HBCUs have continued producing graduates, making significant impacts nationally and internationally.

Since the end of segregation, but perhaps even more in the early twenty-first century, Black college leaders have consistently faced the question "Are HBCUs still relevant?" Unfortunately, this question is typically being raised by the very people who could do most to address the funding problems I've just been talking about: legislators, government officials, and sometimes even benefactors. Interestingly, while state governing bodies are raising this question, 25 percent of African American graduates with STEM degrees earned them from a Black college. According to the United Negro College Fund, Black colleges graduated 46 percent of Black women who earned degrees in STEM disciplines between 1995 and 2004. Moreover, eight Black colleges were among the top twenty institutions to award the most science and engineering bachelor's degrees to Black graduates from 2008 to 2012. Black colleges are the institutions of origin among almost 30 percent of science and engineering doctoral program graduates. Notably, Black colleges only account for 3 percent of the nation's colleges and universities, both public and private.

I believe these statistics provide a compelling answer to anyone who questions the ongoing relevancy of HBCUs and their role in advancing American democracy. These schools have long provided a nurturing environment for young Black men and women to find their footing in the world and gain the skills they need to be productive members of society. They still provide such an environment, and America is now—and will continue to be—a better place thanks to the existence of Black schools.

With that, in this era, it is time for America to invest in Black colleges as never before. Black colleges have always—to borrow a phrase from the retired radio personality and Tuskegee alum Tom Joyner—super-served the Black community. Imagine being a young person of color, from an urban or a rural area, being dropped off at a college at the age of eighteen—being surrounded by thousands of folk who look like you—but from different parts of the nation or even the diaspora—folk who perhaps are more or less liberal or conservative than you. Imagine walking into your first class, and your English professor is a woman of color, and your biology professor is as well. Imagine when you attend your first college-wide meeting, and the dean of your college is a middle-aged man of color. His team of deans is composed of Black administrators who are compassionate yet firm in their desire to ensure your success.

Now, imagine if those institutions did not exist. Who provides the opportunity for development and growth in a space that allows these young people of color to grow into the next Kamala Harris, Stacey Abrams, or Andrew Gillum? Which institution consistently mentors the next generation of Black MDs, lawyers, and scholars? America should consider the historic value of Black colleges—not just the historical value, but what the nation will be if we truly invest in these gems that have provided a bridge over America's troubled water for over 150 years. In essence, Black colleges have historically and presently served as the portal to the American dream for Black folk in America for nearly two hundred years.

Notes

1. Eddie Glaude, *Begin Again: James Baldwin's America and Its Urgent Lessons for Our Own* (New York: Crown, 2020).
2. The author notes that Derek Chauvin was prosecuted and found guilty in the murder of George Floyd and sentenced to twenty-two and a half years on June 25, 2021.

3 While Chaney State University was established on February 25, 1837, they were not degree granting until 1855.
4 Carter G. Woodson, *The Education of the Negro Prior to 1861: A History of the Education of the Colored People of the United States from the Beginning of Slavery to the Civil War* (Washington, D.C.: ASALH Press, 2023).
5 American Missionary Association Annual Report 1862, Constitution of the American Missionary Association (hereafter AMAA); *The Lancet Baltimore*, May 20, 1903; John G. Riley and Leedell Neyland, *History of Florida Agriculture and Mechanical University* (Gainesville: University Press of Florida, 1956), 12.
6 Reginald K. Ellis, "Florida State Normal and Industrial School for Coloreds: Thomas DeSaille Tucker and His Radical Approach to Black Higher Education," in *The Seedtime, the Work, and the Harvest: New Perspectives on the Black Freedom Struggle in America*, ed. Jeffrey L. Littlejohn, Reginald K. Ellis, and Peter B. Levy (Gainesville: University Press of Florida, 2018), 10–27.
7 Ellis, "Florida State Normal and Industrial School."
8 Riley and Neyland, *History of Florida Agricultural and Mechanical University*, 14; James D. Anderson, *The Education of Blacks in the South, 1860–1935* (Chapel Hill: University of North Carolina Press, 1988), 65. To gain a greater understanding of the day-to-day operations of the college, see Neyland and Riley's work. For the purpose of this essay, the focus is geared more toward the influence of Tucker and the Black middle class of Florida than on the institution.
9 Riley and Neyland, *History of Florida Agricultural and Mechanical University*, 14; Anderson, *Education of Blacks*, 65.
10 Anderson, *Education of Blacks*. According to Anderson, "much" of the curriculum of the early Black colleges was rudimentary instruction at best—not truly providing a standard college curriculum. Thus, the rigid standards set forth by Tucker in this targeted liberal arts curriculum were clearly beyond the standard of the day for Black higher education.
11 Riley and Neyland, *History of Florida Agriculture and Mechanical University*, 16.
12 Questions around the rationale of equal pay for both Black and white college instructors during this area have arisen. Based on my research, during the early 1890s—particularly prior to Booker T. Washington's address at the Atlanta Cotton Exposition in 1895 and the Supreme Court decision in *Plessy v. Ferguson* in 1896—there was no precedent for unequal pay in the state of Florida regarding higher education.
13 *Florida Times-Union*, September 1, 1889.
14 Booker T. Washington, *Up from Slavery* (New York: Random House, 1999), 70–78; *The College Arms*, June 1895.
15 AMAA Annual Report 1862; *The Lancet Baltimore*, May 20, 1903; Riley and Neyland, *History of Florida Agriculture and Mechanical University*.
16 In the late nineteenth century, model departments consisted of basic liberal arts instruction.
17 James E. Shepard to James E. Stagg, March 20, 1899, James E. Stagg Papers, Rare Book, Manuscript, and Special Collections Library, Duke University.

18 *Chicago Defender,* July 10, 1919.
19 *Afro-American,* October 15, 1910.
20 Beverly Jones, *James Edward Shepard, The Founder: An Educational and Community Analysis* (Durham: North Carolina Humanities Committee, 1985), 19–23.
21 Association of Public Land-Grant Universities, Office for Access and Success Policy Brief, "Land-Grant but Unequal: State One-to-One Match Funding for 1890 Land-Grant Universities," September 2013, https://www.aplu.org/wp-content/uploads/land-grant-but-unequal-state-one-to-one-match-funding-for-1890-land-grant-universities.pdf.

6

The Seamstress and the Counselor

Evelyn T. Butts, Joseph Jordan Jr., and *Butts v. Harrison* (1966)

JEFFREY L. LITTLEJOHN AND CHARLES H. FORD

The expansion of voting rights in Virginia is popularly associated with the ratification of the Twenty-Fourth Amendment to the U.S. Constitution in 1964 and the passage of the federal Voting Rights Act in 1965. Yet discriminatory obstacles to voting in state and local elections lingered on in Virginia even after these crucial changes to federal election law were made. In fact, it took the confidence and tenacity of two local activists in Norfolk, Virginia— attorney Joseph Jordan Jr. and seamstress Evelyn Butts—to challenge the state's discriminatory voting restrictions and secure democratic rights for all. Accordingly, this chapter traces the development of the unlikely professional partnership between this attorney and housewife, their landmark litigation, and their efforts to shape public opinion to support their side. Indeed, Jordan and Butts's most important contribution to civil rights history may have been their efforts to build independent Black leadership to challenge white political domination in the Old Dominion. Framed in the tradition of John Dittmer's landmark study, *Local People: The Struggle for Civil Rights in Mississippi* (1995), this chapter privileges grassroots activism over the national narrative and organizations. In other words, the anniversary of the expansion of voting rights should be more complicated and extended than merely honoring President Lyndon B. Johnson's response to demonstrations in Selma, Alabama. In Virginia, it must include everyday people who challenged the status quo to introduce a new era of American democracy.[1]

Over the past two decades, the historiography of the civil rights movement has become longer in chronology and more inclusive in terms of its advocates and actors. For this study, the recent scholarship on Evelyn Butts has been particularly useful in spotlighting her efforts to abolish the poll tax in Virginia. Nevertheless, we must not forget another local figure, Joseph Jordan Jr., who was often dismissed during his lifetime as a radical gadfly and promoter of lost causes. Our study shows that both Jordan and Butts played crucial roles in overturning Virginia's poll tax at the U.S. Supreme Court. At the same time, we also put Butts and Jordan in a wider context by showing that their eventual reliance on the Fourteenth Amendment proved to be persuasive to the Warren court, rather than the race-neutral New Deal arguments put forward by white moderates for at least a generation before.[2]

* * *

The first large-scale African American effort to vote in Virginia occurred during the U.S. Civil War. The Union's quick occupation of Norfolk in 1862 facilitated African American advocacy. Accordingly, Thomas Bayne, a Norfolk slave who had escaped to Boston in 1856 via the Underground Railroad, returned to the port city to work as a dentist. With numerous allies, Bayne launched a challenge to Virginia's 1864 constitution, which limited voting rights to whites, by sponsoring a citywide voting experiment on Election Day, May 25. After white officials at the city's polling stations refused to allow Blacks to vote that day, Bayne and his colleagues called a mass meeting for June 5 at Norfolk's Catherine Street Baptist Church. There, more than two thousand Black participants elected eight men, including Bayne, to draft a document expressing their desire for equal rights. Historian Earl Lewis has called the resulting *Equal Suffrage Address* a "classic Afro-American jeremiad."[3] While it showcased the idealistic promise of American liberty and equality, the address simultaneously pointed out the hypocrisy and shortcomings of the American system as it existed.

Although the *Equal Suffrage Address* has received extensive coverage from historians, few have noted its truly radical tone and implications. In a series of resolutions that make up the body of the document, its authors declared that "political, or legal distinctions, on account of color merely," were inconsistent with "sound political economy, . . . patriotism, humanity and religion." To overturn such distinctions, the members of Norfolk's Black elite called for the franchise and "equal political and civil rights." They wanted, in essence, a true revolution in the local and statewide political system that would allow Black men to vote, hold office, and play a role in their own government. To achieve their ends, they promised continuous political and economic pressure, declaring further, in their most defiant statement, that "traitors shall not dictate or prescribe to us the terms or conditions of our citizenship."[4]

Shortly after signing the *Equal Suffrage Address*, one of Bayne's Norfolk allies, George Cook, attended the August 1865 Colored State Convention in Alexandria. Speaking to the convention in its opening session, Cook encouraged the various delegates to stand strong and forthright in their convictions. Had they "not only supported themselves" during their time of enslavement, he asked, but "also their masters, 'many of them in idleness'"? Now the time had arrived to discuss the "subject of freedom." They were no longer slaves or free Blacks, but citizens of the United States, and Cook told them that he and his allies from Norfolk were determined to "secure the right of franchise in every way that is honorable and just." Ultimately, Cook's militant advocacy for voting and civil rights was adopted by the convention, which issued its own controversial address on August 15, 1865.[5]

As a result of African American and Republican Party pressure, Black men in Virginia began voting in 1867.[6] Three years later, the Fifteenth Amendment to the U.S. Constitution was ratified. It stated that the right to vote could not be abridged because of race, color, or previous condition of servitude. As a result, Black men in Virginia turned out by the thousands and elected a new slate of "Readjusters" to office. By the late 1870s, the Readjusters had pursued a biracial settlement to the Civil War and Reconstruction by allowing ambitious African American men a place at the political table. Led by former Confederate general and railroad magnate William Mahone, the group also included Norfolk's mayor William Lamb and other politicians from around the state. Named for its supporters' effort to "readjust" the massive debt of Virginia in order to reduce the tax burden on small farmers, the Readjuster Party highlighted the shared economic interests of poor whites and Blacks and offered for a brief time a populist alternative to the restoration of the gentry. Their emergence was primarily fueled by resentment over the high taxes that were levied to satisfy war debts to elite bondholders and, in Norfolk, over the city's growing reputation as a sinkhole of vice and corruption. The party gained power over the state legislature in 1879 and elected its leader, Mahone, to the U.S. Senate the following year. But the "Lost Cause" refused to lose, and entrenched racism soon doomed any efforts at class-based solidarity. As historians have shown, opponents of the Readjusters used "fraud, violence, and gerrymandering of political boundaries" to break up the Black-white coalition that had once seemed so promising.[7]

Soon, white Democrats returned to office in a movement popularly known as "Redemption." The Democratic Party ensured its "domination of Virginia politics through enactment of the Anderson-McCormick Act of 1884." Specifically, the "administrative machinery of all elections was firmly placed in the hands of Democratic election boards, judges, and clerks at the local level. With few exceptions, Republican and Negro election campaigns became exercises in futility."[8] Then, in 1902, Virginia's white Democrats established the poll tax at the state's constitutional convention. At that time, Carter Glass, a prominent delegate to the convention and later a U.S. congressman and senator, exclaimed, "Discrimination! Why that is precisely what we propose; that . . . is what this Convention was elected for—to discriminate to the very extremity of permissible action . . . with a view to the elimination of every Negro voter who can be gotten rid of, legally, without impairing the numerical strength of the white electorate."[9] Glass and his Democratic colleagues proved remarkably successful. The poll tax system that they established required that people seeking to vote pay a $1.50 registration tax every year. The cost of the tax proved to be only one small part of the system, however. Since the tax was due six months before Election Day, many Virginians failed to pay it on time. As a result, potential voters could be barred from participating in elections, and back taxes might accumulate each year the taxes remained unpaid.

In addition, Virginia Democrats added a new literacy test—more popularly known as the "understanding clause"—to state law. It required that eligible citizens make an application to vote in their own hand, including their details about their contact information that were not always explicitly prompted by the form. In fact, potential Black voters often received blank forms and were asked to read the registrar's mind in terms of what specifically the registrar wanted at that point in time. Virginia law also required that potential voters answer "on oath any and all questions *affecting [their] qualifications as an elector.*" In many localities, white registrars used these opaque questions and implicit assumptions to disfranchise Black voters. Just such an occurrence happened when Thomas C. Allen, the white registrar in Hampton, refused to accept W. E. Davis's voter registration application. Davis filed suit in 1929, and the Virginia Supreme Court later ruled that "neither [Davis's] knowledge or lack of knowledge . . . , nor his proficiency or deficiency in education as disclosed by his answers to . . . questions, has any bearing on whether he is, or is not, entitled to register and vote." Historian J. Douglas Smith has shown the significance of Davis's critical case, which "placed the law firmly on the side of black voters" regarding the use of blank sheet voting and registrar questions.[10]

In contrast, the poll tax in Virginia and other southern states received U.S. Supreme Court approval in 1937, when the justices issued a unanimous ruling in *Breedlove v. Suttles,* finding that Georgia's poll tax was constitutional. The court ruled that voting rights were conferred by the states and that the states might therefore determine voter eligibility as they saw fit, as long as their rules did not conflict with the Fifteenth Amendment (race) or the Nineteenth Amendment (sex). The court also ruled that the poll tax on voting did not violate the privileges or immunities protected by the Fourteenth Amendment. Indeed, because the tax applied to all voters, it did not violate the Fourteenth or Fifteenth Amendment.[11] The court's approval of the poll tax meant that most southern states would continue the practice, even though North Carolina ended its poll tax in 1920.[12] In fact, an analysis by the National Committee to Abolish the Poll Tax in 1940 showed that just 22 percent of potential voters in Virginia voted in that year's presidential election, compared to 71 percent of potential voters in states that did not have a poll tax.[13]

The poll tax effectively cut off the African American vote in Virginia and enabled Harry F. Byrd Sr. to organize and run a Democratic political machine that managed white supremacy in the state for four decades. Byrd, a newspaper publisher and apple grower, built a formidable conservative coalition dedicated to low taxes, limited government, and racial segregation. Byrd served as governor of Virginia from 1926 to 1930 and then won election to the U.S. Senate, where he served from 1933 to 1965. He opposed national Democratic campaigns, like Franklin Roosevelt's New Deal, Harry Truman's Fair Deal, and Lyndon Johnson's Great Society. Byrd also helped organize the Southern Manifesto of 1956, which 101 U.S. senators and congressmen from the South signed to oppose the U.S. Supreme Court's decision in *Brown v. Board of Education of Topeka, Kansas* (1954). He was among the most prominent of the South's Massive Resisters to racial desegregation, and his longtime rule in Virginia was made possible in part by the poll tax.[14]

* * *

Despite the contributions that Black soldiers, shipyard workers, and industrial laborers made to the military effort in World War II, Virginia's white political establishment deepened its support for the poll tax, which forced many African Americans to endure absurdities and hassles just to cast a ballot.[15] For example, Mrs. Florine Smith, a middle-aged African American housewife from Norfolk, wanted to register to vote in the summer of 1963. She followed all of the officious and, at times, contradictory rules, but it took her ten frustrating days, a court order, and a media splash in order to sign up and be counted. In the beginning of this ordeal, she had thought that she could just pay any outstanding poll tax balances from previous years and then she would be allowed to register. But there was an unexpected, if not unprecedented, wrinkle. As the *Virginian-Pilot* reported, "officials let her pay the 1961 and 1962 taxes, plus penalties, but said she would have to go to Richmond to pay the 1960 tax since the books had been closed for that year." Smith did not have the time and money necessary to go to Richmond in person, but she was aware of advocacy groups such as the biracial Tidewater Voter Registration Project (TVRP). Accordingly, she turned to the TVRP for support, which, in turn, called in attorney and soon-to-be-delegate Henry Howell Jr., Norfolk's most prominent white critic of the Byrd political machine. Howell went with Mrs. Smith to the revenue commissioner's office, who then called the state tax commissioner, who then begrudgingly allowed her to pay her 1960 tax in Norfolk and not in Richmond, as previously directed. But then the registrar, Miss Dudley, said that "no one could be registered in the six months before the election," citing the strictures of the state code. But Howell pointed to the Virginia Constitution of 1902, which had no "six-months" language, and got Circuit Court Judge Clyde H. Jacobs to rule ironically that the Virginia Constitution, which, of course, had been expressly written to reduce Black voting, overrode the state code and that Mrs. Smith should be registered immediately. Ten minutes after Jacobs's decision, Smith was in line to register at city hall, and her attorney Henry Howell promptly joined her.

A reporter showed up too, as well as James M. Wolcott and James E. Baylor, Byrd organization men who ran the Norfolk Electoral Board. In fact, these last two gentlemen had at least one more bureaucratic trick to play. Smith immediately noticed that the form she was completing was different from the one her daughter Olivia had filled out a week before. The new form was actually less accessible than the previous one because it assumed that registrants would place basic info in the blank two-thirds toward its bottom: name, date of birth, age, and so on. The old form had explicit prompts for this information. Howell insisted that Smith be allowed to fill out both forms in part to avoid any confusion, but the officials "flunked" Smith on the new form because she had forgotten to place her age in the blank space.

Wolcott told Smith that her registration would be delayed until he could get an opinion from the state attorney general about the forms issue. Howell then went back to Judge Jacobs that morning and drafted a contempt of court order for the judge to issue. Wolcott gave up in the face of contempt charges, and he wanted this matter over as soon as possible. So when Smith and Howell came back to city hall, Wolcott and the registrar intercepted them in the parking lot, gave Smith a clean "old form" to complete and sign, and then "Miss Dudley had her read a sworn statement"—the last remaining piece of business—and she was registered to vote in any election six months from July 25, 1963. This meant the old guard got their "six months" provision in anyway, though: Smith remained technically ineligible to vote in the state and local elections of November 1963.[16]

* * *

Most African Americans trying to vote did not have the connections or persistence that Smith did in her runaround with the Byrd machine. But another ordinary Black housewife from Norfolk, Evelyn T. Butts, did focus her considerable energies and abilities to get rid of these voter suppression policies, teaming up with the most militant of the NAACP's lawyers in the port city, Joseph Jordan Jr., to accomplish what Henry Howell and white members of Norfolk's delegation in Richmond had wanted to do for at least a generation: abolish these poll taxes that hurt poor whites as well as Blacks. Popular memories of civil rights narratives from the 1960s usually include African American activists pressuring well-intentioned white policymakers to do the right thing. Most memorable would be the March on Washington leading to the Civil Rights Act of 1964, or Bloody Sunday in Selma, Alabama, leading to the Voting Rights Act of 1965. But the elimination of discriminatory state and local poll taxes in Virginia took a much more delicate and nuanced dialectic between direct action and legal remedy in the strategies of African American leaders, while similar and contemporary efforts by moderate whites and minority Republicans in Virginia, such as Henry Howell and Edward Breeden, to get rid of these taxes for their own reasons stalled in the state's legislature. Butts and Jordan did not shrink away from their experience as protestors or directors of street theater in their patient legal battle in the courts: it was a pragmatic "whatever worked" for them.[17]

A native of Norfolk, Joseph Jordan Jr. (1923–1991) had attended the city's Booker T. Washington High School before venturing off to Virginia Union University and Brooklyn Law School. A stint in the army during World War II left him paralyzed, after his jeep ran over a land mine in 1945, but Jordan returned to the home front determined to make things better for his family, friends, and broader community. He fought to desegregate the schools in Virginia and to register Black voters as part of the Norfolk Alliance of Political Action Committees. But his most important contribution to civil rights history may have been his effort to create a "Third Force" of "20th CENTURY, ATOMIC AGE NEGROES" to challenge white political domination in the Old Dominion. Following the passage of the Voting Rights Act of 1965, Jordan worked with Evelyn Butts to bring down the poll tax in 1966, and their successful campaign opened the way for a new era in Virginia politics.[18]

Evelyn Thomas Butts (1925–1993) was also a native of Norfolk and a member of its Greatest Generation. She was born Evelyn Thomas and came from a much poorer family than did Jordan. Her mother died when she was just ten at the height of the Great Depression. Her aunt then stepped in and became Evelyn's surrogate mother, inculcating her with the strength, leadership, and survival skills that she would display in the upcoming decades. Like Jordan and every other eligible African American child in Norfolk, Evelyn Thomas would go to overcrowded Booker T. Washington High School, but, unlike Jordan, she would drop out. Instead of graduating, she married a just-drafted solder in the army, Charles Herbert Butts, who, like Jordan, later became injured during World War II. After Charles was discharged, the couple began their first advocacy effort: a private agency to coordinate local efforts to help injured African American veterans and their families.[19]

Times remained tough for the Buttses throughout the late 1940s and 1950s, however, as they tried to help others. Evelyn worked several part-time seamstress jobs, while Charles had a disability pension. They had several children and, at times, had to rely on public and state assistance just to get by. But that marginality did not prevent Evelyn from becoming a force in the local Oakwood Parents Teacher Association, where she insisted on facility and curricular improvements in the separate and unequal Norfolk school system. Indeed, her daughters went on to be some of the first Black transfer students to formerly all-white schools after the Norfolk district initiated desegregation measures in February 1959. As her children reached high school age, Butts continued to serve as one of the loudest voices pushing for an African American representative on the school board. She met attorney Joe Jordan while trying to assist high school and college students who had been harassed and arrested by the police for participating in the sit-ins of 1960 and 1961.[20] And, most dramatically, she, along with other parents and some student leaders, helped organize one of the most dramatic demonstrations in Norfolk's history: the walkout from Booker T. Washington High School in September 1963 to complain about the all-Black school's cramped classrooms and inadequate resources, just after the nation's March on Washington.[21]

* * *

It was in that fall—on Friday, November 29, 1963—that Joseph Jordan, along with his colorful and more famed colleague, Leonard Holt, filed a class action lawsuit with Butts as lead plaintiff that sought the appointment of a three-judge panel to consider the poll tax's constitutionality as well as the legitimacy of the 1902 Virginia State Constitution, which had mandated poll taxes to reduce the electorate. The respondents included the usual Byrd machine stalwarts—from Governor Albertis Harrison through William "Billy" Prieur, clerk of the corporation court in Norfolk and Harry Byrd's right-hand man in the port city. While Butts did claim that the poll taxes were intended to discriminate on the basis of race, her contentions via her legal counsel were largely economic. Butts claimed that, despite fitting all of the eligibility requirements for voting in Virginia, she could not afford the $1.50 levy—which was true. The courts did not dismiss Butts's suit out of hand, and indeed Clement F. Haynesworth, acting chief of the Fourth Circuit Court of Appeals, appointed a special three-judge court to hear Butts's suit a few weeks later. On this panel were U.S. District Court judge Walter E. Hoffman of Norfolk, Judge Albert Bryan of the Fourth Circuit Court of Appeals, and U.S. District Court judge John D. Butzner Jr. of Fredericksburg.[22]

Meanwhile, at the General Assembly, the efforts of the all-white Norfolk delegation to abolish or to lower the poll tax had come to an impasse. A decade earlier, it had seemed that the poll tax would go away legislatively and not judicially, largely as Butts's suit tried to do on populist, New Deal lines that transcended race. Indeed, in 1952, repeal legislation sponsored by Norfolk delegate Walter A. Page actually passed the state house, only to be defeated in the state senate. In 1954, another attempt by Page lost by only a few votes. Massive Resistance to public school desegregation after 1956 poisoned the political well for any kind of reform, however, and poll tax support was linked explicitly to defending the entire Jim Crow system of separate and unequal. Accordingly, in November 1963, when Norfolk legislators such as Edward Breeden again introduced bills to repeal or reduce the tax in order to complement the pending Twenty-Fourth Amendment to the U.S. Constitution that would abolish federal poll taxes by November 1964, these pieces of legislation garnered their least amount of support ever.[23] Indeed, Governor Harrison was proud of the poll tax, maintaining that "Virginia has the simplest system of registration and voting." Once one paid one's $1.50 every year, Harrison maintained, a voter was on the rolls forever and would never be purged. Thus, following Harrison's lead, the Assembly reaffirmed that, despite the unfortunate Twenty-Fourth Amendment, the poll tax would be kept for state and local elections, and "a certificate of residency requirement" would be established for those contrarians who wanted to vote in federal elections yet did not want to pay their poll tax for whatever reason.[24]

The most critical voices against the poll tax in the Assembly were not from Norfolk, however, but from the northern and western Appalachian outposts of the Republican Party in the Old Dominion, where $1.50 a year disqualified many poorer whites who had voted Republican since Reconstruction. Accordingly, the GOP in Virginia sued to abolish the poll tax, alongside Evelyn Butts, in the spring of 1964, and the judges in the case consolidated the suits on the basis that they all challenged Virginia's latest electoral laws. The attorney general for the Commonwealth, Robert Y. Button, confronted this consolidation head-on, claiming that Butts's case rested on race and that the Republican Party's case was motivated purely by partisan reasons. They were different, and they were wrong for different reasons, argued Button.[25]

Button's counterattack fell on deaf ears, even if Butts's first lawsuit was dismissed by the three-judge panel on May 12, 1964, because it failed to move forward with "due diligence." Judge Walter E. Hoffman was a stickler for deadlines being met and was the one who gave the Eastern Virginia District Court the reputation for having a "Rocket Docket." Meanwhile, the plaintiff's failure to get the state to provide statistical voting data on time was not his or the state's problem. Judge Butzner allowed the filing of the second tax suit later that same month on May 19, and its claims and citations were essentially the same as those in the first rendition. In order to speed up the processing of data, however, Jordan and Holt were joined by two seasoned midwestern lawyers: Robert L. Segar and Max Dean of Flint, Michigan. Chief Judge Simon E. Sobeloff of the Fourth Judicial Circuit put together a second three-judge-panel—this time without the impatient Hoffman—of Butzner, Bryan, and now Oren R. Lewis.[26]

Further consolidation of similar poll tax cases led to the suit being moved from Norfolk to Alexandria in the summer of 1964 for everything to be ready for trial by September. The Republican challenge was still in play, plus a new suit brought forth by plaintiff Annie E. Harper on behalf of herself and twenty other African American domestic workers in Fairfax County. Butzner combined them because they all had the same target with the same array of facts at stake, but, after another year of legal maneuvering, he, along with his colleagues, found that these Virginia restrictions and levies on voting did not violate the U.S. Constitution and therefore did not discriminate on the basis of race. A $1.50 tax each year was not an undue burden for most people, and it was a barrier for all, whether white, Black, or racially mixed. Disgusted with this race-neutral defense of discrimination endorsed by federal judges, Butts and her legal team appealed the case to the U.S. Supreme Court, whose members heard the oral arguments in January 1966.[27]

Here Jordan was much more explicit in the deleterious and direct effects that the poll tax had on African Americans' voting: he definitely played the race over the class card before the more sympathetic Warren court. He stressed the fact that the state poll tax and its accompanying 1902 Constitution had deliberately eradicated African Americans from positions of political power throughout the Old Dominion, "as if with the waving of a wand." He showed charts and graphs, demonstrating this drop-off and its continuance after the Second World War—even with the growth of the middle class in Virginia, both white and Black, thanks largely to public and military employment. His Michigan-based colleague, Robert Segar, compiled and presented even more data, both anecdotal and quantitative, to show the tax's disproportionate effects on Black as opposed to white voting, and he tied this undue burden to the Fifteenth Amendment to the U.S. Constitution, which had barred states from denying the vote on racial grounds. But even more appealing to the plaintiff's team was the relatively novel use of the Fourteenth Amendment's "equal protection" clause to attempt to attack discriminatory and irrational voting policies that suppressed poor and minority turnout and representation. Voting is a universal civic practice that guarantees democracy, and everyone should get equal access, regardless of income or race or gender, argued Jordan and his team, now joined by attorney Alison W. Brown of the American Civil Liberties Union.[28]

It was this last argument—the appeal to the Fourteenth, not the Fifteenth, Amendment—that carried the day. In a landmark 6–3 decision, Justice William O. Douglas cited the equal protection clause as grounds to strike down all provisions of Virginia's poll tax. Douglas wrote most famously: "Voter qualifications have no relation to wealth nor to paying or not paying this or any other tax." The majority sidestepped the more fundamental question of whether voting was a form of speech guaranteed by the First Amendment, and did not mention race except as a sidebar of protected qualities—"Wealth, like race, creed or color, is not germane to one's ability to participate intelligently in the electoral process." The court also pointed to a most famous precedent that both Jordan and Butts were trying to get fully implemented: *Brown v. Board of Education* (1954). Hence, the part-time seamstress with her disabled husband from Norfolk had proven her point—with the help of her main attorney Joseph Jordan Jr., described accurately, if condescendingly, by the daily newspaper in town as usually "a champion of lost causes."[29] The U.S. Supreme Court's ruling was not effective immediately, however, and primaries for city council seats in Portsmouth, Virginia Beach, and Newport News slated for the week after the decision were still governed by the previously legal poll tax.[30]

Indeed, as the case wound itself through the panels to the Supreme Court, Butts and Jordan did not cease their other activities. They organized protests, one against a Be-Lo grocery store that had refused to hire Black workers, one against bringing the remains of segregationist general Douglas MacArthur to the old city hall building in 1964 to have a permanent memorial there, another against various local holdouts to the Civil Rights Act of 1964 and its prohibition against overt discrimination in public accommodations. They teamed up with other civil rights advocates to urge both faster and more comprehensive desegregation and better, more modern facilities and curricula within the still largely dual system. It was never a question of dropping direct action in favor of waiting for the courts to act or society to change. And that dynamism and pragmatism served them well in their ultimate legal triumph.

But for Jordan, running for local office meant distancing himself from "movement lawyering." In July 1967, he ran again for the House of Delegates. He explicitly asked for local NAACP support and endorsement. He also sought the blessing of the venerable *Journal and Guide,* Norfolk's historic Black newspaper, which proved surprising because Jordan and his law partners had sparred with editor P. B. Young Sr. over the merits of "movement lawyering" earlier in the decade. For its part, the *Journal and Guide* had always preferred Jordan's courtroom efforts in favor of school desegregation and poll tax reforms over what Young and others considered stunts and counterproductive street theater. When Young passed away in 1962, however, it was time to end any lingering friction over Jordan's embrace of direct action, which had disturbed the newspaper and its publishers. Unfortunately for Jordan, Dr. William P. Robinson Sr., professor of political science at the Norfolk Division of Virginia State College, also pursued the same political path, and they ended up splitting the Black vote. Yet Jordan was not discouraged, finishing eighth among twelve candidates for seven seats. And even though Robinson lost this time too, Jordan and Robinson had attracted white votes.[31] For his part, Robinson would eventually get to the House of Delegates in 1970 and serve admirably until his death from bone cancer in 1981.[32]

Jordan then realized that he needed to reach out to moderate whites and particularly downtown business leaders worried about urban unrest in order to win. On January 11, 1968, he declared his candidacy for city council, and systematically went about courting the most progressive components of the courthouse crowd. Jordan had learned to do this from his poll tax initiative, and the prestige of winning before the Supreme Court did not hurt his confidence. At first, though, he was seemingly rebuffed: Advance Norfolk, a nonpartisan elite and self-appointed watchdog group, deemed Jordan unqualified in April, and Mayor Roy Martin seemed to see Jordan behind any racial tensions or problems in the port city. Nevertheless, after an outcry over Advance Norfolk's preliminary judgment in April, the group issued a revision in May seeing Jordan as the most business-friendly and forward-thinking of all of the candidates. Jordan was also successful in getting the Young Democrats' McDuffie and Tonelson to form an active volunteer core of white Old Dominion college students.[33]

Events almost stopped Jordan's momentum. The assassinations of Martin Luther King Jr. and Robert F. Kennedy polarized the electorate by exacerbating racial tensions in Norfolk. While Virginia stayed relatively calm, local Black leaders such as the Reverend Milton Reid agreed to host the traveling Poor People's March in Norfolk in May 1968. This had been the kind of event that "movement lawyering" would have embraced, but Jordan as candidate distanced himself and did not participate. The civic leadership initially agreed to all of the organizer's logistical demands, just to get the event over with, and then once the march had passed, Mayor Roy Martin publicly exploded. He let loose a brusque tirade on Reverend Reid and accused Jordan of using Reid as a vehicle to threaten the white establishment. This ungentlemanly attack did not sit well with the *Pilot*'s editorial board or the well-connected business supporters of Jordan. For his part, Jordan did not respond to Martin's broadside, allowing his new allies to disapprove of such an unprofessional display of temper.[34]

The evidence of Jordan's success in building a pro-business coalition could be seen in the fancy fundraiser put on by Senator Peter Babalas and his wife, Lilly, for the Black candidate. At their riverfront property on the west side of town, which was described by the paper as "graceful and tree-shaded," on Sunday afternoon, May 19, "about 500 men and women attended the function on the shade-dappled grass, where long white-clothed tables were set for barbecue." As the *Pilot* reporter noted, "Jordan arrived early with his wife." They were two of the four Black people in attendance. Jordan made a joke about using barbecue for bait, as "power boats hummed off-shore" and "a slight breeze fluttered the hems of the ladies' dresses as they sought protection from the glare beneath magnolias." Frederick Stant, Democratic candidate for Congress, said the Babalases' lawn party showed that Blacks could belong to "our" society; City Treasurer Vincent Wyatt, "in a rakish red sport coat," reasoned that, since Blacks made up over 30 percent of Norfolk's population, they should get a representation of at least one-seventh on the council. Both Republicans and Democrats showed up at this event to show their "tolerance" for African Americans. "The party was still going strong at 4 pm, when strains of Jerome Kern's *Showboat* drifted from a speaker through the crowd."[35]

Accordingly, Jordan's eventual victory in June 1968 stemmed from two factors, according to the *Pilot*: "He picked up the support he needed in predominately white precincts and he received a tremendous single-shot vote in the Negro precincts." Single-shot voting meant that all Black votes in a district were cast for one Black candidate. In a field of eight candidates going after three seats, he had finished second—only William P. Barfield of the pro-administration slate of 1960 received more votes. The incumbent Paul Schweitzer lost his seat to Jordan, and said his defeat marked a new era for the port city, even if "only time can indicate whether this is good or not." Schweitzer had been seen as the pragmatic yet still segregationist chair of the school board during Massive Resistance, and his departure was a sad one for those, like Roy Martin, who had gotten a moderate image from standing up to the excesses of that moment still fresh in the minds of many. They had thought that they could keep change at bay by not overreacting but through delay, indifference, and inertia. They had not seen African Americans as leaders in themselves, and this was all new to the municipal leadership. William Barfield said: "I've worked with Negroes all my life and I think we can work with them. I'm sure I can."[36]

The rest of the Jordan-Butts story is full of poignant ironies: from that one successful shining moment, both would go on to be seekers and givers of civic patronage and power in the new dawn of competitive Virginia politics. From being a marginal militant champion of lost causes in the early 1960s, Jordan would go on to become the first African American councilman elected in Norfolk since Reconstruction in 1968, and then vice mayor in the 1970s. He subsequently became a law-and-order circuit judge in the 1980s and was plagued by accusations of corruption and hypocrisy. He went from outsider to insider with the help of his own key contributions to the ending of the poll tax. Butts would go on to serve on the local housing board as well as the Model Cities and Citizens' Advisory Commissions, but when she tried to run for city council in the early 1980s, both the white and Black establishments abandoned her because of her lack of education or professional accomplishments. Wealth may not be a qualification for voting anymore, but it was seen as an informal prerequisite for holding municipal office. She was too Black or grassroots for male leaders whom she had mentored and collaborated with—including, most tragically, Joseph Jordan. Her determination and strength was also now characterized by some as abrasive, undignified, or unprofessional, and they were used against her to frustrate her three attempts to become a councilwoman. In the 1990s, after their deaths, the reputations of Jordan and Butts again changed—this time for the better—as another of Jordan's lost causes, the long-stalled Martin Luther King memorial on Brambleton Avenue, came to completion, and as a street in her Oakwood neighborhood was named after Evelyn Butts. But their biggest triumph has really never been fully appreciated until now—against the context of our new century's spate of voting restrictions and suppressions.[37]

Notes

1 John Dittmer, *Local People: The Struggle for Civil Rights in Mississippi* (Urbana: University of Illinois Press, 1994).

2 For the most complete biographical information on Butts, see her daughter's study: Charlene Butts Ligon, *Fearless: How a Poor Virginia Seamstress Took on Jim Crow, Beat the Poll Tax and Changed Her City Forever* (Bellevue, NE: Smallwood Charlotte Press, 2017). See also Kenneth Cooper Alexander, *Persistence: Evelyn Butts and the African American Quest for Full Citizenship and Self-Determination* (Wilmington, OH: Orange Frazer Press, 2021). For a recent look at Joseph Jordan Jr., see Jeffrey L. Littlejohn and Charles H. Ford, "'In the Best American Tradition of Freedom, We Defy You': The Radical Partnership of Joseph Jordan, Edward Dawley, and Leonard Holt," *Journal of African American History* 106, no. 3 (Summer 2021): 496–520.

3 Earl Lewis, *In Their Own Interests: Race, Class and Power in Twentieth-Century Norfolk, Virginia* (Berkeley: University of California Press, 1991), 11.

4 "Equal Suffrage Address from the Colored Citizens of Norfolk, Va., to the People of the United States," in *Proceedings of the Black National and State Conventions,*

1865–1900, vol. 1, ed. Philip S. Foner and George E. Walker (Philadelphia: Temple University Press, 1986), 80–103.
5 "Proceedings of the Convention of the Colored People of VA., Held in the City of Alexandria, August 2, 3, 4, 5, 1865," in *Proceedings of the Black State Conventions, 1840–1865*, vol. 2, ed. Philip S. Foner and George E. Walker (Philadelphia: Temple University Press, 1980), 256–74.
6 Jane Dailey, *Before Jim Crow: The Politics of Race in Postemancipation Virginia* (Chapel Hill: University of North Carolina Press, 2000); Richard L. Morton, "The Negro in Virginia Politics, 1865–1902" (PhD diss., University of Virginia, 1918), 15–49.
7 Dailey, *Before Jim Crow*; Thomas C. Parramore with Peter C. Stewart and Tommy L. Bogger, *Norfolk: The First Four Centuries* (Charlottesville: University of Virginia Press, 1994), 242–45; Ronald E. Shibley, "Election Laws and Electoral Practices in Virginia, 1867–1902: An Administrative and Political History" (PhD diss., University of Virginia, 1972), 1–2.
8 Shibley, "Election Laws and Electoral Practices," 1–2.
9 Harold Wilson, "The Role of Carter Glass in the Disfranchisement of the Virginia Negro," *Historian* 32, no. 1 (November 1969): 69–82.
10 J. Douglas Smith, *Managing White Supremacy: Race, Politics, and Citizenship in Jim Crow Virginia* (Chapel Hill: University of North Carolina Press, 2002), 230, 231, 232–33.
11 *Breedlove v. Suttles*, 302 U.S. 277 (1937).
12 Sarah Wilkerson-Freeman, "The Second Battle for Woman Suffrage: Alabama White Women, the Poll Tax, and V. O. Key's Master Narrative of Southern Politics," *Journal of Southern History* 68 (May 2002): 333–74.
13 National Committee to Abolish the Poll Tax, "The Poll Tax Repeal Handbook," Washington, D.C., September 1943, Franklin Delano Roosevelt Presidential Library, Hyde Park, New York, OF 1113, Poll tax 1943.
14 Smith, *Managing White Supremacy*.
15 Kevin M. Kruse and Stephen Tuck, eds., *Fog of War: The Second World War and the Civil Rights Movement* (New York: Oxford University Press, 2012).
16 Ed Frede, "Mrs. Smith Registered at Last—10 Day Struggle Ends," *Virginian-Pilot*, July 26, 1963, 29, 34.
17 Parramore et al., *Norfolk*, 362–91.
18 Littlejohn and Ford, "In the Best American Tradition of Freedom"; see also Jeffrey L. Littlejohn and Charles H. Ford, *Elusive Equality: Desegregation and Resegregation in Norfolk's Public Schools* (Charlottesville: University of Virginia Press, 2012).
19 Ligon, *Fearless*; Alexander, *Persistence*.
20 Ligon, *Fearless*; Alexander, *Persistence*.
21 Jeffrey L. Littlejohn and Charles H. Ford, "Booker T. Washington High School: History, Identity, and Educational Equity in Norfolk, Virginia," *Virginia Magazine of History and Biography* 124, no. 2 (2016): 134–62.
22 On earlier challenges to the poll tax in Virginia, see Peter Wallenstein, *Blue Laws and Black Codes: Conflict, Courts, and Change in Twentieth-Century Virginia* (Char-

lottesville: University of Virginia Press, 2004), especially chapter 7; "Suit Challenges State Poll Tax: Constitution, Too," *Norfolk (VA) Ledger-Star,* November 29, 1963, 1.

23 Tom Reilly, "Norfolk Solons Led Fights: Poll Tax Attacks Nearly Succeeded," *Norfolk (VA) Ledger-Star,* November 21, 1963, 29; "Governor Harrison Would Keep Va. Poll Tax," *Norfolk Journal and Guide,* September 1, 1962, C1.

24 Tom Reilly, "Vote 'Purity' at Stake, Harrison Tells Assembly: Legislative Nod Likely," *Norfolk (VA) Ledger-Star,* November 19, 1963, 1, 2. See also "Governor Harrison Would Keep Va. Poll Tax."

25 "Poll Tax Suits Attacked," *Charlottesville Virginian-Pilot,* April 29, 1964, 15.

26 "Michigan Attorneys Battle $1.50 Poll Tax in Virginia," *Detroit Free Press,* October 22, 1964, 1.

27 Alexander, *Persistence,* 182–92.

28 John I. Brooks, "Norfolkian Tells Court of Tax 'Ills,'" *Charlottesville Virginian-Pilot,* January 27, 1966, 1, 10; "Top Court Hears Jordan: Few Negroes in Office, Va. Poll Taxes Blamed," *Norfolk Journal and Guide,* January 29, 1966, C2.

29 John I. Brooks, "Virginia Poll Tax Killed by Court: 6-3 Decision Cites Equality," *Charlottesville Virginian-Pilot,* March 25, 1966, 1, 10. See also "Helped to Kill VA Poll Tax," *Norfolk Journal and Guide,* March 26, 1966, B1.

30 "Seeks Immediate Action: Court Asked to Lift Poll Tax on Local Elections," *Norfolk Journal and Guide,* April 2, 1966, D1.

31 On movement lawyering, see Tomiko Brown-Nagin, *Courage to Dissent: Atlanta and the Long History of the Civil Rights Movement* (New York: Oxford University Press, 2011), 187–94; Littlejohn and Ford, "In the Best American Tradition of Freedom."

32 John Q. A. Chadwick, "Demos Split, but Robinson Wins Assembly Seat," *Norfolk Journal and Guide,* November 15, 1969, 8; Derek T. Dingle, "Virginians Mourn Loss of Powerful Politician," *Norfolk Journal and Guide,* January 21, 1981, 1.

33 Littlejohn and Ford, "In the Best American Tradition of Freedom."

34 See "Understanding the Mayor," *Charlottesville Virginian-Pilot,* May 23, 1968, 14.

35 Lawrence Maddry, "Sen. Babalas Honors Jordan at Party," *Charlottesville Virginian-Pilot,* May 20, 1968, 22.

36 Lawrence Maddry, "Jordan's Election—New Era: Schweitzer," *Charlottesville Virginian-Pilot,* June 12, 1968, 21.

37 "Legendary Local Activist Evelyn Butts Dies at 68," *Charlottesville Virginian-Pilot,* March 12, 1993, A1, A4; Earl Swift, "For All She Meant to Norfolk, Butts Deserved Better," *Charlottesville Virginian-Pilot,* March 12, 1993, D1; Littlejohn and Ford, "In the Best American Tradition of Freedom."

7

Who Killed Ralph Featherstone?

A Case Study in the Repression of the Long Black Freedom Struggle

Peter B. Levy

A bit over a half century ago, just before midnight on March 9, 1970, a bomb demolished a car carrying two young men approximately twenty miles north of Baltimore and two miles south of the courthouse in Bel Air, Maryland, where civil rights activist H. Rap Brown was set to go on trial the following day. The explosion was so severe that authorities could not identify the remains of one of the car's passengers. At first, many speculated that Brown, who was being tried for inciting a riot in Cambridge in 1967, had been in the car. It was quickly announced that Ralph Featherstone, a veteran Student Nonviolent Coordinating Committee (SNCC) activist, had been killed by the blast. Based on a small sampling of skin fragments, medical examiners subsequently identified William "Che" Payne, another SNCC veteran, as the second victim.[1]

Almost immediately, two opposing explanations for their deaths emerged. Framing the incident as part and parcel of a wave of terrorist acts, authorities, the national media, and most local news outlets cast Featherstone as a "bitter revolutionary" and uniformly concluded that Featherstone and Payne had inadvertently blown themselves up with a device that they intended to use to disrupt Brown's trial. Numerous press outlets, including *Time*, the *Washington Post*, and the *NBC Nightly News*, punctuated this interpretation of the Bel Air bombing by quoting a poem allegedly found on Featherstone's body, which read: "To Amerika: I'm playing heads-up murder. When the deal goes down I'm gon [sic] be standing on your chest screaming like Tarzan. Dynamite is my response to your justice."[2]

In contrast, virtually everyone who knew them, from family members to movement colleagues, as well as the Black press, insisted that Featherstone and Payne had been assassinated, most probably by those who sought to kill Brown. Concomitantly, they lambasted the national press's coverage of the incident. Local activists and Brown's attorney, William Kunstler, contended that Featherstone and his yet-to-be-identified passenger had been victims of an "ambush laid by the KKK." Perhaps not so coincidentally, days before the bombing, Kunstler had argued in favor of moving the trial from Bel Air because of the poisonous pretrial coverage by the local press and the danger posed to his client by hundreds of local whites who had begun to arm themselves. Charlotte Orange-Featherstone, Featherstone's wife of just a few weeks, expressed outrage over the way the white press "took the side of the police and the FBI." "They never talked to me," she told the reporters from the *Pittsburgh Courier*, one of the nation's most esteemed African American newspapers. "They accepted the white man's lies and they deliberately attempted to destroy Ralph's character." As to motive, movement veteran Vincent Harding explained at a memorial for Featherstone and Payne at Spelman College that their murderers aimed "to make us afraid to speak, to act, and to be seen with the people who work for equal rights for black people."[3]

Initially, when I began my research, I sought to answer the question: "Who killed Ralph Featherstone?" Making use of heretofore classified government material, especially Featherstone's FBI files, this chapter will suggest that Featherstone's death, alongside the better-known assassination of Black Panther Fred Hampton, and the national media's coverage of it, offers a cautionary tale, reminding us of the dangers of unchecked state power and the risk of relying on the national press to ferret out the truth about the repression of Black dissidents—a lesson we dare not forget as states across the country enact laws to ban teachers from discussing systemic racism in America. The further I pursued this topic, however, the more curious I became about how two such diametrically different explanations of Featherstone's death emerged in the first place. I came to recognize that Featherstone's case sheds light on three important and intertwined themes: first, the long pattern of racial repression in American history, one properly termed the long repression of the Black freedom struggle; second, the resilience of Black folk in the face of this repression and their commitment to democracy nonetheless; and third, the segregation of public memories about this history. In sum, while direct evidence suggests that Featherstone did not blow himself up, indirect evidence of centuries of repression of Black dissenters and white amnesia about this history lends further credence to the contemporary claim that Featherstone's death was part and parcel of broader efforts to cripple the modern civil rights movement.

* * *

Before investigating Featherstone's case, it is imperative to provide a brief survey of this pattern of repression and resistance because it was a story that a coterie of Black Americans had dedicated themselves to unearthing at the time of his death. Indeed, Featherstone stood at the nexus of veteran activists, educators, artists, and public historians who were involved in a project that sought to counter the dominant progressive or exceptionalist narrative of American history, one that largely left out Black men and women. As we shall see, J. Edgar Hoover, the director of the FBI, among others, saw this project as a threat, one as dangerous, if not more so, than radicals with bombs or ties to the Communist Party.[4]

Even before the first Africans arrived in the New World, Black men and women resisted enslavement in every way they could, from running away to mutinying, and their enslavers employed new and unique methods of repression to crush them. According to one source, approximately "one slave ship in ten experienced some form of resistance."[5] On the seas, slave ship captains and crews heavily armed themselves and imposed inhuman conditions on their "cargo." To guard against revolts, newly established colonies enacted strict legal and social distinctions between Blacks and whites, which had not existed in England. These laws, writes Herbert Aptheker, provided for "patrols, no arms to slaves, no resistance to whites, no antislavery agitation, and a policy of divide and rule."[6] Slave patrols, which are the forerunner of today's police forces, searched slave quarters for runaway slaves, weapons, and "evidence of literacy, such as books, paper, and pens." They did so without regard to traditional protections of personal liberties, such as search warrants, a practice akin to the stop-and-frisk policies of modern police forces, which view virtually all Black males as a threat to the social order.[7]

While the egalitarian ideals of the revolution, reinforced by various religious developments, resulted in the gradual emancipation of slaves in northern states, as well as the manumission of some slaves in the Upper South, paradoxically, these very same ideals precipitated a retrenchment of the racial social order. The successful slave insurrection in Haiti (Saint-Domingue), sparked in part by the American Revolution, sent shock waves throughout the United States. It would not be a stretch to suggest that the

American response to the Haitian insurrection represented its first red/black scare, one that set the mold for future challenges to white supremacy. Writes Robin Blackburn, "The awesome scale of the events in Santo Domingo instilled a sort of permanent panic in the minds of New World slave owners." Describing Haitian rebel Toussaint-Louverture and his supporters as "Cannibals of the terrible Republic," Thomas Jefferson, for one, jettisoned whatever remaining reservations he had about the institution of slavery. Fearing that the contagion of liberty would spread, southern states restricted the ability of white Haitians (and their slaves) to migrate to America, limited and/or prohibited the manumission of all slaves, and required free Blacks to register with the state and/or denied them the right to remain in their states upon manumission. Freedom of the press and freedom of religion, two of the cornerstones of the recently enacted Bill of Rights, also suffered, as authorities and slave owners outlawed public discussion of the rebellion and/or other anti-slavery views and barred Black men and women from worshipping from dusk to dawn, even if whites were present. In sum, the Haitian revolt, writes Winthrop Jordan, turned a "noble vision" into a "mirage."[8]

This retrenchment, however, did not snuff out anti-slavery sentiments or actions as evidenced by the emergence of a movement to immediately abolish slavery. Led by free Black persons and runaways, such as David Walker, Frederick Douglass, Harriet Tubman, Sojourner Truth, and Frances Watkins, who wrote powerful autobiographies, delivered spell-binding lectures, and organized networks that physically and legally contested efforts to capture and return slaves to bondage, this movement encountered a fierce counterresponse. In reaction to David Walker's call for slaves to "arise" as well as Nat Turner's rebellion (1832) and the debut of William Lloyd Garrison's *Liberator* (1833), white southerners enacted a panoply of totalitarian-like laws, including prohibitions against the possession or distribution of Walker's or "similar materials," some of which allowed for the death penalty for violators. Fearing that southern bounty hunters would abduct him, Walker's compatriot Henry Highland Garnet recommended that he flee to Canada. Undeterred, Walker pledged to stand his ground, even if it meant that he might be "doomed to the stake and the fire, or to the scaffold tree." Within a year he was, in fact, "found dead near the doorway of his shop" (much like civil rights activist Medgar Evers, who would be shot dead on his front stoop in Jackson, Mississippi, in 1963). While some suggest that Walker died of natural causes, Garnet wrote, "It was the opinion of many that he was hurried out-of-life by means of poison," a view that more than one historian views as plausible.⁹ Perhaps not so coincidentally, similar differences would develop over the untimely deaths of many other Black activists, from Malcolm X and Martin Luther King Jr. to Ralph Featherstone and Fred Hampton.¹⁰

Beyond legislation that limited assembly, speech, the press, and the ability of masters to teach their slaves to read and write (as well as the rights of free Blacks), white mobs terrorized abolitionists and their sympathizers. In 1834 a mob destroyed abolitionist Lewis Tappan's New York City home and set fire to the home and church of Peter Williams, the first Black priest of the American Episcopal Church. In 1835 alone, there were an estimated forty-six cases of mob attacks on abolitionists, virtually all with impunity. In 1836 a white mob targeted James G. Birney and his Cincinnati *Philanthropist*, and in 1837 in Alton, Illinois, another mob attacked Elijah Lovejoy and his *Observer*, and after he rebuilt his press, they killed him. "For all practical purposes," Manfred Berg writes, "mob violence and lynching became officially condoned instruments of defending slavery." Or as South Carolina's James Henry Hammond put it, abolitionism "can be silenced in but one way. Terror and Death." Such sentiment was not reserved to the South. "Many Northerners, especially Jacksonian Democrats," adds Berg, "despised abolitionists as self-righteous and hypocritical fanatics who jeopardized sectional peace and undermined white supremacy. Many Northern newspapers echoed Southern demands for banning anti-slavery activities and openly encouraged mob violence, insinuating that the troublemakers were asking for it."¹¹ Years later, polls would suggest that much of the public shared similar sentiments when white mobs attacked Black students who sought to legally desegregate public schools, from Little Rock, Arkansas, to Boston, Massachusetts, or when the police, state troopers, and national guardsmen deployed lethal force against looters during the Great Uprising.¹² Or as Alabama governor George Wallace (and more recently President Donald Trump) put it, when the looting starts, the shooting starts.

Though they often cast themselves as advocates of states' rights, defenders of slavery significantly increased the power of the federal government to suppress abolitionism. The 1850 Fugitive Slave Law established a federal police force authorized to capture (or kidnap) alleged runaways and enlarged the reach of the federal courts, while simultaneously stripping defendants of their right to jury trials, not to mention the presumption of innocence. The act imposed stiff penalties on those who aided or abetted runaways and prodded many, including those who had been born and raised free, to flee to Canada. While southern politicians led the charge for the act, the law enjoyed the support of numerous northerners, including "Union Safety Committees," which historian Eric Foner has described as abolitionist groups in reverse. Often comprised of judges, jailers, and law enforcement officials, these "safety committees" actively participated in the capture and return of runaways and/or the illegal kidnapping and enslavement of free Blacks.[13]

This is not to argue that these repressive measures stamped out the antislavery movement. On the contrary, more than one historian has convincingly shown that the overreach of the defenders of slavery produced fears that the southern "slave power" was undermining white liberties in the north, which gave political abolitionists additional ammunition to make the case that the spread of slavery needed to be contained.[14] Nonetheless, the fact that slavery lasted longer in the United States than in any other nation in the Western Hemisphere except for Brazil, and that it came to an end only because of the Civil War rather than through a political solution, reminds us of the breadth, depth, and efficacy of these repressive efforts, a lesson that those who sought to maintain white supremacy after the Civil War did not forget.

While the Civil War brought, as President Lincoln put it, "a new birth of freedom," southern whites displayed their determination to minimize its impact. Even before the Thirteenth Amendment went into effect, southern legislators enacted Black codes, and private citizens established paramilitary or terrorist organizations, most infamously the Ku Klux Klan, with state sanction. These laws and organizations aimed, as Confederate general and the KKK's first grand wizard, Nathan Bedford Forrest put it, to "keep the niggers in their place." President Andrew Johnson not only allowed southern states to pursue this end, he impeded Republican efforts to fully implement and execute their "radical" agenda. Often termed "radical reconstruction," this agenda was relatively tame by international standards, limited largely to establishing political and civil equality. It did not meet the economic demands of Black citizens for land, nor did it result in the desegregation of the military or public education or the abolition of antimiscegenation laws (or gender equality). And even during Reconstruction, all too often federal forces proved unable (or unwilling) to protect Black men and women from white mobs who were determined to strip them of their political voice and power, as evidenced by the Colfax massacre of 1873, the "bloodiest single instance of racial carnage" of the era. Even the name given by contemporary whites—who termed it the Colfax "riot" rather than a massacre, demonstrated, as LeeAnna Keith has written, "the success of the reactionary white establishment in controlling the history of the Civil War and Reconstruction." Its story, Keith continues, "vanished from national and even state histories of Reconstruction."[15]

Reconstruction's demise, sealed by the deal of 1877, unleashed an era of repression so widespread and severe it deserves comparisons to Stalin's gulags, Mao's Cultural Revolution, and the worst days of apartheid in South Africa. In violation of the Fourteenth and Fifteenth Amendments, the years that followed Reconstruction included the disfranchisement of Black persons and the establishment of separate and unequal facilities in all walks of life, from schools and public transportation to parks and eating and lodging establishments. Nowhere, historian Leon Litwack reminds us, "was the reassertion of power over black lives more evident than in the machinery of the police and criminal justice system," marked by bigoted police, judges, juries, coerced confessions, "petty prosecutions, the leniency shown white offenders; the impossibility of securing a fair trial . . . disparate sentences; and the terrors of imprisonment, the chain gang, and convict labor."[16]

The era also witnessed waves of racially based riots or pogroms, characterized by white mob attacks on Black persons and property. A case in point was Wilmington, North Carolina, where Black residents maintained a degree of political power through the 1890s. In 1898, a mob of two thousand white men went on a violent rampage, destroying Black property, killing between sixty and three hundred primarily Black men and women, and throwing out the legitimately elected leaders of the city. Neither the state nor federal government made any attempt to counter this coup d'état.[17] Amazingly, whites memorialized this riot by justifying the violence as a righteous response to the alleged corrupt and vindictive actions of Black Americans and the Republican Party since the end of the Civil War.[18]

This does not mean that Black folks in the South acquiesced to a revival of essentially the antebellum racial status quo. Building on efforts and networks that predated the Civil War, as Steven Hahn makes clear in *A Nation under Our Feet*, they deployed an assortment of political tools, broadly defined, to combat white supremacy. They created political organizations, sometime secret ones, such as the Union Leagues, to pursue the implementation of Reconstruction measures, and after northern troops withdrew from the South in 1877, to resist its dissolution. When these failed, they orchestrated emigration efforts and labor strikes and forged biracial political alliances that challenged the dominance of the Democratic Party. Time and time again, however, these political efforts revealed the boundaries of democracy, as whites employed their economic and political power to strangle them. During Reconstruction, the KKK and other white paramilitary organizations targeted Black schools and churches because they saw them as locales of political activism, and they assassinated prominent Black political leaders and their allies, including "Republican congressmen, state legislators, former delegates to constitutional conventions, and county officeholders: not least armed sheriffs and constables, magistrates and solicitors." In North Carolina, for instance, the Union League's entire political infrastructure "were almost wholly destroyed," through acts of violence and intimidation. Potential Exodusters (those who sought to migrate to Kansas and other points west) who gathered on the banks of the Mississippi River encountered "intimidation, paramilitary violence, and the instruments of state power." Emblematically, when Jack Turner, a political activist from Choctaw County, Alabama, sought to work with whites to challenge the domination of the all-white Democratic Party, he was arrested and ludicrously "charged with conspiring to massacre all of the whites in Choctaw County," and hung by a white mob.[19]

Time and space do not permit anything close to an adequate discussion of lynching, which took place at a rate of one person every four days from 1889 to 1929—motivated to a large degree, according to Hahn, in reaction to the upsurge in biracial political organizing. The website of the Equal Justice Initiative (EJI) provides a succinct summary of the impact and legacy of lynchings, terming them "violent and public acts of torture that traumatized black people throughout the country" and "were largely tolerated by state and federal officials." These lynchings, EJI continues, were acts of terrorism that "profoundly impacted race relations in this country and shaped the geographic, political, social, and economic conditions of African Americans." In addition to documenting 4,085 lynchings in twelve southern states from 1877 to 1950, the EJI makes clear that lynchings did not take place "as punishment of an alleged perpetrator for a crime." As suggested above, southern states already had plenty of legal ways to severely punish Black men and women accused of breaking the law. Rather, the EJI asserts, "racial terror lynching was . . . a tactic for maintaining racial control by victimizing the entire African American community."[20]

Just as important for our purposes, those who spoke out against lynching found themselves silenced and/or their protests diminished by legal and extralegal means. Ida B. Wells, the most prominent contemporary critic of lynching, who refuted the "old threadbare lie that Negro men rape White women," stands as a case in point. In response to Wells's well-documented arguments that lynching had nothing to do with the sexual transgressions of Black men, the *Daily Commercial,* Memphis's white-owned and largest newspaper, labeled Wells a "Black scoundrel" who was lucky to be alive and urged readers to silence her. Not long after, the office of Wells's newspaper, the *Free Speech,* was ransacked; her business partner was forced, under threat of death, to retract her story; and she was forced to flee Memphis forever. If she had remained in Memphis, there can be little doubt that white mobs would have consummated the *Daily Commercial*'s call to "perform . . . a surgical operation" on her "with a pair of tailor's shears." While Wells, operating first in New York and later in Chicago, raised national and international awareness about lynching, at the time of her death in 1931, lynchings continued to take place, and neither the federal government nor state authorities proved willing to prevent them either by enacting federal anti-lynching laws or prosecuting participants under state laws.[21]

The oppressive conditions of the South, along with the allure of more economic and social opportunities in the North, catalyzed the migration of hundreds of thousands of Black folks to the North and West. The North and West, however, did not prove to be the promised land, as Jim Crow, especially in the form of housing and employment discrimination and persistent mistreatment by the police, reigned. To overcome Jim Crow in the North, African Americans established new social movements and political organizations, from the NAACP to Marcus Garvey's Universal Negro Improvement Association (UNIA). No sooner had these organizations established a toehold, however, than they too became the target of state and extra-state forms of repression. Writes Theodore Kornweibel, particularly with the United States' entry into World War I in 1917, federal, state, and local agencies set out to "suppress any dissent against the war and require 100% patriotism from the black population." This repression continued after the war's end. J. Edgar Hoover, who saw the Black freedom struggle as a threat to his "personal racial preferences," played a particularly prominent role in the government's efforts to stop what he perceived "as continued threats to white supremacy" from his earliest days with the "Bureau of Investigation" to his last years as the director of the FBI. Very early in his career, Hoover committed himself to destroying Marcus Garvey and the UNIA. Much to their chagrin, Black activists who cooperated with Hoover's crusade against Garvey soon found themselves targeted, because, as Kenneth O'Reilly puts it, "Government authorities saw every Black dissenter as a subversive, every criticism of American policy as un-American." No Black activists, O'Reilly concludes, "from the *Chicago Defender* to the African black Brotherhood," proved "immune."[22]

Moreover, the post–World War I red scare coincided with a wave of race riots, perhaps more properly termed massacres, from Chicago and East Saint Louis to Tulsa, Oklahoma, two years after the war's end. Combined, the red scare and riots helped dampen the hope that the war would usher in an era of freedom. As Cameron McWhirter puts it, "After World War I, black Americans fervently hoped for a new epoch of peace, prosperity, and equality. Black soldiers believed their participation in the fight to make the world safe for democracy finally earned them rights they had been promised since the close of the Civil War. Instead, an unprecedented wave of anti-black riots and lynchings swept the country."[23]

Simultaneously, local and state authorities, from police forces to investigatory bodies, demonstrated whose side they would be on when Black persons resisted such repression. In Chicago, writes Simon Balto, "the police department revealed itself as an institution that would not work well for black people. Members of the CPD [Chicago Police Department] repeatedly proved themselves defenders of whiteness and the color line, rather than as protectors of life and livelihood."[24] Concomitantly, state legislatures established commissions that investigated and persecuted "radicals." New York's Lusk Committee, primarily remembered for its investigations of Bolshevik sympathizers, did its best to silence critics of the racial order, with New York's Lusk Committee treating "all black leaders who were to the left of Booker T. Washington as potential Bolsheviks."[25]

While government suppression of Black activists waned during the 1930s, it never disappeared. Moreover, the failure of the government to protect Black men and women and to pursue state, local, and extralegal violators of their legal and civil rights, in other words acts of omission as opposed to commission—remained pervasive. When FDR's attorney general, Frank Murphy, established a civil rights division of the Justice Department in 1939, Hoover essentially refused to investigate allegations of police brutality. At the same time, Hoover enthusiastically pursued FDR's directive to surveil possible Communist Party connections to a wide range of Black celebrities and organizations, from the National Negro Congress to Olympic champion Jesse Owens. During World War II, when the struggle for racial equality gained new momentum, Hoover stretched FDR's directive to surveil countless organizations that publicly opposed Jim Crow, including the March on Washington Movement, which had successfully prodded the president to desegregate the defense industry.[26]

In the decade following the end of World War II, the cold war at home (also termed the red scare or McCarthyism) stultified dissent about racism in America, sapped the energy of civil rights organizations, and depleted and/or debilitated the corps of potential civil rights leaders. If East-West tensions had not increased or if "McCarthyism" or the red scare had been less severe, the civil rights movement would have blossomed earlier and taken on different characteristics than that which it eventually did.[27] A brief survey of the repression of a single civil rights organization, the Civil Rights Congress (CRC), helps illustrate this.

Established in late April 1946, the CRC brought together members of "various left-wing, black, labor, and progressive organizations," many of whom had rallied around the Scottsboro Boys and/or had been members of the National Negro Congress (NNC).[28] The CRC, which historian Susan Glenn has termed the "Black Lives Matter" movement of its time, focused on providing legal aid to Black persons, particularly on the local level, protesting against racially biased cultural productions such as minstrel shows and the film *Birth of a Nation*, lobbying for civil rights legislation, and broadcasting the plight of Black Americans to an international audience. In "We Charge Genocide" the CRC petitioned the United Nations to investigate the United States and its human rights violations. Cosigned by a who's who of intellectuals and civil rights activists, from W.E.B. Du Bois and Paul Robeson to George Crockett and Mary Church Terrell, the petition "sought to demonstrate that the government was in violation of the U.N. Genocide Convention." It did so by carefully laying out the definition of genocide, namely, "causing seriously bodily or mental harm to members of [a] group ... in time of peace or in time of war," and then delineating literally hundreds of instances of such harm to Black men and women in the United States. Though it received a favorable reception internationally, U.S. authorities dismissed it as a piece of communist propaganda or as hyperbole, and rather than investigating or doing something about its charges, vilified and persecuted its accusers for being "un-American."[29]

Displaying the segregation of public memory, for years white critics of McCarthyism tended to downplay or entirely overlook its impact on Black Americans, focusing instead on its effect on prominent diplomats, scientists, and celebrities, especially Alger Hiss, the Rosenbergs, and the Hollywood Ten. For instance, *Senator Joe McCarthy*, the 1959 best-selling work by journalist Richard Rovere, extensively described McCarthy's impact on American foreign policy, government employees, and American politics but contained virtually nothing on the ways it derailed the civil rights movement.[30] Even though *New York Times* writer Walter Goodman acknowledged that the modern red scare originated with the Dies Committee, named for its white supremacist chairman, Texas congressman Martin Dies, Goodman's 564-page book *The Committee* (1964) failed to discuss the lasting impact that the House Un-American Activities Committee had on the Black freedom struggle beyond this seemingly coincidental origin story.[31]

Black Americans, who in general felt that less attention should be directed toward fighting communist subversion and more to fighting injustice at home, developed a different memory of McCarthyism, one that was reinforced by and which in turn reinforced a broader critique of the dominant progressive narrative of American history. As Gerald Horne put it, during the 1950s and 1960s, white commentators underappreciated "the leftist tilt of the Black community generally" and virtually ignored or misrepresented the long history of Black dissent, revolts, and the repression of both throughout the course of American history.[32] Not surprisingly, some of the earliest and sharpest critics of McCarthyism came from organs of Black protest, such as *Freedomways, The Liberator,* and *Liberation* magazine.[33] Building on their different views, these journals, as well as the work of pioneering Black historians—a broad array of activists, artists, public historians, professionals, and amateurs—engaged in a project to recapture or reconstruct the history of African Americans, to un-erase the history of resistance and repression. This included Malcolm X, who as Pero Dagbovie observes, like Marcus Garvey before him, "shared the idea that the history of African Americans' mistreatment could be used to simultaneously indict their oppressors while motivating their people." Other key figures in advancing this project were Lerone Bennett, the public historian Margaret Taylor-Burroughs and her husband, poet Charles Burroughs, and Amiri Baraka (Leroi Jones).[34]

* * *

As noted above, among those involved in unearthing or reconstructing Black history and developing it as a tool to upset the racial status quo was Ralph Featherstone. This project was central to Featherstone's life, though few would have gathered this based on the reporting of either the national press or smaller white-owned regional papers following his death. Born in 1939, Featherstone grew up in Washington, D.C., at the time one of the most segregated places in America. Featherstone graduated from Roosevelt High School and the District of Columbia Teacher's College and went on to work as a speech pathologist in the city's schools. In 1964, along with many other Black and white civil rights activists, he traveled to Mississippi to participate in Freedom Summer, where he played a prominent role in establishing and running Mississippi's Freedom Schools. In doing so, noted one retrospective piece, he consistently "placed his life in peril," because in his own words, these schools were "inspiring the people to lend a hand in the fight" for freedom and equality. "The Mississippi educational system," Featherstone explained at the time, "is geared to teach the Mississippi Way of Life. Dissent is heresy." The "only thing our kids know about history," he continued, "is about Booker T. Washington and George Washington Carver and his peanuts," and he was especially proud of the work he and his colleagues did to develop an African American history curriculum.[35]

Pam Parker Allen, who met Featherstone at Holly Springs, Ohio, when the two of them attended SNCC's training for Freedom Summer volunteers, recalled "he had a wonderful smile" and was "kind and gentle, and unlike many of the other men of the project, very respectful of women." Several years later, when she reencountered Featherstone, she recalled that "Feather," as he was known, was proud of the Freedom School artwork he had brought back to D.C. to exhibit to the public. On hearing of his death a few years later, she dismissed the idea that he had blown himself up, agreeing with others that he and William Payne were killed by those who were intent on killing H. Rap Brown. While the white press asserted that Featherstone had grown into a "bitter revolutionary," Allen adamantly disagreed. "Always my memory of Ralph is that twinkle in his eye and how he showed me one could laugh and still struggle for justice." Likewise, Daphne Muse, who worked alongside Featherstone at the Drum and Spear bookstore, emphasized that he "commanded the full respect of everyone he worked with," from SNCC veterans to publisher Arthur Wang and the investigative journalist I. F. Stone. Ironically, Muse added, one of the first things Featherstone told her was to "never talk to the F.B.I.," because it was not to be trusted. Multiple people, from Allen to Charlotte Orange, Featherstone's wife of only a few weeks, also emphasized Featherstone's drive to tell and spread the history of Black people, as well as his reverence for Carter G. Woodson, the famous pioneer Black historian, and his desire to build on Woodson's work.[36]

Featherstone's commitment to countering the dominant/exceptionalist narrative of American history also emerged during his incarceration in Dallas County, Alabama, in the early spring of 1965. Echoing the sentiments of Martin Luther King Jr.'s "Letter from a Birmingham Jail," Featherstone noted that one of the advantages of "being in jail" is that it allowed people to do a lot of talking, thinking, and listening. While the Battle of Selma raged outside, he and the other inmates discussed the history and nature of racism in America. They even set up a temporary freedom school, where "people talked about how Negroes got into the situation in which we found ourselves," which in turn led to discussions about the history of slavery, the accumulation of wealth, and the contemporary control of it and the nation's natural resources.[37]

In between Freedom Summer and 1970, Featherstone worked alongside Stokely Carmichael and other activists in Lowndes County, Alabama, and rose within SNCC's ranks. In 1966 he became its program director and, along with SNCC's other leaders, coauthored a sharp critique of the increasingly influential claim that contemporary Black problems were rooted in their dysfunctional behavior—a view often associated with Daniel Patrick Moynihan—rather than European and American efforts to "exploit and dehumanize the descendants of Africa for monetary gain." He also participated in the making of *Still a Brother*, a 1968 film narrated by Ossie Davis, that tackled one of the central debates among Black intellectuals, namely, the history and place of the Black bourgeoisie.[38]

Prior to moving back to Washington, D.C., Featherstone helped Black men and women in the Mississippi Gulf develop a catfish collective so that they could attain a degree of economic self-sufficiency. Following his death, several members of this collective traveled to Washington to pay him their respects. Mrs. Lillie Jones, a seventy-one-year-old from Neshoba County, Mississippi, credited Featherstone with paving the streets of her community, adding that Black people in the area would "never forget him." Several months later, members of the collective paid further tribute to Featherstone by organizing a "Featherstone Black Arts Festival," where movement veteran Fannie Lou Hamer spoke, Bernice Reagon and the Harambee Singers sang, and members of the Free Southern Theater and BLACKARTSOUTH troupe performed. Reagon's "The Ballad of Featherstone and Che" made clear that those who knew him believed he had been assassinated by those who sought to crush Black dissent. "It was not carelessness, and for sure not suicide," Reagon and the Harambee singers harmonized. "Assassination took these lives!"[39]

In the late fall of 1969, Featherstone joined the staff of the Drum and Spear bookstore in Washington, D.C. Founded by SNCC veterans Charlie Cobb, Judy Richardson, Courtland Cox, and Curtis Hayes, the bookstore, along with its affiliates, the Center for Black Education and Afro-American Resources (AAR), sometimes referred to as the Drum and Spear complex, "functioned," to borrow Colin Beckles's words, "as an active political information center where the archiving, production, and distribution of 'Black counterhegemonic' information" took place. To this end, it maintained an extensive list of works about and by Black persons, which collectively sought to refute the dominant and degrading images of Black people that "white controlled institutions of communication" had produced for years. Drum and Spear also published books by Black authors from Africa and the African diaspora and sponsored films and book and poetry readings, such as one by Gwendolyn Brooks, one of Featherstone's favorites.[40]

Strategically located in the Fourteenth Street area—Washington's Harlem—Drum and Spear's founders believed, as Seth Markle put it, "that picking up a book was figuratively equivalent to picking up a gun. . . . Black book publishers, in particular viewed the act of reading not as a leisure exercise, but as arming the black community with knowledge of their history, culture and Third World radical ideas." As an extension of this belief, many of those who worked for Drum and Spear, including Featherstone, played an active role in promoting the development of the Black Student Movement and Black studies curriculum and programs. This included the establishment of the Center for Black Education, initially housed by Federal City College in Washington, D.C., and subsequently independently operated by one of Drum and Spear's associates. Ironically, as we will see below, J. Edgar Hoover may have shared a similar view about the power of books, which helps explain his absolute antipathy to Drum and Spear and its continued existence.[41]

In addition to stocking bookshelves and manning the cash register, Featherstone spent much time and energy seeking funds for the bookstore, including establishing a comprehensive program of Black education and community development. Beginning in September 1969, Featherstone solicited a grant from the Domestic and Foreign Missionary Society of the Episcopal Church, which itself was run by the National Council of Churches. Running thirty-five pages long, this proposal read much more like a traditional grant application to the Ford Foundation than a revolutionary manifesto. It set out a very ambitious agenda of creating a community-oriented library, promoting an Afro-American News Service, an Afro-American Cultural Education Center located adjacent to the Drum and Spear, an Institute of Urban Studies, and a "Community Skills and Service Corps." If granted, the proposal had the added advantage that it could help regenerate business in one of the neighborhoods hit the hardest by the racial uprising that had erupted in Washington, D.C., following Martin Luther King Jr.'s assassination in April 1968. In other words, it should have received the support of the Nixon administration, because it meshed with the president's promotion of Black capitalism. But none of these facts or internal reports showing that Drum and Spear was a legitimate business mattered to Hoover.[42]

On the contrary, Hoover was so concerned with the rise of Black bookstores that in the wake of Featherstone's death he directed his agents to increase surveillance of them and develop counterintelligence measures lest they become a "ready outlet for inflammatory racial literature" and activism.[43] The fact that this directive appeared on a classified memo about Featherstone's recent death provides us with a serendipitous opportunity to return to one of the initial questions posed by this chapter, namely, who killed Ralph Featherstone. Before we do so, however, let's first learn a bit more about William Payne, who died in the car with him.

Far less is known about Payne than Featherstone, but a partial biography can be constructed from a variety of sources. Born in Covington, Kentucky, in 1943, Payne graduated from the still segregated (all-Black) Lincoln-Grant High School in 1963. He then enlisted in the U.S. Naval Reserves, serving two years of active duty in the Vietnam War. After receiving an honorable discharge, he enrolled at Xavier University in Cincinnati and became involved in the SNCC. He joined other SNCC activists in Selma and Atlanta in 1967 and 1968, and he rose to be the number-one assistant to the head of SNCC's Atlanta branch. There is some evidence that Payne may have used an alias; for instance, when his body was recovered at the scene of the car bombing, he had several different IDs on him, adding to the confusion about who the second victim was. Payne participated in the National Black Economic Development Conference (NBEDC), which took place in Detroit in April 1969. This event brought together a variety of activists, from clergy members to members of the Black Panther Party, with the aim of addressing how to "implement Black Power not just socially but economically." The most notable outcome of this conference was the "Black Manifesto," which SNCC's longtime executive secretary James Forman thrust on members of Riverside Church in New York City, and by extension the national media, the following month.[44] Perhaps not so coincidentally, many attendees of the NBEDC attracted considerable attention from the FBI, including Muhammad Kenyatta, who presented the eulogy at Payne's funeral.[45]

Well before this conference, the FBI had stepped up its efforts to repress the Black freedom struggle by establishing the Counterintelligence Black Nationalist Hate Group program in August 1967, better known simply as COINTELPRO. Seeking to "expose, disrupt, misdirect, discredit, or otherwise *neutralize* [my emphasis] the activities of black nationalist, hate-type organizations and groups, their leadership, spokesmen, membership," this operation was directed to miss no opportunity to achieve these goals. While the best-known COINTELPRO actions involved the surveillance of Martin Luther King Jr. and its efforts to crush the Black Panther Party, which included the murder of Chicago Panther leader Fred Hampton, the FBI closely monitored H. Rap Brown and Stokely Carmichael, two of Featherstone's closest SNCC associates, and considered ways to neutralize them. Indeed, from the date he delivered a fiery address in Cambridge, Maryland, on July 24, 1967—for which he was charged with inciting a riot—and through and long after the car bombing in Bel Air, where his trial was slated to begin, Brown was one of the FBI's most wanted men. (Technically, he wasn't added to the Most Wanted list until after he went underground the day after the car bombing.)[46]

Less famous than these COINTELPRO initiatives was Hoover's directive to investigate and disrupt or discredit the Drum and Spear bookstore and its workers—including Ralph Featherstone. By early 1969, this involved the recruitment of informants and the persistent surveillance of the bookstore's phone and bank records. None of this counterintelligence work uncovered any evidence suggesting that Featherstone or any of his associates were making or intending to use a bomb to disrupt the trial slated to begin on March 10, 1970. On the contrary, as noted above, this surveillance revealed that Featherstone was busy trying to obtain funding from the Episcopal Church.[47]

Concomitantly, the FBI and state authorities displayed little if any interest in protecting Brown or his cohorts from potential threats, ranging from reported KKK activity near the Bel Air courthouse to inflammatory statements by public officials (often broadcast verbatim by the press), which, as Brown's lawyer William Kunstler put it, made a fair trial of his client impossible to achieve.[48] Rather, from the moment that the bombing took place, the FBI's primary concerns were to locate (and arrest) Brown and to help drive the narrative that Featherstone was a "bitter revolutionary" who had intended to disrupt Brown's trial and mistakenly blew himself up instead. It did this by selectively leaking information from classified documents that emphasized Featherstone's connections to the antiwar movement, his participation in the 1967 National Black Power Conference in Newark, and his travel to Cuba in 1968. Information about Featherstone's work as a dedicated speech therapist in Washington, D.C.'s schools before he joined SNCC 1964, his near-death experiences in Mississippi and Alabama in the mid-

1960s while working for the Freedom Schools and Black enfranchisement, and his reputation for being a soft-spoken and somewhat shy person were conveniently omitted from the same covertly leaked reports.[49]

Somewhat along the same lines, the FBI followed one bizarre lead after another to prove that Featherstone had constructed the bomb. This included pursuing a tip provided by a confidential informant who alleged that Featherstone had arranged to meet with a neo-Nazi to obtain twenty cases of dynamite. Rather than revealing that agents found no evidence to corroborate this story, or any other that cast Featherstone as the culprit, the FBI kept such exculpatory evidence hidden from public view. Simultaneously, they squelched reports, which emanated from their own informants, that Featherstone and Payne had gone to Bel Air to meet with Kunstler to prepare for Brown's trial and that they may have even met with him before heading back to Washington, D.C.[50]

On March 16, one week after the bombing, the FBI issued a press release that contained its "Final Report" on Featherstone's case. In it, Hoover stated that FBI forensic experts had determined that the "dynamite which killed Featherstone and Payne was intended for use in Black extremist activities." He added that the "dynamite bomb was prepared in Washington, D.C. and was transported to the State of Maryland." How he knew that it was prepared in D.C., transported to Maryland, and intended for use in Black extremist activities remains a mystery, because nowhere in this release, or in any previous and/or future statements, did Hoover and/or any of his representatives present any proof of these assertions. They simply made them, sans support, and the national press and other government officials accepted them without question. Instead of providing proof, the press release presented a number of ad hominem statements, such as the tidbit that Payne was known as "Che" because he had visited Cuba, and that Black militants were seeking to exploit Featherstone's death "to increase racial tension and misunderstanding." Indeed, rather than address the key question, how the FBI knew that the bomb was not planted in their car, Hoover practiced his own form of jujitsu by accusing militants of spreading misinformation, when in fact it was the FBI's COINTELPRO program that had and would continue to spread misinformation about Black militants.[51]

Sensing something fishy, Featherstone's family wrote to Maryland governor Marvin Mandel to express their extreme bitterness "about the handling of the death . . . and related statements made by the state of Maryland," the press, and federal authorities. Why had they advanced "a conclusive theory even before the fire from the explosion had been extinguished"? "The investigation, such as it was," they continued, "was only a rubber stamp of the original statement made by the MSP [Maryland State Police]." Featherstone's family also raised questions about several key discrepancies or holes in the case, ranging from "unexplained skid marks at the scene of the explosion" to the fact that their car was headed away from Bel Air and its courthouse when the bomb exploded. This, they and others emphasized, undercut the government's claim that they were driving toward the courthouse to disrupt Brown's trial. The family and others also wondered if the presence of a state trooper within eyesight of Featherstone's car when the bomb went off was a coincidence or not. Had he been following them all along? The governor told his top aid to inform the Featherstone family that he refused to answer these questions in writing but was amenable to setting up a personal meeting. None ever took place.[52]

As noted above, others joined Featherstone's family in challenging the view that Ralph Featherstone and William Payne had blown themselves up. The National Council of Negro Women, hardly a radical organization by most accounts, headed by Dorothy Height, termed Featherstone's and Payne's deaths part of a "continuing trend of genocide—official and unofficial—against those who raise their voices." Associates of Featherstone and Payne declared that "the real intent" of the bombing "was to encourage fear, to paralyze black people and to make us afraid to take action in our own interests." Somewhat similarly, Ralph Abernathy, who succeeded Martin Luther King Jr. as the head of the Southern Christian Leadership Conference, suggested that Featherstone's and Payne's deaths provided further evidence of "forces at work in this country" who sought "to destroy black leadership," a claim that might have garnered greater attention had the nation known about the FBI's COINTELPRO program. (Abernathy's statement was only reported in the *Atlanta Daily World*, a lesser-known Black newspaper.)[53]

Building on such doubts, upward of twenty Black leaders, including Congressmen John Conyers and Ronald Dellums, of Michigan and California, respectively; Mayor Richard Hatcher of Gary, Indiana; and Georgia state senator (and SNCC veteran) Julian Bond, released a statement demanding a "full scale impartial investigation of the bombing." Rather than blowing himself up, they asserted that Featherstone had been killed by those who sought to "kill H. Rap Brown." Along the same lines, those who worked with Featherstone at Drum and Spear reasoned that "the presence of Ralph and Che in Bel Air was certainly known by their enemies," including the fact that they were "responsible for transporting Rap Brown into Bel Air.

A cold and calculated decision was made to eliminate them . . . [when] a high explosive bomb was placed in their car." And they declared that Black people should protest against this crime.[54]

When the government failed to heed Dellums's call for an investigation, Floyd McKissick told readers of the *New Amsterdam News* that the government's desire to save money and recalcitrance to convict whites for acts of violence against Blacks lay behind its actions.[55] But the FBI's files suggest otherwise. To reiterate, maintaining cover for the FBI CONINTELPRO operations, in general, and the government's involvement in the murder of Black Panther Fred Hampton, more specifically, lay at the center of their response to Featherstone's death. (One might suggest that they viewed Featherstone and Payne as collateral damage in the broader war against the New Left.) On the morning of March 10, less than twelve hours after Featherstone's death, Daniel Moynihan, one of President Nixon's top advisers, informed the FBI that the president was "concerned over the situation." To counter rumors that a bomb may have been thrown into their car, the Justice Department prodded the FBI to pursue evidence that might counter this claim. Moynihan also urged his colleagues at the Justice Department to stifle rumors of government persecution of Black militants and prodded FBI agents to bolster the claim that the bomb that killed Featherstone was connected to other recent bombings.[56]

The following day, fearing that Featherstone's death might strengthen the case for the government's involvement in the murder of Black Panther Fred Hampton, Jerris Leonard, the head of the Civil Rights Division of the Justice Department, circulated a memo that made clear that his office did not want this connection to be made. Shortly thereafter, a Chicago grand jury exonerated government officials of any involvement in Hampton's death. As many know, years later the government acknowledged that it had participated in Hampton's death. But this acknowledgment only came in response to countless lawsuits, led by Jeffrey Haas and Flint Taylor, and the emergence of classified material about COINTELPRO and other secret operations. Reflecting on Leonard's actions, Jeffrey Haas observed that Leonard "was supposed to be looking into civil rights violations against the Panthers" and other civil rights organizations at the time of Featherstone's death, "yet he . . . help[ed] the FBI and other law enforcement agencies monitor and destroy them, to which Haas's longtime colleague, Flint Taylor, declared: 'Talk about the fox watching the chickens.'"[57]

The response of Maryland officials echoed those of the FBI. Ironically, in its initial press release, Maryland colonel Thomas Smith, who headed the formal investigation, expressed some ambivalence about the cause of the bombing. He informed reporters that Featherstone's vehicle was headed away from Bel Air, a fact, as suggested above, that did not mesh with the notion that Featherstone intended to blow up the court where Brown was to be tried. In this initial release, Smith also stated that he could not "eliminate the possibility that it [the bomb] had been planted in the car by someone else." But in all subsequent statements, Colonel Smith, Governor Mandel, and other government spokespersons uniformly echoed the claims made by Hoover in his March 16 press release, sans elaboration on their initial reports. When Clarence Davis, a local Black activist, delivered a speech that questioned the state's version of events, Colonel Smith, with the governor's knowledge and approval, initiated efforts to squelch Davis's protests—rather than see if they were valid.[58] In other words, like the FBI, Maryland's officials did everything possible to frame Featherstone as a victim of his own actions and to avert investigating leads that might suggest otherwise.

Governor Mandel's papers also reveal the close ties—one might call it a revolving door—between the FBI and the state police, which, in turn, helps explain why Maryland law enforcement authorities so closely toed the FBI's line. For instance, on June 30, 1970, the governor announced that Colonel Lally, formerly of the FBI, had been appointed as the secretary of the newly created Department of Public Safety and Corrections and that Colonel Smith, also a one-time FBI agent, had been promoted to succeed him as the superintendent of the Maryland State Police. When asked if it was problematic that both had worked for the FBI, Mandel replied no. Unfortunately, no one from the press followed up by asking Mandel if Smith's past association with the FBI and his ongoing work with them had influenced his investigation of the Featherstone case.[59]

To make matters worse, authorities and the press bent over backward to directly implicate Featherstone in a separate bombing of the Dorchester County Courthouse in Cambridge, Maryland, which took place the day after Featherstone was killed. A widely circulated Associated Press story showed a photograph of Ralph Featherstone followed by a brief claim, made by an unidentified state official, that the two blasts were "directly connected." The *Chicago Tribune* reported that the "former site" of Brown's trial had been blown up by a "2d Blast within 24 hours of the bomb that had blown up in Featherstone's car," implying that both bombings were part of a bigger scheme. The newspaper provided no evidence to support this connection. Citing FBI sources, the *Baltimore Sun* reported that forensic experts had found "similarities" in the bombings. The *New York Times* more subtly linked Featherstone to the Dorchester County bombing by reminding readers that Cambridge "was to have been the site of Mr. Brown's trial." None of these news sources noted that it was the state, not Brown, that had requested the shift in venue, ever identified the state officials who claimed that the bombings were directly connected, or, in the weeks that followed, investigated and/or reported on their alleged link.[60]

Worse still, authorities and the press directly and indirectly implicated Featherstone in a spate of bombings that took place across the nation in the days before and after his death. Most notably, three days before Featherstone's death, several members of the Weathermen, an offshoot of the Students for a Democratic Society (SDS), blew themselves up in a townhouse in Greenwich Village. Taking place in the middle of New York City, this bombing garnered headlines across the country (and mention in histories of the era). While Featherstone had absolutely no connection to this bombing, press coverage suggested otherwise. Stories about Featherstone and the Greenwich Village bombing often shared the same page, making it seem that they were directly related. *Time* magazine's March 23 issue, for instance, included a story titled "Protest and Death" that showed photos of Featherstone alongside those of Ted Gold and Cathy Wilkerson, two of the SDS members involved in the Greenwich Village bombing. News analysis and editorials about the long history of radical bombers who killed themselves helped cement this point of view. So too did reportage that Featherstone had attended and/or participated in SDS conferences in the past, though there was no evidence that either he or his colleagues supported the Weathermen, the SDS offshoot that was responsible for the Greenwich Village bomb.[61] Conveniently, authorities never held a press conference to retract their earlier statements of Featherstone's connections to these bombings, and there is some evidence that they chose not to pursue leads showing that he had not been involved.[62]

One story that epitomized the press's biased reporting and revealed the government's pleasure with these pieces (if not direct connection) was penned by Daniel Breasted. In his story, Breasted, a white reporter for the *New York Daily News,* fumed at Black activists for refusing to allow him into Featherstone's memorial services. "It was a far and chilling cry from the benign days of the civil rights fellowship in the nation's capital when the late Dr. Martin Luther King, Jr. could lead a march of 250,000 black and white Americans down Constitution Ave. to a mass rally at the Lincoln Memorial, as he did in August 1963," Breasted complained. Put somewhat differently, in his estimation, Featherstone and Payne had gotten what they deserved by ejecting whites from the movement and rejecting nonviolence and the civility of the "benign years" of the movement. Breasted was so pained by the experience of being denied access to Featherstone's memorial service that he failed to notice that many of those who had helped King organize that march, from John Lewis to Dorothy Height, had joined the mourners at the service in challenging the state's and the national press's explanation of who had killed Featherstone.[63] Perhaps not so coincidentally, Breasted's story, along with another *Daily News* headline, titled "Own Bomb Slew Rap's Pals," ended up on Hoover's desk and was widely circulated among his top associates.[64]

The one exception to this national frame were two stories written by Charlayne Hunter-Gault. She not only described Featherstone's memorial service in a favorable light but also presented claims by SNCC veterans and Featherstone's longtime friends that the government had rushed to judgment and mischaracterized Featherstone as an embittered person, sans editorial commentary. One person Hunter-Gault quoted, for instance, was the onetime SNCC activist and future U.S. congressman John Lewis, who described Featherstone as a person who "believed in people being able to determine their own destinies," hardly a characteristic of a bomber. That Hunter-Gault wrote these two stories was not a coincidence. At the time she was one of the few Black journalists employed by a major white newspaper, and she had her own history of activism (she was one of the first two Black students to desegregate the University of Georgia in 1961). Years later, Hunter-Gault explained the unusual circumstances that led her to write these stories. Knowing many of Featherstone's colleagues, she attended his service. She was so moved by Charlotte Orange's presence and Courtland Cox's eulogy, in which he warned that the "danger zone is everywhere," that she asked for Cox's permission to report on it. Cox, who had kept all of the press out of the service, including Breasted, allowed her to do so. Looking back, Hunter-Gault added that white reporters tended to portray Featherstone through "a prism" that did not reflect the Black experience, including assumptions about his guilt.[65]

* * *

For most Americans, as far as we can tell, Featherstone's "Death to America" poem, which ended with the line, "Dynamite is my response to your justice," served as all the proof they needed that he was a bomber (and had blown himself up). At the time, none of the newspapers, magazines, or television stations entertained the possibility that the poem might have been planted on him. Prior to public revelations about COINTELPRO, perhaps this was to be expected. But given what we know about the FBI's authorship of fake material aimed at neutralizing Black dissent, including one that sought to undermine Muhammad Kenyatta, who was a close associate of William Payne, it should not be beyond our imagination that the poem was forged. What we do know is that none of the fourteen FBI memos dated March 10, 1970, nor the detailed inventory of Featherstone's possessions compiled at the site of the bombing, made any mention of Featherstone's alleged "Death to America" suicide note. Rather than release these memos to the press, the FBI maintained them as classified records until I obtained them through a FOIA request, nearly fifty years after his death. Why they stayed classified remains a mystery.66

The question of who killed Ralph Featherstone will probably never be definitively answered. As suggested by Featherstone's family, many holes in the government's case remained unexplored, and the government and national press clearly displayed a rush to judgment. Regardless, the vastly different explanations of his death cannot be understood simply as a manifestation of those who knew him and those who did not. Rather, as suggested above, we must consider the segregated memories and understandings that Blacks and whites have about the long history of the repression of Black freedom. At the time of Featherstone's death, most whites maintained a historical amnesia or denied that a pattern of undemocratic repression existed; for many Black Americans, in contrast, as Dorothy Height maintained, Featherstone's death represented a "continuing trend of genocide." As states across the nation ban the teaching of critical race theory (CRT), the 1619 Project, and other discussions of systemic racism, Featherstone's death and the history behind the different interpretations of it deserve our attention to help us better understand how important and divisive history is, or, as William Faulkner remarked, "The past is never dead. It's not even past."67

Notes

1 For an image of the scene, see Peter Levy, "Who Killed Ralph Featherstone?" History News Network, March 8, 2020, https://historynewsnetwork.org/article/174474.
2 "Protest and Death," *Time*, March 23, 1970, 9–10; David Brinkley, *NBC Evening News*, March 11, 1970, Vanderbilt Television News Archive, file:///F:/Lexar/featherstone/NBC%20Evening%20News%20for%201970-03-11%20_%20Vanderbilt%20 Television%20News%20Archive.html; Carl Bernstein, "Bomb Blast Victim Was a

Bitter Rights Activist," *Washington Post*, March 11, 1970; "Rap Brown May Have Been Explosion Victim: Trial Recessed," *Redlands Daily* (UPI), March 10, 1970; "Is Rap Brown 2nd Victim," "1 in Wreck Friend of Brown," and "Guard Is Alerted by Mandel," *New Journal* (UPI), March 10, 1970; "Explosion Theory Told by Police," *Baltimore Evening Sun* (AP), March 11, 1970; Philip D. Carter, "'Fooling Around' Held Cause of Fatal Blast," *Washington Post*, March 11, 1970, 10; "Friend of Rap Brown Dies with 2nd Man in Auto Blast in Bel Air," *New York Times*, March 11, 1970, 1; Peter Jay, "Car Blast Kills 2 Near Trial of Rap Brown," *Washington Post*, March 11, 1970; "Negro Killed in Blast of Car Described as Revolutionary," *Arizona Republic*, March 11, 1970; Peter Jay and John Hanrahan, "Fatal Blast Laid to Dynamite," *Washington Post*, March 15, 1970; "Own Bomb Slew Rap's Pals: FBI," *Sunday Daily News*, March 15, 1970; Nathan Miller, "The Bomb Never Got the Barons in the Terror of America's Past," *Baltimore Sun*, March 29, 1970. The *Baltimore Sun*, Maryland's most widely read newspaper, was on strike in the immediate weeks following the bombing; thus, its reporting on the event was delayed.

3 "Motion for Remand of Trial to Dorchester County," H. Rap Brown Case File, Circuit Court of Maryland, Dorchester County, Maryland State Archives (henceforth Brown Case File); Victor S. Navasky, "Right On! With Lawyer William Kunstler," *New York Times*, April 19, 1970, 217; *Hilltop* [Howard University], March 13, 1970; "Nat'l Leader of NCNW Condemns Last Week's Senseless Bombing," *Philadelphia Tribune*, March 17, 1970; "Bomb Deaths of Rap Brown's Friends Called 'Political Assassinations,'" *Philadelphia Tribune*, March 17, 1970; "SNCC Head Condemns Death of Payne and Featherstone," *Atlanta Daily World*, March 17, 1970; "'Feather' Was Bridegroom of Three Weeks," *Baltimore Afro American*, March 21, 1970; "'Feather's Ashes Going to Nigeria," *Baltimore Afro-American*, April 4, 1970; "Mrs. Featherstone Tells Doubts, Fears," *Pittsburgh Courier*, May 23, 1970; "Black Brothers Cut Down by 'Establishment,'" *Spelman Spotlight*, May–June 1970, 7.

4 On the project to develop a counternarrative, see Pero Dagbovie, "Making Black History Practical: Carter G. Woodson, the Proto Black Studies Movement, and the Struggle for Black Liberation," *Western Journal of Black Studies* 28, no. 2 (July 1, 2004): 372; Jonathan Scott Holloway, *Jim Crow Wisdom: Memory and Identity in Black America since 1940* (Chapel Hill: University of North Carolina Press, 2013); Jeffrey Aaron Snyder, *Making Black History: The Color Line, Culture, and Race in the Age of Jim Crow* (Athens: University of Georgia Press, 2018); James Edward Smethurst, *The Black Arts Movement: Literary Nationalism in the 1960s and 1970s* (Chapel Hill: University of North Carolina Press, 2005); Pero Dagbovie, "History as a Core Subject Area of African American Studies: Self-Taught and Self-Proclaimed African American Historians, 1960s–1980s," *Journal of Black Studies* 37, no. 5 (May 2007): 602–29; James E. West, *Ebony Magazine and Lerone Bennet Jr.: Popular Black History in Postwar America* (Urbana: University of Illinois Press, 2020); Ian Rocksborough-Smith, *Black Public History in Chicago* (Urbana: University of Illinois Press, 2018); Ian Rocksborough-Smith, *Black Public History in Chicago: Civil*

Rights Activism from World War II into the Cold War (Champaign: University of Illinois Press, 2018).

5   Lorenzo J. Greene, "Mutiny on the Slave Ships," *Phylon* 5, no. 4 (1944): 346–54; "Slave Ship Mutinies," Slavery and Remembrance, Colonial Williamsburg, http://slaveryandremembrance.org/articles/article/?id=A0035, accessed June 5, 2024.

6   Herbert Aptheker, "American Negro Slave Revolts," *Science and Society* 1, no. 4 (Summer 1937): 513.

7   On slave patrols, see Sally E. Hadden, *Slave Patrols: Law and Violence in Virginia and the Carolinas* (Cambridge, MA: Harvard University Press, 2001); Phillip L. Reichel, "Southern Slave Patrols as a Transitional Police Type," *American Journal of Policy* 7 (1985): 51–63; Victor Stolberg, "Slave Patrols," in *The Social History of Crime and Punishment in America: An Encyclopedia*, ed. William Miller (London: Sage, 2012), 1678–79. The literature on the tools that slave masters used to maintain control over their slaves is enormous. Among the most important recent works are Ira Berlin, *Many Thousands Gone: The First Two Centuries of Slavery in North America* (Cambridge, MA: Belknap Press of Harvard University Press, 1998); Walter Johnson, *River of Dark Dreams: Slavery and the Empire of the Cotton Kingdom* (Cambridge, MA: Belknap Press of Harvard University Press, 2013). Johnson shows how white southerners even constructed a carceral landscape to maintain social order. On the evolution of the first urban police units from essentially state-sanctioned vigilante forces that sought to patrol a large number of free Blacks, who were seen as a particularly dangerous class, see Adam Malka, *The Men of Mobtown: Policing Baltimore in the Age of Slavery and Emancipation* (Chapel Hill: University of North Carolina Press, 2018).

8   Robin Blackburn, "Haiti, Slavery, and the Age of Democratic Revolution," *William and Mary Quarterly* 63, no. 4 (October 2006): 643–74; Michael L. Nicholls, "Strangers Setting among Us: The Sources and Challenge of the Free Black Population in Early Virginia," *Virginia Magazine of History and Biography* 108 (2008): 155–79; Winthrop Jordan, *White over Black: American Attitudes toward the Negro, 1550–1812* (New York: Norton, 1968), 354.

9   Hasan Crockett, "The Incendiary Pamphlet: David Walker's Appeal in Georgia," *Journal of Negro History* 86, no. 3 (Summer 2001): 305–18; Michael Gorup, "Subverting the American Paradox: Race, Redemption, and Revolution in David Walker's Appeal," *Law, Culture and the Humanities* 17, no. 2 (December 2017): 355–76; Kenneth Greenberg, ed., *Nat Turner: A Slave Rebellion in History and Memory* (New York: Oxford University Press, 2004).

10 George Bretman, Herman Porter, and Baxter Smith, *The Assassination of Malcolm X* (New York: Pathfinder, 1991); William F. Pepper, *The Plot to Kill King: The Truth Behind the Assassination of Martin Luther King, Jr.* (New York: Skyhorse, 2016); Jeffrey Haas, *The Assassination of Fred Hampton: How the FBI and the Chicago Police Murdered a Black Panther*, rev. ed. (Chicago: Lawrence Hill, 2019); Michael Vinson Williams, *Medgar Evers: Mississippi Martyr* (Fayetteville: University of Arkansas Press, 2013).

11 Manfred Berg, *Popular Justice: A History of Lynching in America* (Chicago: Ivan R.

Dee, 2016), 34–35; David Bryon Davis, ed., *Antebellum American Culture: An Interpretive Anthology* (State College: Pennsylvania State University Press, 1979), 297–98; Jeff Rutenbeck, "Partisan Press Coverage of Anti-Abolitionist Violence: A Study of Early Nineteenth-Century 'Views Flow,'" *Journal of Communication Inquiry* 19, no. 1 (Spring 1995): 126–41; Nicholas Wood, "'A Sacrifice on the Altar of Slavery': Doughface Politics and the Black Disenfranchisement in Pennsylvania, 1837–1838," *Journal of the Early Republic* 31, no. 1 (Spring 2011): 75–106. On the slow death of slavery in New Jersey and the dearth of pro-abolitionist sentiment, see James Gigantino II, "The Whole North Is Not Abolitionized: Slavery's Slow Death in New Jersey, 1830–1860," *Journal of the Early Republic* 34, no. 3 (Fall 2014): 411–37.

12 I use the term "Great Uprising" in my study of the race revolts of the 1960s. See Peter B. Levy, *The Great Uprising: Race Riots in Urban America during the 1960s* (New York: Cambridge University Press, 2018).

13 Eric Foner, *Gateway to Freedom: The Hidden History of the Underground Railroad* (New York: Norton, 2015), 137. Manisha Sinha emphasizes that running away and other forms of slave resistance lay at the heart of the abolitionist movement, shaping its goals and tactics. Manisha Sinha, *The Slave's Cause: A History of Abolition* (New Haven, CT: Yale University Press, 2016), 1–2.

14 See, for example, Corey Brooks, *Liberty Power: Antislavery Third Parties and the Transformation of American Politics* (Chicago: University of Chicago Press, 2016).

15 Charles Lane, *The Colfax Massacre, the Supreme Court, and the Betrayal of Reconstruction* (New York: Henry Holt, 2008); LeeAnna Keith, *The Colfax Massacre: The Untold Story of Black Power, White Terror, and the Death of Reconstruction* (New York: Oxford University Press, 2008). Keith notes that even W.E.B. Du Bois, who termed orthodox treatments of Reconstruction "propaganda," missed the Colfax massacre in his pioneering revisionist study of the era. See W.E.B. Du Bois, *Black Reconstruction: An Essay toward a History of the Part Which Black Folk Played in the Attempt to Reconstruct Democracy in America, 1860–1880* (New York: Harcourt, Brace, 1935).

16 Leon Litwack, *Trouble in My Mind: Black Southerners in the Age of Jim Crow*, Kindle ed. (New York: Vintage, 2010), location 4832 (chapter 5).

17 Ida B. Wells, "Lynching, Our National Crime," Black Past, September 22, 2008, https://www.blackpast.org/african-american-history/1909-ida-b-wells-awful-slaughter/.

18 Laura F. Edwards, "Captives of Wilmington: The Riot and Historical Memories of Political Conflict, 1865–1898," in *Democracy Betrayed: The Wilmington Race Riot*, ed. David Ceselski and Timothy Tyson (Chapel Hill: University of North Carolina Press, 1998), 113.

19 Steven Hahn, *A Nation under Our Feet: Black Political Struggles in the Rural South from Slavery to the Great Migration* (Cambridge, MA: Harvard University Press, 2003), 287, 356, 393.

20 Equal Justice Initiative, *Lynching in America: Confronting the Legacy of Racial Terror*, 3rd ed., https://lynchinginamerica.eji.org/report/.

21 Richard Wormser, *The Rise and Fall of Jim Crow* (New York: St. Martin's, 1999);

Ida B. Wells, *Southern Horrors: Lynch Law in All Its Phases* (New York: New York Age, 1892). For a recent study that documents government complicity well into the 1930s, see Charles L. Chavis Jr., *The Silent Shore: The Lynching of Matthew Williams and the Politics of Racism in the Free State* (Baltimore, MD: Johns Hopkins University Press, 2022).

22 Theodore Kornweibel Jr., *Investigate Everything: Federal Efforts to Ensure Black Loyalty during World War I* (Bloomington: Indiana University Press, 2002); Theodore Kornweibel Jr., *Seeing Red: Federal Campaigns against Black Militancy, 1919-1925* (Bloomington: Indiana University Press, 1998); Tony Martin, *Race First: The Ideological and Organizational Struggles of Marcus Garvey and the Universal Negro Improvement Association* (Westport, CT: Greenwood, 1976), 174-200; Kenneth O'Reilly, *Racial Matters: The FBI's Secret File on Black America, 1960-1972* (New York: Free Press, 1989), especially chapter 1, "The Negro Question: Origins of a Private War."

23 Cameron McWhirter, *Red Summer: The Summer of 1919 and the Awakening of Black America* (New York: Henry Holt, 2011); Jan Voogd, *Race Riots and Resistance: The Red Summer of 1919* (New York: Peter Lang, 2008).

24 Simon Balto, *Occupied Territory: Policing Black Chicago from Red Summer to Black Power* (Charlotte: University of North Carolina Press, 2019), 29-30, 37-39.

25 Legislative Committee of the People's Freedom Union, *The Truth About the Lusk Committee: A Report* (New York: Nation's Press, 1920); J. M. Pawa, "Black Radicals and White Spies: Harlem, 1919," *Negro History Bulletin* 35, no. 6 (October 1972): 2.

26 O'Reilly, *Racial Matters*, chapter 1; Merle Reed, "The FBI, MOWM, and CORE, 1941-1946," *Journal of Black Studies* 21, no. 4 (1991): 465-79. On the FBI and Owens, see "Jesse Owens Reportedly Was Target of FBI Probe," *Los Angeles Times*, January 20, 1985.

27 Mary L. Dudziak, "Desegregation as a Cold War Imperative," *Stanford Law Review* 41, no. 1 (November 1988), 61-120; Mary L. Dudziak, *Cold War Civil Rights: Race and the Image of America* (Princeton, NJ: Princeton University Press, 2000); Renee Romano, "No Diplomatic Immunity: African Diplomats, the State Department and Civil Rights, 1961-64," *Journal of American History* 85, no. 2 (September 2000): 546; George Lewis, *The White South and the Red Menace: Segregationists, Anticommunism, and Massive Resistance, 1945-1965* (Gainesville: University Press of Florida, 2004); Peter B. Levy, "Painting the Black Freedom Struggle Red: Southern Anticommunism and the Civil Rights Movement," in *Cold War Culture and Society: The Cold War* vol. 5, ed. Lori Bogle (New York: Routledge, 2001); Jeff R. Woods, *Black Struggle, Red Scare: Segregation and Anti-Communism in the South, 1948-1968* (Baton Rouge: Louisiana State University Press, 2003). On the interrelationship between the Cold War and American foreign policy, particularly as it relates to African Americans and policies toward Africa and other developing nations, see Jonathan Rosenberg, *How Far the Promised Land? World Affairs and the American Civil Rights Movement from the First World War to Vietnam* (Cambridge, MA: Harvard University Press, 2006); Brenda Gayle Plummer, *Rising Wind: Black Americans*

and U.S. Foreign Policy, 1935–1960 (Chapel Hill: University of North Carolina Press, 1996); Brenda Gayle Plummer, *Window on Freedom: Race, Civil Rights and Foreign Affairs, 1945–1988* (Chapel Hill: University of North Carolina Press, 2003); Penny Von Eschen, *Race against Empire: Black Americans and Anticolonialism, 1937–1957* (Ithaca, NY: Cornell University Press, 1997); J. H. Meriweather, *Proudly We Can Be Africans: Black Americans and Africa, 1935–1961* (Chapel Hill: University of North Carolina Press, 2002); Thomas Borstelmann, *The Cold War and the Color Line: American Race Relations in the Global Arena* (Cambridge, MA: Harvard University Press, 2001); Carol Anderson, *Eyes Off the Prize: The United Nations and the African American Struggle for Human Rights, 1944–1955* (New York: Cambridge University Press, 2003).

28 Erik Gellman, *Death Blow to Jim Crow: The National Negro Congress and the Rise of Militant Civil Rights* (Chapel Hill: University of North Carolina Press, 2012).

29 Susan A. Glenn, "We Charge Genocide—The 1951 Black Lives Matter Campaign," Mapping American Social Movements Project, https://depts.washington.edu/moves/CRC_genocide.shtml, accessed June 5, 2024.

30 Richard Rovere, *Senator Joe McCarthy* (New York: Harcourt, Brace, Jovanovich, 1959). Contemporary conservative works on McCarthy and the House Committee on Un-American Activities proved even less useful because they cast the Cold War red scare as warranted and a force for good. See, for example, William F. Buckley, *The Committee and Its Critics: A Calm Review of the House Committee on Un-American Activities* (New York: Putnam, 1962).

31 Walter Goodman, *The Committee: The Extraordinary Career of the House Committee on Un-American Activities* (New York: Farrar, Straus & Giroux, 1964). Not so coincidentally, Goodman, whose intellectual journey was taking him from the Left to the Right, joined neoconservatives in presenting a sharply critical view of the advocates of Black Power. For instance, Goodman's *New York Sunday Times Magazine's* piece on the National Conference for New Politics lambasted Black nationalists for hijacking the gathering of new leftists and left liberals who hoped to develop an alternative to the established parties, perhaps by kick-starting a Martin Luther King Jr.–Dr. Benjamin Spock third-party ticket. These "new Jacobians," Goodman's term for Black nationalists like H. Rap Brown, promoted antisemitic resolutions (truly pro-Palestinian) and made outrageous demands that won the support of white new leftists, who were, in Goodman's words, "dripping with guilt" and "open appearing Communists." Walter Goodman, "Yessir, Boss, Said the White Radicals: When Black Power Runs the New Left," *New York Times*, September 24, 1967, 257.

32 Born in 1949, as the red scare was eviscerating the Black Left, Horne, who turned to writing in the late 1980s after working as a political activist and attorney for radical and left-wing causes, produced a literal library of works on this subject matter. Indeed, his scholarship generated what he and younger scholars termed the "Horne thesis," namely, "the argument that white supremacy and anti-communism were the major forces shaping post–World War II life and politics in the United States, with significant implications for African-descended and colonized people globally." See

Gerald Horne, *Black and Red: W. E. B. Du Bois and the Afro-American Response to the Cold War, 1944–1963* (Albany: State University of New York Press, 1985); Gerald Horne, *Communist Front? The Civil Rights Congress, 1946–1956* (Rutherford, NJ: Fairleigh Dickinson University Press, 1988); Gerald Horne, *Black Liberation/Red Scare: Ben Davis and the Communist Party* (New York: International, 2021); Gerald Horne, *Red Seas: Ferdinand Smith and the Radical Black Sailors in the United States and Jamaica* (New York: New York University Press, 2009); Gerald Horne, *Paul Robeson: The Artist as Revolutionary* (London: Pluto Press, 2016). For an extensive examination of Horne and his works, see *Journal of African American History* 96, no. 2 (Spring 2011), especially Erik S. McDuffie, "Black and Red: Black Liberation, The Cold War, and the Horne Thesis," 236–47, and Gerald Horne, "One Historian's Journey," 248–54. In addition to Horne's work, see Manning Marable, *Race, Reform and Rebellion: The Second Reconstruction and Beyond in Black America, 1945–2006* (Jackson: University Press of Mississippi, 2007), 22–32; Thomas A. Krueger, *And Promises to Keep: The Southern Conference for Human Welfare* (Nashville: Vanderbilt University Press, 1967); Robert R. Korstad, *Civil Rights Unionism: Tobacco Workers and the Struggle for Democracy in the Mid-Twentieth Century South* (Chapel Hill: University of North Carolina Press, 2003): Michael Honey, *Southern Labor and Black Civil Rights: Organizing Memphis Workers* (Urbana: University of Illinois Press, 1993); Robin D. G. Kelley, *Hammer and Hoe: Alabama Communists during the Great Depression* (Chapel Hill: University of North Carolina Press, 1990); Horace Huntley, "The Red Scare and Black Workers in Alabama: The International Union of Mine, Mill and Smelter Workers, 1945–1953," in *Labor Divided: Race and Ethnicity in United States Labor Struggles*, ed. Robert Asher and Charles Stephanson (Albany: State University of New York Press, 1990), 29–45; Barbara S. Griffith, *The Crisis of American Labor: Operation Dixie and the Defeat of the CIO* (Philadelphia: Temple University Press, 1988).

33 Christopher M. Tinson, *Radical Intellect: Liberator Magazine and Black Activism in the 1960s* (Chapel Hill: University of North Carolina Press, 2017).

34 See Peter W. Bardaglio, review of *Democracy Betrayed, American Historical Review* 105, no. 2 (April 2000): 554–55.

35 "Freedom Schools in Mississippi," *Student Voice*, August 5, 1964; "Underground Education: The COFO Friends of Freedom Schools," Bay Area Friends of SNCC, January 1965, http://freedomarchives.org/Documents/Finder/DOC40_scans/40.Movement.Jan.1965.pdf; Courtland Milloy, "A Namesake Worthy of His Name," *Washington Post*, May 30, 1999, C1.

36 Charlotte Orange-Featherstone, "Brothers and Sisters—The World in an Uproar and the Danger Zone Is Everywhere," 1970, https://www.crmvet.org/mem/feather.htm; Mariama Nzinga Orange, "Now She Flies: Dr. Charlotte Orange-Featherstone," December 2009, https://www.crmvet.org/mem/feathers.htm; Claude Pam Parker Allen, "Would You Marry One?," https://www.crmvet.org/info/marryone.htm; Daphne Muse, "Drum and Spear Bookstore (1968–1971)," SNCC Legacy Project, https://sncclegacyproject.org/drum-spear-bookstore-and-press/, accessed June 5, 2024.

37 Ralph Featherstone, "The Stench of Freedom," *Negro History Bulletin*, March 1965, 130.
38 "SNCC Statement on White House Conference," May 23, 1966, https://snccdigital .org/wp-content/uploads/digitalcollections/66_sncc_whitehouseconf.pdf, accessed June 28, 2023; *Still a Brother: Inside the Negro Middle Class*, directed by William Greaves, William Greaves Productions, 1968; for information on the film see NET Journal, American Archive of Public Broadcasting, https://americanarchive.org/ catalog/cpb-aacip_516-kd1qf8kh4s, accessed June 5, 2024.
39 Charlayne Hunter, "Blast Victim Regarded as Top Rights Organizer," *New York Times*, March 11, 1970, 34; Charlayne Hunter, "Negroes Mourn Car Blast Victim," *New York Times*, March 15, 1970, 39; "West Point Honors Featherstone," *New Pittsburgh Courier*, June 20, 1970, 2; "The Ballad of Featherstone and Che" *Give Your Hands to Struggle: The Evolution of a Freedom Fighter*, Paredon Records, 1975.
40 Ralph Featherstone as remembered by Daphne Muse, October 2012, "Drum and Spear Books Founded," Digital SNCC Gateway, https://snccdigital.org/events/drum -and-spear-books-founded/; Colin Beckles, "Black Bookstores, Black Power, and the FBI: The Case of Drum and Spear," *Western Journal of Black Studies* 20, no. 2 (Summer 1996): 63; Joshua Davis, *From Headshops to Whole Foods: The Rise and Fall of Activist Entrepreneurs* (New York: Columbia University Press, 2017); Joshua Clark Davis, interview of Charles Cobb, October 16, 2015, https://www.crmvet.org/ nars/cobb2015.pdf.
41 Seth Markle, "'Book Publishers for a Pan-African World': Drum and Spear Press and Tanzania's 'Ujuama' Ideology," *Black Scholar* 37, no. 4 (Winter 2008): 16–26; Ibram Rogers, "Remembering the Black Campus Movement: An Oral History Interview with James P. Garrett," *Journal of Pan African Studies* 2, no. 10 (June 2009); Ibram Rogers, "The Black Campus Movement: An Afrocentric Narrative History of the Struggle to Diversify Higher Education, 1965–1972" (PhD diss., Temple University, 2009); James P. Garrett, "Creating a Black Studies Department at Federal City College (UDC)," Black Power Chronicles, SNCC Legacy Project, 2020, https:// blackpowerchronicles.org/cool_timeline/creating-a-black-studies-department-at -federal-city-college-udc-1968-1969/.
42 The full proposal can be found in Drum and Spear's FBI file. See SAC, New York to Hoover, September 5, 1969. While Drum and Spear requested over $400,000, the Episcopal Church granted far less, between $30,000 and $60,000. See WFO to Hoover, December 5, 1969; SAC, WFO to Hoover, February 20, 1970, February 28, 1970, and June 30, 1970; SAC, NY to Hoover, September 2, 1970.
43 J. Edgar Hoover (Director, FBI) to SAC, WFO, April 8, 1970, Drum and Spear, FBI.
44 Theodore H. Harris, "William Herman Payne," in *The Kentucky African American Encyclopedia*, ed. John A. Hardin, Karen Cotton McDaniel, and Gerald L. Smith (Lexington: University of Kentucky Press, 2015), 399; G. C. Moore to W. C. Sullivan, March 11, 1970; L. M. Walters to Tolson, March 11, 1970, with attachment dated March 12, 1970, FBI's Drum and Spear File. On NBECD see "Jim Forman Delivers Black Manifesto at Riverside Church," SNCC Digital Gateway, https://snccdigital .org/events/jim-forman-delivers-black-manifesto-at-riverside-church/, accessed

June 30, 2023. On Payne's aliases, see also Stanley Wise to Mrs. Emma Payne, March 20, 1970, SNCC Papers.

45 On the FBI's efforts to "neutralize" Kenyatta, see John M. Crewdson, "Black Pastor Got F.B.I. Threat in '69," *New York Times*, March 17, 1975, 61.

46 Hoover Memos, August 25, 1967, and February 23, 1968, in FBI: Black Extremists Part I, available online at the FBI's "Vault," https://vault.fbi.gov/cointel-pro/cointel-pro-black-extremists/cointelpro-black-extremists-part-01-of/view. See also Ward Churchill and Jim Vander Wall, *Agents of Repression: The FBI's Secret Wars against the Black Panther Party and the American Indian Movement* (Boston: South End Press, 2002); O'Reilly, *Racial Matters;* U.S. Senate, Select Committee to Study Governmental Operations with Respect to Intelligence Operations, *Final Report*, Book II: *Intelligence Activities and the Rights of Americans* (Washington, D.C.: Government Printing Office, 1976). On the government's long pursuit of Brown, see Obaid H. Siddiqui, "The Prosecution of a Revolutionary: The Trials of H. Rap Brown (Jamil Al-Amin)," Medium, January 4, 2018, https://medium.com/@ohsiddiqui/the-prosecution-of-a-revolutionary-the-trials-of-h-rap-brown-jamil-al-amin-d19aed200bd9.

47 For a sense of the network of Black activists that Drum and Spear was part of, and which raised alarm bells at the FBI, see Drum and Spear Bookstore/Racial Matters, FBI-DOCID-7000264.PDF, DOCID-70001034.PDF, and DOCID-70001078.PDF (in author's possession). Thanks to Josh Davis for sharing these files with me. See especially SAC, WFO to Director, FBI, March 27, 1970; Director, FBI to SAC, WFO, April 8, 1970; Robert E. Weems Jr. and Lewis A. Randolph, "The National Response to Richard Nixon's Black Capitalism Initiative: The Success of Domestic Détente," *Journal of Black Studies* 32, no. 1 (September 2001): 66; Joshua Clark Davis, "The FBI's War on Black-Owned Bookstores," *Atlantic*, February 19, 2018, https://www.theatlantic.com/politics/archive/2018/02/fbi-black-bookstores/553598/.

48 SAC, NY to Hoover, September 5, 1969, SAC, NY to Hoover, September 25, 1969; NY FBI to Hoover, December 5, 1969, in Featherstone FBI file (in author's possession); Hoover to SAC, WFO, August 18, 1969, and FBI: Drum & Spear Files; Arthur Murphy to Governor Mandel, March 3, 1970, Judge E. Dyer Jr., "Order of Court in Case of H. Rap Brown" and "Motion for Remand of Trial to Dorchester County," March 9, 1970, Brown Case File.

49 FBI Baltimore to Hoover, WFO, March 10, 1970; SAC, WFO to Hoover and WFO, March 1970; FBI Baltimore to Hoover, March 10, 1970, FBI Jackson (Mississippi) to FBI Washington and Baltimore, March 10, 1970; FBI Atlanta to Hoover, March 10, 1970; FBI Jackson to Director, Baltimore, WFO; FBI Washington to Hoover et al., March 10, 1970; FBI Baltimore to Hoover, March 10, 1970; A. Rosen to DeLoach (Memo), March 10, 1970; C. S. Walker to Mr. Walter, March 10, 1970; FBI Jackson to Hoover, March 10, 1970; FBI Baltimore to Hoover, March 10, 1970, all in Ralph Featherstone's FBI File (in author's possession); Ralph Featherstone, "The Stench of Freedom."

50 SAC, WFO to Hoover et al., March 11, 1970; SA Harry Ervin to SAC, WFO, March 20, 1970; SAC, Alexandria to SAC WFO, March 20, 1970; SAC, Baltimore, to Direc-

tor, March 24, 1970; SAC, WFO to SAC, Baltimore, March 25, 1970; SAC, WFO to SAC, Alexandria, March 25, 1970, all in Featherstone Files; Peter Jay, "Report Puts Brown in Md. Last Sunday," *Washington Post,* March 14, 1970; Rowland Evans and Robert Novak, "Administration Aides Delude Selves About Having Curbed Civil Disorders," *Washington Post,* March 30, 1970; "Rate of Violence on Left Side Increasing," *Daily Chronicle,* April 1, 1970.

51 M. A. Jones to Mr. Bishop, memo, March 14, 1970, regarding Director's Statement; FBI, "Press Release: Destruction of Automobile on Route," March 16, 1970, both in Ralph Featherstone File.

52 James Featherstone to Governor Marvin Mandel, April 15, 1970; Governor Marvin Mandel to James Featherstone, April 25, 1970, both in Governor's Files, S1046-126, "Trial of H. Rap Brown," Maryland State Archives.

53 "SCLC Head Comments Death of Payne, Featherstone," *Atlanta Daily World,* March 17, 1970.

54 "Explosion Deaths 'Murder,' Says Women's Group Proxy," *Michigan Chronicle,* March 28, 1970, 3; "'Feather' Was Bridegroom of Three Weeks," *Afro-American,* March 21, 1970, 1. Press release is reprinted in its entirety in Cleveland Sellers, *The River of No Return: The Autobiography of a Black Militant and the Life and Death of SNCC* (New York: William & Morrow, 1973), 263-64.

55 Floyd McKissick, "16 Years Too Late," *New Amsterdam News,* March 28, 1970, 7.

56 A. Rosen to DeLoach, re: call of Daniel Moynihan, March 10, 1970, FBI Featherstone Files.

57 Haas, *Assassination of Fred Hampton,* 248-49; Churchill and Vander Wall, *Agents of Repression;* O'Reilly, *Racial Matters;* Church Committee, *Report,* http://www.aarclibrary.org/publib/contents/church/contents_church_reports.htm.

58 Hoover to Col. Smith, March 14, 1970; Col. Smith to Governor Mandel, March 25, 1970; Governor Marvin Mandel, Press Conference (Transcript), March 16, 1970; Governor Marvin Mandel, Press Conference (Transcript), March 26, 1970; Howard Moore to Governor Mandel, April 2, 1970, and Russell Fisher, April 16, 1970. In these letters, Moore, who represented the Featherstone family, complained that his family had not been able to get the autopsy reports yet. Neither Fisher nor the governor apologized for this. All in Governor Marvin Mandel Papers, General File, S1641-1912, 1969-1970, Post-Mortem, and Governor, Subject File, S1046-126, A-G, "Trial H. Rap Brown," Maryland State Archives; "Church Orders Activist Probe," *Baltimore Sun,* March 21, 1970.

59 Governor Mandel, Press Conference (Transcript), June 30, 1970.

60 Homer Bigart, "Friend of Rap Brown Dies with 2nd Man in Auto Blast," *New York Times,* March 11, 1970, 1; *Redlands Daily,* March 10, 1970; *Chicago Tribune,* March 13, 1970; "Police Seek Woman in Blast," *Ironwood Daily,* March 11, 1970; "Women Sought in Bombing at Cambridge," *Washington Post,* March 12, 1970; "White Woman Sought in Connection with Cambridge Blast," *Danville Register,* March 12, 1970; "Terrorist Bombing," *Chicago Tribune,* March 13, 1970; "Step Up Hunt for Bombers," "Annapolis Edgy After Blasts," *Washington Post,* March 13, 1970; AP, "Bombings Hit Brown Riot Trial," *Daily Reporter,* March 11, 1970, 1; "FBI Notes Similari-

ties in Bombings," *Baltimore Sun*, March 19, 1970; "Police Seek Woman in Blast," *Spokesman*, March 12, 1970.
61 "Protest and Death," *Time*, March 23, 1970, 9–10; Rowland Evans and Robert Novak, "Rate of Violence on Left Side Increasing," *Daily Chronicle*, April 2, 1970, 6 (Evans's and Novak's column was widely syndicated); Peter Jay, "Bomb Threats in the Area," *Washington Post*, March 13, 1970; Nathan Miller, "The Bombs Never Got the Barons in the Terror of the American Past," *Baltimore Sun*, March 29, 1970.
62 "FBI Notes Similarities in Bombings," *Baltimore Sun*, March 19, 1970; "Police Seek Woman in Blast," *Spokesman*, March 12, 1970.
63 David Breasted, "FBI: Rap Pals Killed by Own Bomb Device," *New York Daily News*, March 15, 1970. Insight into Breasted can be gleaned by examining his news stories, and their placement in the *Daily News*, in the year leading up to the bombing. In July 1969, for instance, Breasted wrote an unfavorable story on unrest at UC Berkeley. Adjacent to his article was one titled "Hoover Warns U.S. of Extremism Peril," in which the FBI director "blasted . . . 'unprecedented' waves of black and new left extremism" who "seek to overthrow our system of government." The following November, Breasted wrote a piece on the New Mob's massive antiwar rally in Washington, D.C., titled "Form Human Shield Between Cops and Crooks," in which he reported on "Yippies, Crazies, and other radicals [who] hurled bottles, bricks and rocks through the windows." In contrast, his article "Agnew Is Confident of Haynsworth Okay" accepted the vice president's assertion that he was not guilty of reports of corruption, without question. In 1973, Agnew resigned due to these charges.
64 Ralph Featherstone's FBI Files.
65 Charlayne Hunter, "Blast Victim Regarded as Top Rights Organizer," *New York Times*, March 11, 1970, 34; Charlayne Hunter, "Negroes Mourn Car Blast Victim," *New York Times*, March 15, 1970, 1; Charlayne Hunter-Gault, interviewed by Larry Crowe, June 15, 2006, The HistoryMakers, session 1, tape 6, story 5, https://www.thehistorymakers.org/sites/default/files/A2006_092_EAD.pdf.
66 FBI Baltimore to Hoover, WFO, March 10, 1970; SAC, WFO to Hoover and WFO, March 1970; FBI Baltimore to Hoover, March 10, 1970, FBI Jackson (Mississippi) to FBI Washington and Baltimore, March 10, 1970; FBI Atlanta to Hoover, March 10, 1970; FBI Jackson to Director, Baltimore, WFO; FBI Washington to Hoover et al., March 10, 1970; FBI Baltimore to Hoover, March 10, 1970; A. Rosen to DeLoach (Memo), March 10, 1970; C. S. Walker to Mr. Walter, March 10, 1970; FBI Jackson to Hoover, March 10, 1970; FBI Baltimore to Hoover, March 10, 1970; all in Ralph Featherstone's FBI File. Forty-six years after the car bombing, Dr. Vincent Di Maio, who in 1970 was "finishing his one-year fellowship in the Office of the Chief Medical Examiner of Maryland," recalled finding "a kind of manifesto, half suicide note and half warning" in Featherstone's pockets. Di Maio, who went on to become one of the nation's most famous/infamous forensic witnesses—for instance, he participated in George Zimmerman's murder trial, on the side of the defense—proclaimed that Featherstone and Brown had "forcibly transformed the SNCC from a nonvio-

lent integration group into a full-fledged black power movement that promoted violence," and tarred him with having traveled to Cuba to "celebrate the anniversary of Castro's Cuban revolution," though he did not explain how the note made its way from the examiner's office to the press. Nor did Di Maio respond to my written query about his memory of this incident. See Dr. Vincent Di Maio and Ron Franscell, *Morgue: A Life in Death* (New York: St. Martin's Press, 2016), 90–94.

67 William Faulkner, *Requiem for a Nun* (New York: Knopf Doubleday, 1975).

8

A Movement of Movements

The Making of the Maryland Anti-Lynching Federation
and the Fight for Democracy in the Free State

CHARLES L. CHAVIS JR.

In late January 1932, nearly two months after the lynching of Matthew Williams in Salisbury, Maryland, a white Johns Hopkins University professor named Dr. Broadus Mitchell published a report of his investigation into the lynching.[1] He wrote:

> The impression was received by the inquirer that the public spirit of Salisbury is far below what is desirable. Those whom one would expect to be leaders in a crisis decided to fall in with the ignorant, the prejudiced, the frightened, the sullenly boastful. Salisbury has given proof of its lack of civic morality—not only in lynching and burning, but even more pointedly in the childish defenses offered for the lynching afterward. One feels that the business organizations stand for nothing better than mere town boosting, the churches have neglected the application of religion to life.

Supported by corroborating evidence from Black witnesses, journalists, and organizers, Mitchell concluded that individual lynchers were not the sole perpetrators of the Williams lynching; he also demonstrated how public officials, institutions, legal bodies, and economic regimes directly supported the lynching. In the aftermath, these same systems aided the lynchers in their successful, yearslong scheme to displace and dispossess Williams's family, descendants, and community. In 1934, following the publication of his report, Mitchell—a socialist and racial egalitarian—launched an unsuccessful campaign for governor of Maryland; that same year, he testified on behalf of the Maryland Anti-Lynching Federation (MALF) at the Punishment for the Crime of Lynching hearings in Washington, D.C., before the U.S. Senate.[2]

Much like Dr. Broadus Mitchell, the multiracial members of MALF—including Juanita Jackson Mitchell, Asbury Smith, Elisabeth Gilman, and George B. Murphy, among others—trace their radical roots to the Eastern Shore lynchings of Matthew Williams (Salisbury, 1931) and George Armwood (Princess Anne, 1933).[3] Unfortunately, scholars have only recently begun to expand on the work of MALF's multiracial, intersectional founders.[4] The Williams and Armwood lynchings, together with dozens of other lynchings that occurred in Maryland across the nineteenth and twentieth centuries, firmly rebuked the myth that racial terror violence—in frequency and in cruelty—was confined to the Deep South.[5] Indeed, Maryland's Eastern Shore, where tidewater slavery persisted longer than anywhere else in the state through the racialization, commodification, and exploitation of thousands of people of African descent, deserves particular attention for how its lynching regime functioned precisely as intended: to support anti-Black violence, while denying Black life, dignity, and due process. Addressing these failures—or features—of the law in Maryland and the nation was the very premise of MALF.

In addition to drawing national and international condemnation, the Williams and Armwood lynchings illustrated how lynching functioned in conjunction with systems in Maryland to persecute and dehumanize Black people.[6] In both cases, the families of Williams and Armwood were ignored by the state; it was journalists from the *Baltimore Afro-American*, not local officials or law enforcement, that informed the families of the lynchings.[7] Furthermore, Albert Ritchie, Maryland's governor from 1920 to 1935, conspired with local state's attorneys in Somerset and Wicomico Counties to downplay the lynchings, protect the lynchers and their allies, and avoid political fallout.[8] Indeed, despite numerous law enforcement agents stepping forward to identify the perpetrators of the Matthew Williams lynching, together with corroborating evidence from clandestine investigations authorized by Ritchie himself, none of the lynchers was held accountable. This absence of swift intervention compounded the long-term implications of the Williams and Armwood lynchings, allowing the lynchers and their systemic allies to terrorize, dispossess, and displace Black Marylanders for decades thereafter.

The aftermath of the Williams and Armwood lynchings was thus instructive for the MALF radicals. It was during this time, in the early 1930s, that four broad legalistic principles emerged, each foundational to MALF's future proposed anti-lynching legislation. The four principles were (1) protecting African American legal and civil rights and their birthrights; (2) holding lynchers, their allies, and culpable institutions to account through federal intervention, thus circumventing states and localities that had historically supported lynchings; (3) preventing lynchings and subsequent physical, psychological, and economic violence targeting Black people; and (4) atoning for lynchings through reparations and the like. Their proposition was simple: it was not enough, though certainly a start, to punish acts of lynching on an individualized basis. In addition to punishment, proactive and reparative actions were needed.

The Case of Matthew Williams

On December 4, 1931, following a dispute over pay discrepancies between Matthew Williams, a young Black man from Salisbury, Maryland, and his employer, Daniel Elliot, witnesses heard two shots fired. When authorities arrived, Elliot was dead, and Williams, incapacitated and unconscious, was lying in a pool of blood. Shortly thereafter, Williams was taken to the segregated wing of Peninsula General Hospital located in downtown Salisbury. After discovering that he was alive, a crowd of more than a thousand people demanded that the hospital turn Williams over.[9]

Eventually, the mob reached Williams, who was straitjacketed in the hospital. Mob members threw him out of the window to the angry crowd below. White thugs, including local law enforcement officers, then stabbed and dragged Williams three blocks to the courthouse lawn, where they hung his unconscious body twenty-five feet above the ground, with an oil-soaked rope provided by the local fire chief.[10] A piece of that rope now resides in the Smithsonian National Museum of African American History and Culture.[11]

Shortly thereafter, onlookers witnessed the traditional conclusion to such a ritual, which historian Donald Mathews names "the southern rite of human sacrifice," as ruffians cut Williams's toes from his body as souvenirs. Finally, as if they had not done enough, the white mob anointed Williams's lifeless corpse with oil and gasoline and set his mutilated body ablaze directly in front of Salisbury's Black business district, known as Georgetown.[12]

In the background, Maryland's politically ambitious governor, Albert C. Ritchie would, in an attempt to position himself as a viable challenger to President Franklin Roosevelt, become one of the first governors in the

United States to investigate the lynching death of a Black person. Ritchie tasked Patsy Johnson, a member of the Pinkerton National Detective Agency and a former prizefighter, with going undercover in Salisbury and infiltrating the mob that murdered Williams. Johnson would eventually befriend a young local who admitted to participating in the lynching and who also named several local law enforcement officers as ringleaders. Despite this, after hearing 124 witness statements, a grand jury declined to indict the perpetrators.

The Case of George Armwood

Ritchie's silence following the failed investigation concerning Williams's lynching stands in stark contrast to how outspoken and concerned he was regarding the lynching of George Armwood, which took place two years later, and the subsequent failure to obtain an indictment, even with eyewitness statements from state police officers identifying the culprits.

Armwood was lynched after being accused of the attempted assault of seventy-one-year-old Mary Denston on October 16. Reminded of the handling of the Williams investigation, Ritchie did not trust the local authorities, including Judge Duer and the state's attorney, and ordered Attorney General Preston Lane to conduct a secret investigation into Armwood's lynching. Just as in the case of Williams, the investigation revealed the identity of members of the mob, including the statements of state police officers who were eyewitnesses to the lynching. In contrast to his reaction to Williams's lynching, Ritchie was extremely vocal concerning the performance of the local authorities, who had failed to keep Armwood safe. Nonetheless, in the end Judge Lynch still prevailed as the system of silence was too strong, and the all-white grand jury returned no bill, claiming that they could not identify anyone in the mob.

This is where Ritchie departed from his response in 1933 following the lynching of George Armwood, disregarding the grand jury, displacing State's Attorney John Robins, and officially taking over the investigation. Ignoring the jury's decision, Ritchie ordered the National Guard to arrest the four men who had been identified as members of the lynch mob. The next day in Somerset County, four men were on trial for the lynching in Princess Anne in a habeas corpus hearing. Nevertheless, in the end Judge Lynch again prevailed. One thousand white supporters cheered as the jury ordered the release of the accused and dismissed the case permanently.[13]

Maryland's Eastern Shore—both Princess Anne and Salisbury—had been, and would continue to be, a hotbed for anti-Black violence in the Depression-era Upper South. Fantasized notions of Black people as inherently criminal, hypersexual, inferior, and economically subordinate—widely held among white Eastern Shore Marylanders—collided with the reality of Black economic resilience, even prosperity, despite Jim Crow impositions. It was under these conditions, in the immediate aftermath of the Williams and Armwood lynchings, that MALF was born—originated by those who mourned yet persisted in the face of racial terror and violence.

Galvanized around the Depression-era lynchings of Matthew Williams (1931) and George Armwood (1933) on Maryland's Eastern Shore, MALF was one of the nascent forces in Maryland's early civil rights movement during the early years of the Great Depression and helped construct the foundations of the nationwide anti-lynching movement of the 1930s.

This essay investigates the impact of national forces on MALF; raises critical questions about how race, religion, and politics affected it; and provides a framework to analyze Depression-era African American commissions in other localities. MALF was made up of individuals, including notable politicians, attorneys, educators, activists, and religious leaders responsible for investigating racial disparities within the state, including the lynching of Williams and Armwood. This essay will examine MALF's dynamic groups of interracial leaders and the organizations they represented, specifically focusing on how members crossed boundaries of race and class, testing their protected status as social and political leaders to challenge the indifferent and racist hypocrisy of the state and the nation.

The Making of the Maryland Anti-Lynching Federation

To white and Black progressive religious leaders, 1933 represented a unique time in the Black freedom struggle in Maryland, the United States, and across the globe. Such a prophetic call galvanized African American civil rights and religious leaders in Maryland to come together and vow to bring an end to lynching in the state. As a result, a little over a week following Armwood's lynching, several civil rights advocates established the Maryland Anti-Lynching Federation at the home of socialist and civil liberties activist Elisabeth Gilman. At this meeting, the officers were first decided; Gilman served as secretary, Rev. Peter Ainslie served as honorary chair, Rev. Asbury Smith was chair, and George B. Murphy and Rabbi Edward Israel were vice chairs. Despite being established only a few weeks following the Armwood lynching, the federation had successfully been able to secure membership from some thirty-five religious and interracial organizations and clearly represented the transition from rhetoric to action.[14]

Through it, liberals took a policy-based approach to combating race lynching in the "Free State." Such an approach was evident during the organization's first meeting, where the participants established four committees, each of which took a progressive approach as they framed their organization's plans. The anti-lynching activists addressed some of the common issues such as the failure to prosecute known vigilantes, as well as what they saw as one of the underlying issues supporting Maryland's race lynching tradition—the role of education. The committees thus focused on developing antilynching legislation, education reform, membership, and fundraising.

As early as 1933, the Maryland state legislature was said to have considered proposing anti-lynching legislation following the lynching of George Armwood during the special session. However, in the last hour, Governor Ritchie pulled his support for the legislation, arguing instead for revising the state's criminal law "to speed up" legal action.[15] Even though neighboring Virginia had led the nation in passing anti-lynching legislation at the state level in 1928, Maryland did not follow suit. Commentary and laws concerning lynching date back to the 1850s when state legislators argued: "We have heard of Lynch law, and every sort of law, which can designate a popular outbreak. We have witnessed enough to teach us that such popular fury sweeps every thing before it, as regardless of opposition from every element in the moral world, as the tempest in the natural. Yet popular prejudice against an individual, does not forfeit his claim to the benefits of the law."[16] Additionally, the Maryland Annotated Code of the Public General Laws makes mention of lynching specifically as it relates to deaths related to negligence, citing the 1898 state court case *Cocking v. Wade,* which stated that if a sheriff is charged with permitting a lynching, his bond cannot be sued.[17] This case would set the precedent for public official immunity in Maryland.[18]

Described by Barbara Jeanne Fields as the "Middle Ground," Maryland is neither completely northern nor southern nor even distinctively a border state. Slaveholding, yet allegedly neutral during the Civil War, the state was the home of many people who significantly influenced national civil rights issues. Where some states saw a decrease in interracial advocacy efforts, Maryland (through Baltimore) would emerge as the epicenter for such collaborations prior to the 1920s.[19] Such collaborations were interracial and ecumenical from their inception, and in Maryland, a pioneer in the space prior to the youthful arrival of Asbury Smith, Edward Israel, Elisabeth Gilman, and George Murphy, Rev. Peter Ainslie III would lay the foundation for MALF.

Rev. Peter Ainslie III

Born in Dunnsville, Virginia, in 1867, Peter Ainslie III was a minister, theologian, and advocate for racial and ethnic unity in the Christian Church (Disciples of Christ) and a leader of the ecumenical movement. Ainslie arrived in Baltimore in 1891 after a short stint in Newport News, Virginia, when he was called to serve as pastor of Calhoun Christian Church of Baltimore. That Calhoun Church congregation would later relocate and become Christian Temple, the congregation he served for the next forty years.[20] Reverend Ainslie was a pioneering pacifist and leader in the international ecumenical movement and emerged as a figure in the Faith and Order movement of the World Council of Churches and served as a trustee of the Church Peace Union founded by Andrew Carnegie.[21]

In 1919, following the Hague Conference of the World Alliance for International Friendship of churches in France, Reverend Ainslie returned to the United States in the midst of racial unrest and was compelled to establish Baltimore's first interracial conference, one of the first in the nation.[22] In his memoir, *Some Experiments in Living*, he discussed his experiences confronting anti-Black racism throughout his time in Virginia and the makeup of the Baltimore Interracial Commission that he established. This included subcommittees focusing on "courts, education, health, housing, industry, family life, recreation, religion and race attitudes."[23]

Reverend Ainslie was one of the first white Christian leaders in Maryland to vocally respond to the lynching of Matthew Williams in 1931 and George Armwood in 1933, in the pulpit and the press, calling out the so-called Christian leaders in the communities who remained silent following the tragic murders. Shortly after the lynching of Matthew Williams, Reverend Ainslie decried from the pulpit that, "Every church in Salisbury ought to hang crepe on its doors and ask itself the question: What have we been teaching through the years to have produced such a result in our quiet community? Is there no sense of alarm in the conscience of those churches?"[24] In naming Reverend Ainslie, MALF was likely honoring his legacy as Reverend Peter was gravely ill and died in February 1934, after two failed medical operations.[25]

With the radical and liberal legacy of Reverend Ainslie, came problematic approaches to leadership that were centered around paternalistic and neo-abolitionist approaches to narrative construction. At the same time, Reverend Ainslie's privilege as a white Christian male allowed him access to white spaces that female leaders were denied. MALF potentially understood this as they considered the youthful Rev. Asbury Smith to serve as the federation's chair.[26]

Rev. Asbury Smith

Ordained in 1924, Rev. Asbury Smith moved to Baltimore where he began serving several congregations including the predominantly African American congregation, McKendree (which later became Arlington).[27] While the interracial and ecumenical movement in Baltimore was progressive and ahead of its time, Asbury's role leading a largely Black congregation in Maryland was not typical for the period. Reverend Smith's role as a radical interracialist can be underscored by the fact that he was regularly listed in *The First Colored Professional, Clerical and Business Directory of Baltimore City*.[28]

His interracial and anti-lynching activism began in 1932, when he authored an article in the *Evening Sun* in response to the lynching of Matthew Williams in Salisbury, his native home. The following year he responded again, this time reflecting on the lynching of George Armwood. He wrote:

> I have lived on the Eastern Shore the greater part of my life. My family and friends are there. To know that these people whom I love almost without exception approved the brutal lynching of Armwood grieves me deeply.... I am ashamed of being an Eastern Shore man. I feel ashamed of being a white man. I feel ashamed of being an ordained minister of the Christian Church. I consider black men my brothers. I am willing to stand beside them in their suffering.... All that is within my power to do I shall do as a protest against this brutal lynching and to make such an occurrence impossible in the future.[29]

Following this, Reverend Smith became directly involved in MALF, which would provide a foundation for his future efforts in the civil rights struggle in Maryland and across the United States. He served in leadership in organizations including the Baltimore Federation of Churches, Maryland's Interracial Commission, the Fair Employment Practices Commission, and the National Urban League.³⁰ Smith, like Israel, was a religious leader who was politically active, consulting local, state, and national political leaders around issues of racism and labor rights. In many ways it was Reverend Smith's unique experiences that compelled him to distance himself from the distinctly southern and racist ideals of the Eastern Shore community where he was born. Smith's conception of the Social Gospel challenged racist tradition and precedents within white Protestant denominations, specifically in the Methodist Episcopal Church. Indeed, Smith's unique approach embodied a liberal and radical religious and political identity that was complemented by the support of two youthful vice chairs: George B. Murphy and Rabbi Edward Israel.

George B. Murphy

Born in Baltimore, George B. Murphy Jr. (1906–86) was reared in one of Maryland's most influential families. He was the grandson of John H. Murphy, founder of the *Baltimore Afro-American Newspaper*. Shortly after a brief stint teaching in South Carolina following his undergraduate education at Dickerson University, Murphy retired to his home town to work for the family business where he would serve as editor of the *Afro-American* in the late 1920s and 1930s.

In the 1930s, while serving as the national correspondent to the NAACP, Murphy began to push back against the policies and practices of the NAACP, specifically in regard to their legalistic approach to combating anti-Black violence—an approach that leaders like Murphy deemed to be unsuccessful. Murphy believed lynching could only be stifled through "mass action," an approach that he argued was proven effective in the case of the Scottsboro Boys after the mothers of the young boys obtained representation from the International Labor Defense (ILD), which spearheaded a nationwide and worldwide campaign that saved them from execution.³¹

It was ILD's proven track record that potentially inspired George Murphy to support communist candidates for public office. He saw both the Democratic and Republican Parties as only concerned about Black issues when it was politically opportune and felt that much of their critique of anti-Black violence was empty and uninformed by the lived experiences of those directly impacted by the racial terror.³²

Following the lynching of George Armwood, Murphy joined forces with the NAACP's top lawyer and the vice dean of Howard University Law School, Charles Hamilton Houston, and began seeking an audience with President Roosevelt to recommend policies and discuss strategies to combat the scourge of lynching. In October 1933, Roger M. Baldwin of the American Civil Liberties Union was able to secure a White House meeting for both Murphy and Houston. However, after waiting for more than two hours, they were told that the president was now refusing to meet with the delegation. FDR's response foreshadowed the "hands-off" approach he would take to lynching for years to come, because he calculated it was too risky politically to be associated with anti-lynching forces as he relied on the support of southern white democrats. As FDR distanced himself, however, his wife, Eleanor, did not, as she increasingly served as a conduit between the White House and the NAACP and spoke out against lynching.[33]

In 1941, Murphy formally resigned from the NAACP and joined the National Negro Congress (NNC), founded in Chicago in 1935 to fight for a bigger share of New Deal programs for African American people.[34] Murphy went on to have a storied career, devoting his life to truth-telling and to justice-centered investigative journalism and advocacy. Murphy went on to become one of the signers of the Civil Rights Congress's "We Charge Genocide" petition, delivered by Paul Robeson at the United Nations in 1951.[35] Much of the evidence provided to make the case for the charge was based on the documented injustices against Black citizens that Murphy had covered while editor of the *Afro*, including the thousands of cases of racial terror lynchings. Murphy would go on to befriend a number of prominent activists and scholars of the civil rights movement including W.E.B. and Shirley Graham Du Bois, Thurgood Marshall, and Paul Robeson. George Murphy's acumen in the areas of investigative journalism and public policy would be supplemented by the reform Jewish leader Rabbi Edward L. Israel.

Rabbi Edward L. Israel

Born in Cincinnati, Ohio, in 1896, Rabbi Edward L. Israel was a Jewish religious leader who would test the limits of the reform movement out of which he was born. He was directly connected with the foundational reform leaders who were integral in establishing the NAACP and served as mentor to Rabbi Stephen Wise, among others. In 1923, Israel was called to become senior rabbi of Har Sinai of Baltimore. He remained in that post until his resignation in 1941, a few months before his death. Before being elected rabbi of the eminent Har Sinai Congregation, Israel had become quite familiar with such instances of racial violence throughout the United States. However, it was not until his post in Baltimore that he would become directly involved in the Black struggle advocating for national anti-lynching legislation and social justice reform alongside civil rights organizations such as the Urban League and the Maryland Anti-Lynching Federation. As he evolved, at the end of his life his devotion to social justice garnered recognition by FDR as "one of the great liberals of our time."[36] While Israel brought the influence of the reform Jewish movement, the Baltimore political and progressive philanthropic community was represented by Elisabeth Gilman.

Elisabeth Gilman

A devout socialist and daughter of John Hopkins University president Daniel C. Gilman, Elisabeth Gilman emerged as a pioneering political figure and financial supporter of social justice organizations, including MALF. In 1928, Gilman began holding some of the first interracial dinners in Baltimore at her Mount Vernon home. There, she honored NAACP pioneer and grandson of William Lloyd Garrison, Oswald Garrison Villard, after the Southern Hotel refused to serve the six Blacks out of more than one hundred individuals invited to attend and she moved the dinner to her home. In the early 1930s, she joined the Socialist Party and even pursued a run for mayor of Baltimore and later governor of Maryland.[37] Gilman's relationship with Villard led him to become a regular speaker at the federation's meetings, where Garrison, like Israel, compared Maryland's and the nation's attitude toward race lynching with the atrocities that were taking place in Germany.[38]

By October, MALF had grown tremendously by taking a big tent approach; the federation sought to connect existing movements that were sympathetic to the anti-lynching cause. The extensive networks of Israel, Gilman, and Smith led to the rapid expansion of MALF. By the final monthly meeting in October, the federation included religious, social, and political organizations. Organizational representatives came from the Park Avenue Friends Meeting, Women's International League for Peace and Freedom, League for Industrial Democracy, Johns Hopkins University Liberal Club, People's Unemployment League of Maryland, Amalgamated Clothing Workers of America, Socialist Party of Maryland, International Ladies' Garment Workers' Union, and the Urban League, as well as the Colored Women's Suffrage Club, Synagogue Youth, Baltimore YMCA, Young People's City-Wide Forum, Maryland Civil Liberties Committee, Federation of Labor, Homewood Friends Meeting, Workmen's Circle, and the Baptist Ministerial Conference.[39]

In November 1933, a few months following the George Armwood lynching, MALF hosted a meeting to discuss a model for a proposed anti-lynching bill. The meeting, held at the Westminster Presbyterian Church, featured presentations from Oswald Garrison Villard of the *Nation*, Walter White, general secretary of the NAACP; Edward S. Lewis, executive secretary of the Baltimore Urban League; and Roger N. Baldwin of the ACLU. Villard, who delivered the most compelling speech, placed the events in a global perspective. He lamented: "We have lived through one of the most disastrous weeks in our history.... Today, if we protest against the horrible brutalities in Germany, the ill-treatment of political prisoners in Poland, Yugoslavia, and Japan's action in Manchuria, what standing are we going to have? Will it not be enough for despots everywhere to point the finger of scorn at us and repeat three words, 'Maryland, Missouri, California.' Hitler himself could make the same reply if there were American protests against anti-Semitic crimes in Germany."[40]

Beyond placing race lynching in Maryland in global perspective, he spotlighted two other cases of lynching that took place just months apart. They included the lynching of Lloyd Warner in St. Joseph, Missouri, and Brooke Hart in San Jose, California. Outside of the lectures, the meeting centered on workshopping and presenting practical models of anti-lynching legislation that the group hoped would be introduced to the Maryland state legislature. The chief presenter of the draft legislation was Baltimore attorney John Henry Skeen, who presented the legislation to the group. Among the primary goals of the meeting was to strategize as to the ways in which an anti-lynching bill could be enacted within the state legislature, exploring the development of education plans designed to address the root causes and attitudes associated with those who participate in lynching.[41]

In December 1933, MALF tested the strength of their advocacy and mobilization efforts. On December 8, for instance, MALF lobbied the state legislature for the passage of two anti-lynching bills, both issued by Senator E. Milton Alfred (Democrat from the Fourth Baltimore District). After successfully obtaining ten thousand signatures, MALF was able to garner the support of thirty-five organizations in favor of the legislation. If passed, both bills would make lynching a statutory crime and allow the collection of damages ranging from $2,000 to $10,000 from the community where one occurs. Rev. Asbury Green, MALF chair, was successful in galvanizing an interracial group of faith leaders, including Father John T. Gillard, chaplain to the Oblate Sisters of Providence and vice chair for MALF, who in his statement pushed back against the prevailing argument that honest tax-paying citizens should not be penalized for the deeds of a few bad apples. He wrote: "The bill to penalize a county where a lynching occurs is not unfair... because the intelligent people of a community are responsible for what happens in the community. Only when the respectable element is aroused can it control the lower elements."[42] Years later Rev. Asbury Smith recalled the day when he was thrust into leadership after just turning thirty years old:

> Well, when I appeared before the State Legislature I was thirty years old.... So many people came to support this bill we had introduced, it was supposed to be held in the Senate room, and they couldn't get in there, so they moved to the House of Representatives, and it was crowded to the deck. We had there the cream of the black community, and we had some of the intellectuals and some of the leaders of the liberal white community, for example Elisabeth Gilman, whose father was the first president of Goucher College, was there. Margaret Carey was there, who was a leading Quaker and a family of multi-millionaires. I mean, they were people highly respected in the community, although they were a little liberal in their points of view. I had the backing of some of the leading citizens of the state. They saw the folly of this, and they were anxious to correct it, as was I.[43]

Costigan-Wagner Anti-Lynching Hearing

One year later, Asbury, Israel, and other MALF members traveled to Washington, D.C., where they were joined by political, civil rights, and religious leaders from throughout Maryland to testify at the federal Costigan-Wagner anti-lynching hearing. The Costigan-Wagner anti-lynching bill was drafted by two Democratic senators, Robert F. Wagner of New York and Edward Costigan of Colorado, following an increase in racial terror lynching during the Great Depression. The Costigan-Wagner bill was a part of a congressional effort dating back to the turn of the twentieth century.[44]

The ten delegates from Maryland included Juanita Jackson Mitchell of the Baltimore City-Wide Young People's Forum, journalists Clarence Mitchell and Louis Azreal, Johns Hopkins professor Dr. Broadus Mitchell, Father John T. Gillard, Maryland attorney general W. Preston Lane, and

Simon E. Soberloff, U.S. district attorney of Maryland. Though the House of Representatives subsequently passed anti-lynching legislation, the Senate would not pass legislation until 2022.[45]

In spite of failing to make any progress as it relates to anti-lynching legislation, Israel continued to work alongside local and national Black leaders in Baltimore. However, his liberal ideals and attitudes were soon to be challenged for a second time when he was forced to confront the racism practiced by members of his own congregation, who owned a number of retail stores and entertainment venues in predominantly Black West Baltimore. Situated along Pennsylvania Avenue, these Jewish-owned businesses failed to provide jobs for their Black customers whose dollars they depended on. By 1936, with Black unemployment rates nearly triple that of the national average, problems such as these had begun to arise throughout northern cities, sparking a movement commonly known as the "Buy Where You Can Work" campaign. For those who valued the role that Jews have historically played in the Black freedom struggle up until this point, such discrimination by Jewish business owners was enraging. Dr. Lillie May Carroll Jackson, president of the Baltimore NAACP, was one such leader, and like Murphy, she found herself challenging the limits of Jewish liberalism, sparking a national discussion concerning anti-Black racism among Jews and antisemitism among Blacks.

Juanita Jackson

Committed to interracial and interfaith work, Israel was a member of both the NAACP and the National Urban League. He also participated in the City-Wide Young People's Forum, an interracial civil rights youth group, founded in 1931 by the daughter of Dr. Lillie May Carroll Jackson, Juanita Jackson (later Mitchell), in response to the lynching of Matthew Williams on Maryland's Eastern Shore.

Of all of the testimony given during the congressional hearing, the testimony of Juanita Jackson was the most compelling argument in favor of the Costigan-Wagner anti-lynching legislation, lifting up the failures of the state and local governments to protect Matthew Williams (1931) and George Armwood (1933) from the hands of white racist mobs. She stated, "Had there been a law such as the Costigan-Wagner anti-lynch bill, which provides for the prosecution in Federal courts of delinquent and negligent officers of the law, the cases would have been removed from the hands of local authorities who, with their eyes on the next election, have proved that in nearly every case they are only too willing to cover up the evidence."[46] Juanita Jackson got at the heart of the issues regarding the need for federal interventions regarding localized and regional anti-Black violence in the United States. These calls for federal protection date back to the Reconstruction era in the United States. In spite of the demise of enslavement in the United States, the system of segregation and racial oppression emerged to replace the racial hierarchy that enslavement made plain, further preserving the system of white supremacy in the United States.

For Jackson the application of such policies was seen firsthand, based on the track record of Governor Ritchie's push for states' rights, reawakened the faith of the progenitors of the former rebellious states and supported the development of conservative southern Democrats (future Dixiecrats).[47]

Less than ten years prior, Ritchie showed signs of hypocrisy, specifically addressing the lynching crisis, when he argued against the Dyer anti-lynching bill. The bill, sponsored by Leonidas C. Dyer, Republican representative from Missouri, was the congressional effort of 1922 to pass federal legislation to address and require federal prosecution for lynchings.[48] In response Ritchie proclaimed: "Dyer Bill in truth is a political measure designed to capture the colored bloc vote, and it extends Federal sovereignty and jurisdiction over every State official—from constable to governor."[49]

Similarly to those who supported secession during the Civil War and fought against anti-lynching legislation in the 1930s, Ritchie used the rhetoric of states' rights. However, his primary goals were maintaining white supremacy, controlling Black bodies, and continuing inaction against anti-Black violence. Jackson provides evidence of such inaction, lifting the failures of the state to hold the lynchers of Matthew Williams and George Armwood accountable, stating: "We can never hope for a republican Government under brutal mob rule. Not only that, the failure to punish lynchers has heretofore always meant another lynching. On the Eastern Shore lawless ones know that there are [sic] no firm determination to prevent lynchers. State police are too polite to shoot at would-be lynchers. State administrators twice proved completely impotent to deal with lynchers."[50]

In the end, Jackson supported the legislation because it was a natural representation of checks and balances as it held state and local law enforcement accountable by proposing federal prosecution of participants in lynch mobs, including public officials and law enforcement officers who failed to protect the victims in their custody. As she concluded her testimony, she prophetically pointed to the role of officers in relation to racial terror lynching, drawing a direct line from the racial terror lynching of old to the modern-day killings of Black people at the hands of police, stating: "Lynching can only be reduced to the minimum when conniving officers come to know that they will be liable, not to local court which is sure to support them, but to Federal law."[51] Roosevelt refused to speak out in favor of the bill. He argued that it would alienate white voters in the South and cause him to lose in the next election. The bill died without ever going to the floor of the Senate for a vote.

Conclusion

Flanked by Michelle Duster, the great-granddaughter of Ida B. Wells, and Kamala Harris, the first Black woman elected to the vice presidency, President Joseph R. Biden signed H.R. 55—the Emmett Till Antilynching Act—into law on March 29, 2022. It defined lynching as a federal hate crime—ensuring that future instances of lynching will not be prosecuted in isolation by states and localities. The bill passed despite initial opposition from southern senators such as Rand Paul (R-KY), who stalled the bill amid nationwide protests over the murder of George Floyd.[52] Following more than a century of debate and hundreds of failed pieces of anti-lynching legislation, Duster described the significance of the passage of H.R. 55: "Since my great-grandmother's visit to the White House 124 years ago, there have been over two hundred attempts to get [anti-lynching] legislation enacted . . . but we finally stand here today, generations later, to witness this historic moment."[53]

Conspicuously missing from H.R. 55 and its subsequent signing ceremony, however, was any mention of some of the earliest pieces of anti-lynching legislation—the Dyer anti-lynching bill and the Costigan-Wagner bill—and their radical originators, such as members of MALF. Also missing from H.R. 55 is a more expansive vision of anti-lynching legislation, adopted by MALF and other early proponents, that goes beyond federalizing the prosecution of lynchings. H.R. 55 does not offer a formal apology from the federal government for its lack of action on lynching; it does not compel states and localities to apologize and atone for their complicity in racial terror; it does not provide trauma-informed, culturally responsive mental health care for descendant communities; and it does not offer economic programs such as reparations to reverse decades of dispossession, displacement, and disfranchisement that targeted descendant communities and communities of color more broadly.

The radical organizing and solidarity following the lynchings of Matthew Williams and George Armwood, perhaps most prominently represented by MALF, dispels the pervasive myth of Black—and multiracial—acquiescence in the aftermath of racial terror violence. Organizers of MALF, alongside their allies, emerged from the dual Eastern Shore lynchings at once mourning and motivated. They were determined, in the immediate aftermath of the worst form of American domestic terrorism, to make the anti-lynching movement not only reactive to lynching but also responsive to the families, communities, and descendants harmed by lynching.

MALF's proposed legislation would have constituted more than a symbolic, largely preventive victory. It would have gone much further: stripping states and localities of their unchecked power to cover up lynchings; imposing standardized penalties as a deterrent to would-be lynchers; holding hyperlocal systems accountable for their role in supporting lynchings; and requiring the public sector more broadly to atone for the extermination of Black life and livelihoods through direct reparations and federal support. Save for the possibility of future policy stemming from the federal government or from state and local entities such as the Maryland Lynching Truth and Reconciliation Commission, MALF's vision for anti-lynching action—sweeping, reparative legislation—is yet to be realized.[54]

Notes

1 Mitchell quoted in "Senator Bruce Joins Defense Eastern Shore," *Salisbury Daily Times*, January 29, 1932.

2 U.S. Senate Committee on the Judiciary, *Punishment for the Crime of Lynching: Hearings Before a Subcommittee of the Committee on the Judiciary, United States Senate, Seventy-Third Congress, Second Session, on S. 1978, a Bill to Assure to Persons within the Jurisdiction of Every State the Equal Protection of the Laws and to Punish the Crime of Lynching, February 20 and 21, 1934* (Washington, D.C.: Government Printing Office, 1934).

3 For the foundational restorative justice text on the lynchings of Matthew Williams and George Armwood, see Sherrilyn A. Ifill, *On the Courthouse Lawn*, rev. ed.: *Confronting the Legacy of Lynching in the Twenty-First Century* (Boston: Beacon, 2018). For a more recent work on Salisbury's Black communities, Black resistance in the aftermath of the Williams lynching, and the politics of lynching in Maryland, see Charles L. Chavis Jr., *The Silent Shore: The Lynching of Matthew Williams and the Politics of Racism in the Free State* (Baltimore: Johns Hopkins University Press, 2022).

4 Andor Skotnes, *A New Deal for All? Race and Class Struggles in Depression-Era Baltimore* (Durham, NC: Duke University Press, 2012); Jeanne Theoharis, Komozi Woodard, and Dayo F. Gore, *Want to Start a Revolution? Radical Women in the Black Freedom Struggle* (New York: New York University Press, 2009).

5 Confining the lynching regime geographically is not only ahistorical; it also prevents us from scrutinizing why lynchings occurred in great numbers—and devastating brutality—outside the Deep South, and dismisses the Black agitators who survived and emerged in the aftermath of racial terror violence. See Lee Ann Fujii, "'Talk of the Town': Explaining Pathways to Participation in Violent Display," *Journal of Peace Research* 54, no. 5 (2017): 661–73; Janice Hittinger Barrow, "Lynching in the Mid-Atlantic, 1882–1940," *American Nineteenth Century History* 6, no. 3 (September 2005): 241–71; Kidada E. Williams, "Regarding the Aftermaths of Lynching," *Journal of American History* 101, no. 3 (December 2014): 856–58; Kidada E. Williams, "Reconsidering the Lynching Archive: A Review of *The End of American Lynching* and *Lynch Mobs: Narratives of Community and Nation*," *Reviews in American History* 41, no. 3 (September 2013): 501–6.

6 A. D. Emmart, "Maryland Finds Way Back to London Press—First Page," *Baltimore Sun*, November 29, 1933.

7 "Mother's Heart Is Broken from Lynch Tragedy," *Afro-American*, October 21, 1933.

8 For more on Ritchie and his communications with local officials, see Charles L. Chavis Jr., "Governor Albert C. Ritchie Confronts Judge Lynch: The Politics of Anti-Black Racism in the Free State and Beyond," in *Silent Shore*, 81–104; also see Newspaper Clippings and Correspondence Relating to the Lynching of Matthew Williams, Courthouse Lawn, Salisbury, MD, December 4, 1931, Governor Albert Ritchie Collection, Maryland State Archives, Annapolis, MD, http://mdhistory.msa.maryland.gov/msaref10/msa_s1048_1_and_10/html/index.html.

9 Ralph Matthews, "Church as Usual for Godfearing Sho' Lynchers," *Afro-American*, December 12, 1931.

10 "Eye Witness to Lynching Tells How Mob Acted," *Afro-American*, December 12, 1931.

11 Handwritten note and rope used to lynch Matthew Williams, December 1931, Gift of the Estate of Paul S. Henderson, National Museum of African American History and Culture, Washington, D.C.; Tulani Salahu-Din, "The Evidence of Things Unsaid," National Museum of African American History and Culture, July 6, 2017, https://nmaahc.si.edu/object/nmaahc_2013.50abc.

12 Mathews contextualizes such a cultural phenomenon: "Given the brutality of lynching and the contempt with which its victims were treated, one might be excused some skepticism that in executing a black victim, whites were actually making him sacred." Donald G. Mathews, "The Southern Rite of Human Sacrifice: Lynching in the American South," *Mississippi Quarterly* 61 (2008): 27.

13 "Get at the Roots," *Afro-American*, October 21, 1933; "Mother's Heart Is Broken from Lynch Tragedy."

14 "Named Honorary Head of Anti-Lynching Group," *Baltimore Sun*, November 7, 1933.

15 "Anti-Lynching Bill Is Urged for Maryland," *Detroit Tribune*, November 11, 1933.
16 Proceedings and Debates of the 1850 Constitutional Convention, vol. 101, no. 2, Debates 477.
17 "Negligence Causing Death," *The Annotated Code of the Public Civil Laws of Maryland, 1911*, Article 67, 1535; *Cocking et al. v. Wade, Sheriff, et al.*, 87 Md. 529 (Md. 1898).
18 Phillip Pickus, "Notes: Torts—Government Immunity—Police Officer Pursuing Suspect Owes Duty of Care to Third Parties Injured by the Fleeing Suspect; Injured Plaintiff Can Recover from State and Political Subdivisions If Officer Was Negligent in Commencing and Maintaining Pursuit. *Boyer v. State*, 323 Md. 558, 594 A.2d 121 (1991)," *University of Baltimore Law Review* 21, no. 2 (January 1, 1992), https://scholarworks.law.ubalt.edu/ublr/vol21/iss2/6.
19 Maryland was an epicenter for such collaboration prior to the 1920s and remained so for a number of years after. See David Taft Terry, *The Struggle and the Urban South: Confronting Jim Crow in Baltimore before the Movement* (Athens: University of Georgia Press, 2019); C. Fraser Smith, *Here Lies Jim Crow: Civil Rights in Maryland* (Baltimore: Johns Hopkins University Press, 2008); Barbara Jeanne Fields, *Slavery and Freedom on the Middle Ground: Maryland during the Nineteenth Century* (New Haven, CT: Yale University Press, 1984), xv.
20 Duane D. Cummins, *The Disciples: A Struggle for Reformation* (St. Louis: Chalice Press, 2009), 169.
21 "Rev. Dr. Ainslie, Liberalist, Dies at Age of 66," *Evening Sun*, February 23, 1934.
22 William R. Hogg, *Ecumenical Foundations: A History of the International Missionary Council and Its Nineteenth-Century Background* (Eugene, OR: Wipf and Stock, 2002), 188.
23 John Jasper, "Virginia Liberalism at Its Best in Dr. Peter Ainslie's New Book," *Afro-American*, June 17, 1933.
24 "Quiet Reigns after Hanging in Salisbury, Should Hang Crape," *Baltimore Sun*, December 7, 1931; "Peter Ainslie: Further Comment on the Lynching," *Evening Sun*, October 22, 1933.
25 "Rev. Ainslie in Baltimore," *Baltimore Sun*, February 23, 1934.
26 Charles Kirk Pilkington, "The Trials of Brotherhood: The Founding of the Commission on Interracial Cooperation," *Georgia Historical Quarterly* 69, no. 1 (1985): 58; Mark Ellis, *Race Harmony and Black Progress: Jack Woofter and the Interracial Cooperation Movement* (Bloomington: Indiana University Press, 2013), 88.
27 "Asbury Smith, Minister, Civil Rights Advocate Dies," *Baltimore Sun*, May 25, 1993.
28 Robert W. Coleman, *The First Colored Professional, Clerical and Business Directory of Baltimore City* (Baltimore, 1913–46).
29 "Comment on the Armwood Lynching: The Rev. Asbury Smith," *Afro-American*, October 28, 1933.
30 "Asbury Smith, Minister, Rights Advocate Dies."
31 Mark Naison, *Communists in Harlem during the Depression* (Urbana: University of Illinois Press, 2005), 85.

32 Kelly Miller, Dr. Edward Wheatley, and G. B. Murphy Jr., "Out for Foster," *Afro-American*, November 5, 1932; Naison, *Communists in Harlem*, 303–4.
33 "Says F.D.R. Can't See Delegation," *Afro-American*, September 2, 1933; Melissa Cooper, "Reframing Eleanor Roosevelt's Influence in the 1930s Anti-Lynching Movement around a 'New Philosophy of Government,'" *European Journal of American Studies* 12, no. 1 (March 7, 2017): 4, https://doi.org/10.4000/ejas.11914; Kenneth O'Reilly, "The Roosevelt Administration and Black America: Federal Surveillance Policy and Civil Rights during the New Deal and World War II Years," *Phylon* 48, no. 1 (1987): 14, https://doi.org/10.2307/274998.
34 Naison, *Communists in Harlem*, 304.
35 William Patterson, "We Charge Genocide: The Historic Petition to the United Nations for Relief from a Crime of the United States Government Against the Negro People," Civil Rights Congress (U.S.), 1952.
36 "Twentieth Anniversary of the Death of Rabbi Israel," Speech Draft, 1962, Har Sinai Collection, Jewish Museum of Maryland, Goodwin Library and Robert L. Weinberg Family History Center, Baltimore, Maryland.
37 "A Testimony to Miss Elisabeth Gilman, the Humanitarian," *Afro-American*, May 24, 1930.
38 "City's 'Nation' Dinner Most Memorable in Series-Villard," *Afro-American*, March 17, 1928.
39 "To Press for Legislation," *Baltimore Sun*, October 23, 1933; "R.N. Baldwin Talks on Mobs Tomorrow," *Baltimore Sun*, October 26, 1933.
40 "Asserts Lynching Increases Crimes," *Baltimore Sun*, December 2, 1933.
41 "Will Present Model Anti-Lynching Bill," *Evening Sun*, November 29, 1933.
42 "Ministers Back Anti-Lynching Acts at Hearing," *Evening Sun*, December 8, 1933; "Anti-Lynching Laws Are Urged by Priest," *Tablet* (Brooklyn, NY), December 23, 1933; State Legislation: December 7, 1933, http://whilbr.org/itemdetail.aspx?idEntry=8620; MSA Bill Info, SM73-20, http://guide.msa.maryland.gov/pages/item.aspx?ID=SM73-20.
43 Asbury Smith, "The Great Depression Series," Washington University in St. Louis Special Collections, Washington University Film and Media Archive, Henry Hampton Collection.
44 Ida B. Wells was among the first advocates for federal anti-lynching legislation, urging William McKinley to propose congressional legislation. However, actual anti-lynching legislation dates to 1900, when the sole African American member of the U.S. Congress, George Henry White of North Carolina, proposed legislation H.R. 6963, "A Bill for the protection of all citizens of the United States against mob violence." By 1918, Leonidas C. Dyer, a Republican representative of Missouri, launched the campaign for the Dyer anti-lynching bill. The fight for anti-lynching legislation would continue for more than 120 years, until Congress passed the Emmett Till Antilynching Act on March 29, 2022. Tianna Mobley, "Ida B. Wells-Barnett: Anti-Lynching and the White House," White House Historical Association, April 9, 2021, https://www.whitehousehistory.org/ida-b-wells-barnett-anti

-lynching-and-the-white-house; Jeffery A. Jenkins, Justin Peck, and Vesla M. Weaver, "Between Reconstructions: Congressional Action on Civil Rights, 1891–1940," *Studies in American Political Development* 24, no. 1 (2010): 57–89, https://doi.org/10.1017/S0898588X10000015; Megan Ming Francis, *Civil Rights and the Making of the Modern American State* (Cambridge: Cambridge University Press, 2014), 86; "H.R. 55—117th Congress (2021–2022): Emmett Till Antilynching Act," March 29, 2022, https://www.congress.gov/bill/117th-congress/house-bill/55.
45 "H.R. 55."
46 U.S. Senate Committee on the Judiciary, *Punishment for the Crime of Lynching*.
47 Indeed, Ritchie's appeal for states' rights was not new. In fact, most southern Democrats were champions of states' rights to avoid federal enforcement of civil rights measures. Indeed, this stance can be tracked from the postbellum period where Democrats fought against Reconstruction-era civil rights laws, to the twentieth century, through anti-lynching legislation and eventually with the Civil Rights Act of 1964 and Voting Rights Act of 1965. See Kari Frederickson, *The Dixiecrat Revolt and the End of the Solid South, 1932–1968* (Chapel Hill: University of North Carolina Press, 2001), 238; Joseph B. Chepaitis, "Albert C. Ritchie in Power: 1920–1927," *Maryland Historical Magazine* 68 (1973): 399.
48 *Journal of the House of Representatives of the United States* 65, no. 2 (1918): 297.
49 "Ritchie, in Virginia, Urges Protection of States' Rights, Calls Dyer Bill, 'Label' to Capture Negro Vote," *Washington Post*, March 6, 1926.
50 U.S. Senate Committee on the Judiciary, *Punishment for the Crime of Lynching*.
51 U.S. Senate Committee on the Judiciary, *Punishment for the Crime of Lynching*.
52 Nicholas Fandos, "Frustration and Fury as Rand Paul Holds Up Anti-Lynching Bill in Senate," *New York Times*, June 5, 2020, https://www.nytimes.com/2020/06/05/us/politics/rand-paul-anti-lynching-bill-senate.html.
53 White House, "President Biden Signs into Law H.R. 55, the 'Emmett Till Antilynching Act,'" YouTube, March 29, 2022, https://www.youtube.com/watch?v=oZBnUftOlfY&t=1606s.
54 The Maryland Lynching Truth and Reconciliation Commission is the first and only body of its kind in the United States. Established by House Bill 307, the commission is authorized to research cases of racially motivated lynchings, hold public meetings and regional hearings where a lynching of an African American by a white mob has been documented, and make policy recommendations to the Maryland General Assembly and Maryland's governor. More information, including updated research and recordings from previous hearings, is available at https://msa.maryland.gov/lynching-truth-reconciliation/.

Epilogue

JACQUELINE JONES

Taken together, the essays in this volume make the case that, throughout American history, Black people have served as the conscience of the nation, living and dying for the ideal of a multiracial democracy. Black activists have defined—and are defining—the contours of U.S. citizenship, employing multiple protest strategies to hold the country accountable for the democratic principles it has professed—but too often thwarted—over the centuries. These activists have demonstrated a striking consistency in their efforts to expand suffrage, challenge the tenets and brutality of white supremacy, and create a full and accurate narrative of the nation's past. In doing so, they have exemplified patriotism's best practices and, in dramatic fashion, furthered the democratic experiment. At the same time, whites' multipronged, often vicious responses to these efforts reveal the angry defensiveness of a people caught in a lie—the blatant falsehood that America is and has always been a democratic nation dedicated to equality and justice for all its citizens.

Certainly, the term "democracy" is problematic, its definition vague and deeply contested. Over the years a substantial proportion of Americans have held that group mission statements, politicians' promises, and laws on the books are sufficient to ensure a democratic society, regardless of whether those statements, promises, or laws have a basis in reality. Questions abound: Does a democratic system depend on broad-based suffrage, or are the interests of the republic served by various restrictions on access to the ballot box? Is a just economic system a key component to democracy, or are extremes of wealth and poverty compatible with this type of political system? How did various rights and privileges—such as universal suffrage, school integration, interracial marriage, equal access to medical care and good jobs—take shape and evolve within the United States? Black men and women have used a variety of means to answer these questions, enriching the ongoing quest for a more just society.

The authors of these essays describe a wide variety of protest strategies, in the process highlighting a wide range of individuals and groups active in the African American freedom struggle for democracy. In a representative, winner-take-all democracy, minority groups face the challenge of securing majority support for even modest reforms, not to mention radical changes. These challenges unfolded on the local, state, and national stages. At the local level, in certain communities where Black people might be able to deploy large numbers of voters, their power might be more formidable than at the national level, where (today) Black people represent just 11 percent of the total population. Black freedom fighters have always contended with inconstant white allies, making the fight for justice a fraught proposition throughout American history.

Here, then, are stories detailing the dynamics of particular tactics in service of change, modest as well as transformational—organizing local communities, launching boycotts, filing lawsuits, creating Black-owned newspapers, founding and leading Black colleges and universities, waging political campaigns, seeking funding for social services, and loudly demonstrating at political conventions and in the streets. The essays highlight the particular skills, temperaments, and political ideologies among a spectrum of Black activists—men and women, young and old, academics and intellectuals, journalists, lawyers, politicians, clergy, members of sororities and women's clubs, full-time workers for civil rights groups, and ordinary men and women. Equally striking is the history of various organizations (some enduring, some fleeting) created to advance the struggle, including the National Council of Negro Women, the NAACP, the Brotherhood of Sleeping Car Porters and Maids, the Urban League, the Student Nonviolent Coordinating Committee, the Black Panthers, and Black Lives Matter, to name just a few. At the grassroots level, networks of kin, church, and community emerged to coordinate efforts to build freedom schools, register voters, assist southern migrants arriving in the North, and offer health and vocational services to impoverished communities.

Despite their overall unity of purpose in seeking to hold the United States accountable for its undemocratic, white supremacist practices and institutions, Black people hardly constituted a political monolith. The essays in this volume indicate ongoing debates and outright conflicts over strategies and targets for protest. In the early 1900s, the integrated NAACP chose to follow a more moderate course of action compared to all-Black groups such as Marcus Garvey's Universal Negro Improvement Association. Black leaders debated whether white allies should serve exclusively as funders of Black-defined projects or as full and equal partners in formal associations. In the 1960s, grassroots organizations such as the Student Nonviolent Coordinating Committee considered themselves more effective and more responsive to ordinary people compared to top-down groups such as the Southern Christian Leadership Conference. People divided along lines of gender and age to answer the question: Should Black Americans' historic faith traditions guide the way, or did the times demand more militant measures?

Specific examples in this volume illuminate some of these clashes over personnel and tactics. Black women struggled to be heard and recognized as leaders as well as sustainers of critical protest-support systems. News media, encouraged by certain Black male leaders, depicted the modern civil rights movement as an all-male club of charismatic clergy, the Reverend Martin Luther King Jr. foremost among them. This narrative ignored the roles of local community members—including, during the Montgomery bus boycott, local teacher Jo Ann Gibson Robinson. Popular accounts of the boycott continue to portray Rosa Parks as just a weary seamstress unwilling to give up her bus seat to a white person, when in fact she had a long history of activism in the NAACP. Dorothy Height objected to the virtually all-male lineup during the rally at the March on Washington in 1963. Media accounts also shaped the public image of the Black Panthers—as militant, armed men—when in fact a majority of its members were Black women and its programs focused on providing food and social services to local communities.

In other examples of intragroup dissent, in the mid-1930s, A. Clement MacNeal criticized the Chicago NAACP's reluctance to take on the Sears Company for its refusal to hire Black workers, for fear of alienating a white patron. In that city, various groups, including the NAACP, the Brotherhood of Sleeping Car Porters and Maids, and the South Parkway branch of the Young Women's Christian Association, all vied for influence. Generational differences among activists have at times produced conflicts over the relative value of reform, defined as piecemeal progress via legislation, and radicalism, defined as challenges to fundamental structures and institutions. And too, at times religious and cultural affiliations shaped strategies, when, for example, Black Muslims rejected the integrationist stance of mainstream civil rights leaders (and Protestant preachers) in the 1960s.

In fact, debates and discussions among Black leaders over tactics have gone far beyond the iconic, early twentieth-century either-or, W.E.B. Du Bois–Booker T. Washington split, one that (in simplified terms) cast principled demands for full civil rights as distinct from "accommodation" to inequality in return for physical safety. Black leaders have discussed, debated, and fought over the most effective channels for change within a resistant society. As a result, as these essays make clear, the Black freedom struggle has penetrated virtually every aspect of American society, yielding pointed challenges that have varied in intensity and focus but have targeted domestic anti-Black terrorism; employment and housing discrimination; disfranchisement; segregated venues and education; inferior health care; and the anti-democratic tendencies of political institutions, from local school boards to the Supreme Court, Congress, and the presidency.

At the same time, these essays remind us that the history of Black people's abundant, variegated protests constitutes only half of the story of American democracy. The other half is told by the reaction that such protests have provoked among entrenched interests that feared the real and implied threats to their own power. That fierce backlash came out through a wide range of individual and institutional behaviors, from horrific violence to seemingly bland bureaucratic policies. Instances of lynchings of individuals and massacres of whole communities have claimed the lives of thousands of African Americans, with hundreds of men, women, and children killed at a time in instances too numerous to mention here. In Black areas, local police units more often resembled occupying military forces, quick on the trigger, than protectors of people and property. National white leaders condemned Black protesters, no matter how peaceful, as communists, terrorists, aliens, and all-around un-American agitators. State governments used voter suppression methods and deployed the criminal justice system as agents of repression. Over the generations, Supreme Court justices have put their stamp of approval on slavery, Jim Crow segregation, poll taxes, and the all-white primary. Indeed, the relatively liberal Warren court of the 1950s and 1960s was an aberration of sorts, a temporary break from the court's routinely conservative practices. Under the leadership of J. Edgar Hoover, the FBI engaged in surveillance of leading civil rights leaders, tarring such leaders as Soviet-controlled revolutionaries fomenting social disorder and dedicated to the overthrow of the U.S. government.

At times reaction came in the form of official boards and other entities withholding resources from Black-run initiatives and institutions. Examples include the defunding of Houston's voter registration drive as part of the War on Poverty in 1967 and the withholding of state-mandated appropriations for Tennessee's public Historically Black Colleges and Universities (an estimated $544 million shortfall, from the 1940s to 2020). In 1964, as part of the process of challenging Virginia's poll tax, state officials derailed a lawsuit by refusing to provide the required statistics for the plaintiffs in a timely manner. In the early twenty-first century, some states revived Jim Crow practices of voter suppression in an effort to limit the political power of Black Americans. Indeed, from the founding of the nation onward, whites have enlisted the machinery of government at all levels to counter Black people's challenges to discrimination in all aspects of American life.

News media such as newspapers and TV programs have pushed false narratives in service to their white owners, reporters, and customers. Attacks on Black servicemen and whole communities at the end of World War I were labeled not massacres, which they were, but "race riots." In March 1970 the FBI, local white reporters, and the governor of Maryland colluded to rush to judgment and declare Ralph Featherstone, who died in a car bombing, a violent, "bitter revolutionary"; this was a young man who taught history to Mississippi schoolchildren and hoped to secure funding for a Washington, D.C., bookstore from the Episcopal Church. In sum, the cases cited in this volume serve as a reminder that, in the fight for democracy, narratives matter: Will truth prevail, or falsehoods and scapegoats capture the public's attention, with disastrous results?

Conspicuous for their absence in these essays are the white allies who might have used their clout—and compassion—to enhance in a meaningful way Black people's drive for civil rights. These potential allies included members of the Republican Party in the nineteenth-century North, members of the Democratic Party after the 1930s, leaders of major labor unions, military veterans in the age of segregation, and academics and other intellectuals who chose to adhere to and promote the tenets of scientific racism. Indeed, except for the short-lived Readjusters in Virginia (1879–85) and the short-lived Populist Party in the 1890s, it is quite striking that the history of the campaign for a multiracial democracy includes so few Black-white coalitions, at least before the 1930s. After that decade, when Black northerners and southerners became a key component of the New Deal coalition, the Democratic Party proved an unreliable ally when it came to promoting fair housing and economic justice. By the 1980s, in a bid to appeal to white working-class voters, Republican leaders were proving adept at introducing cultural and other wedge issues to fracture the Democratic Party. Republicans argued that furthering Blacks' legal rights and disbursing federal relief funds amounted to zero-sum games—in other words, the (false) notion that any rights and material gains that benefited Blacks would necessarily come at the expense of white families and communities. Ironically, these tactics promoting white grievance and resentment proved largely successful in an era when an emerging global economy negatively affected many workers regardless of race, workers who might have found common ground with each other in defiance of persistent Republican fearmongering.

Running throughout these essays is the dramatic conflict over who controls the story of this nation's past. In the 2020s, the "history wars" are the stuff of angry public debates, sensational headlines, and state legislative initiatives—but these wars are not new. In the late nineteenth century, reactionaries sought to recast the Reconstruction era as a time when corrupt Black freedmen, egged on by cynical white Republicans, embarked on a period of outrageous misrule of the former Confederate states. Since that time, an influential segment of the American public has embraced fiction over fact, myth over history. There are obvious reasons for this kind of politicized storytelling. Denying the historical record of Black struggle and protest allows the deniers to justify white supremacy as well as capitalist formations and attendant inequalities, political and economic; in this historical rendering, Black activists are outliers in an arc of unbroken progress and American "exceptionalism." Portraying Black activism as either a shameful or insignificant chapter of the nation's past is part of an effort to discredit those who call attention to structural and systemic forms of racism that have persisted despite the Civil Rights Act of 1964 and Voting Rights Act of 1965. This myth discourages critical thinking and encourages students to engage in a rote pledge of allegiance to the U.S. military and the "Founding Fathers" and other slaveholders. The myth encourages white Americans to blame the victims—of police brutality, of years of underfunding Historically Black Colleges and Universities, of banking practices such as redlining and predatory lending. Emblematic of all these efforts is the 2020 *Report of the 1776 Commission,* pet project of President Donald Trump, a reimaging of U.S. history riddled with errors and marked by falsehoods. It was around this time that conservative state legislatures began to brand any aspect of structural racism ("critical race theory") as dangerous to young minds, and to outlaw the teaching of so-called divisive concepts in the classroom.

History is the story of divisive concepts. Americans would be hard-pressed to find a concept more divisive than the unfulfilled quest for a multiracial democracy. The Black drive for real freedom and equality—and not just a paper freedom and equality—has met with stiff resistance throughout American history. These essays remind us of what is at stake as that drive—and reactionary resistance—remain in full view today. Truly, the struggle continues.

CONTRIBUTORS

Reginald K. Ellis is provost professor of community outreach, engagement, and research at Florida A&M University. His publications include *Between Washington and Du Bois: The Racial Politics of James Edward Shepard* and *The Seedtime, the Work, and the Harvest: New Perspectives on the Black American Freedom Struggle in America*, coedited with Jeffrey L. Littlejohn and Peter B. Levy.

Peter B. Levy is professor emeritus at York College. Publications include *The Great Uprising: Race Riots in Urban America during the 1960s* and *The Seedtime, the Work, and the Harvest: New Perspectives on the Black American Freedom Struggle in America*, coedited with Jeffrey L. Littlejohn and Reginald K. Ellis.

Jeffrey L. Littlejohn is professor of history at Sam Houston State University. Publications include *Elusive Equality: Desegregation and Resegregation in Norfolk Public Schools*, coauthored with Charles H. Ford, and *The Seedtime, the Work, and the Harvest: New Perspectives on the Black American Freedom Struggle in America*, coedited with Reginald K. Ellis and Peter B. Levy.

Kristopher Bryan Burrell is associate professor of history at Hostos Community College in Bronx, New York. Publications include "Black Women as Activist Intellectuals: Ella Baker and Mae Mallory Combat Northern Jim Crow in New York City's Public Schools during the 1950s," in *The Strange Careers of the Jim Crow North: Segregation and Struggle Outside of the South*, edited by Brian Purnell and Jeanne Theoharis with Komozi Woodard, and "Where from Here? Ideological Perspectives on the Future of the Civil Rights Movement," in *Western Journal of Black Studies*.

Charles L. Chavis Jr. is assistant professor of conflict resolution and history and founding director of the John Mitchell Jr. Program for History and Justice at George Mason University. Publications include *The Silent Shore: The Lynching of Matthew Williams and the Politics of Racism in the Free State* and *For the Sake of Peace: African Perspectives on Racism, Justice, and Peace in America*.

Charles H. Ford is professor of history at Norfolk State University. Publications include *Elusive Equality: Desegregation and Resegregation in Norfolk Public Schools,* coauthored with Jeffrey Littlejohn, and "'In the Best American Tradition of Freedom, We Defy You': The Radical Partnership of Joseph Jordan, Edward Dawley, and Leonard Holt," coauthored with Jeffrey Littlejohn, in *Journal of African American History.*

Jacqueline Jones is Ellen C. Temple Chair in Women's History and Mastin Gentry White Professor of Southern History at the University of Texas–Austin. Publications include *Labor of Love, Labor of Sorrow: Black Women, Work and the Family from Slavery to the Present* and *Goddess of Anarchy: The Life and Times of Lucy Parsons.*

Cassandra Newby-Alexander is professor of history and director of the Joseph Jenkins Roberts Center for the African Diaspora at Norfolk State University. Publications include *Virginia Waterways and the Underground Railroad* and *History of the Civil War in Hampton Roads.*

Wesley G. Phelps is associate professor of history at the University of North Texas. Publications include *Before Lawrence v. Texas: The Making of a Queer Social Movement* and *A People's War on Poverty: Urban Politics and Grassroots Activists in Houston.*

Sharlene Sinegal-DeCuir is chair of the Department of African American and Diaspora Studies and associate professor of history, Keller Family Endowed Professor, at Xavier University of Louisiana. Publications include "'Nothing Is to Be Feared': Norman C. Francis, Civil Rights Activism, and the Black Catholic Movement," in "Faith in Action: Historical Perspectives on the Social and Educational Activism of African American Catholics," special issue of *Journal of African-American History.*

INDEX

Abernathy, Ralph, 141
Abolition and abolitionists, 126–28, 149n13
Abrams, Stacey, 103
Adams, John, 91
Advance Norfolk, 118
Africa and African diaspora, 91, 129, 137
African Americans. *See* Black Americans; Black women
Afro, 167
Afro-American Resources (AAR), 136
Agnew, Spiro T., 156n63
"Agnew Is Confident of Haynsworth Okay" (Breasted), 156n63
Ainslie, Peter, III, 162, 164–65
Akron, Ohio, 36
Alabama, 16, 17, 127, 139
Alabama State College, 48, 62, 64
Alexander, Sadie T. M., 36, 40
Alexander, Will W., 59
Alexandria, VA, 108, 115
Alfred, E. Milton, 169
Allen, Earl: background of, 75; establishment of HOPE Development by, 83–84; and Project Freedom, 76, 77, 78–79, 80, 81, 82, 86; strategies and characteristics of, 75–76, 79, 81, 83–84, 85; and War on Poverty, 75–76
Allen, Pam Parker, 135
Allen, Thomas C., 109
Alpha Kappa Alpha (AKA), 58, 60
Alton, IL, 127
American (term), 9, 15–16, 28
American Civil Liberties Union (ACLU), 116, 167, 169
American Civil Rights Association, 51
American Episcopal Church, 127
Anderson, James D., 104n10
Anderson-McCormick Act of 1884, 109

Anthony, Susan B., 39, 51
Antisemitism, 169, 171
Aptheker, Herbert, 125
Arkansas, 44
Arlington/McKendree congregation, 165
Armwood, George: failure to punish murderers of, 159, 161, 172; family of, 159; lynching of, 4, 159, 161, 162, 163, 164, 165, 166, 169, 171–72, 174
"Ar'n't I a woman?" (Truth), 36, 38, 45n3
Ashmun Institute/Lincoln University, 92
Associated Press, 143
Association of Public and Land-Grant Universities, 101
Atlanta, GA, 1, 42, 138
Atlanta Cotton State Exposition, 96, 104n12
Atlanta Daily World, 141
Atlanta University, 101
Atlantic City, NJ, 22
"Attitudinal Structure of African American Women Party Activists, The" (Clawson and Clark), 52
Azreal, Louis, 170

Babalas, Lilly, 118, 119
Babalas, Peter, 118, 119
Baker, Ella Jo, 2, 36, 41–43, 61, 62–63
Baldwin, James: and American democracy, 2, 16, 20, 26, 27, 28–29, 90; and William F. Buckley, 26
Baldwin, Roger N., 167, 169
"Ballad of Featherstone and Che, The" (Reagon), 136
Ballew, William: and Earl Allen, 76; and economic justice, 86; and Houston antipoverty agency, 76, 77, 78, 79, 81, 83; and Louie Welch, 78, 79; and Project Freedom, 77, 78, 79, 81, 83

Baltimore, MD: anti-lynching advocates in, 164, 165, 166, 168, 169; Black leaders in, 171; ecumenical movement in, 165; houses of worship in, 167; interracial movement and activities in, 26, 163, 165, 168; lynching near, 123; political districts in, 169; racial discrimination in, 171; YMCA in, 168
Baltimore Afro-American Newspaper, 159, 166
Baltimore City-Wide Young People's Forum, 170
Baltimore Federation of Churches, 165
Baltimore Interracial Commission, 164
Baltimore NAACP, 171
Baltimore Sun, 143, 146n2
Baltimore Urban League, 169
Balto, Simon, 132
Baptist Church, 99
Baptist Ministerial Conference, 169
Baraka, Amiri (Leroi Jones), 134
Barber, William, 29
Barfield, William P., 119
Barnett, Bernice McNair, 48
Bates, Daisy, 44
Baylor, James E., 111
Bayne, Thomas, 107, 108
BBC, 45
Beckles, Colin, 136
Bel Air, MD, 123, 124, 139, 141
Bell, Derrick, 14
Be-Lo grocery, 117
Bennett, Lerone, 134
Berg, Manfred, 127
Berlin, Ira, 148n7
Bethune, Mary McLeod: on 1946 report by President's Committee on Civil Rights, 41; as activist, 2, 36, 41, 56–58; background of, 41; and Booker T. Washington, 56–57, 68n24; career of, 56–57; and Civil Rights Commission, 58; and collaboration between civil rights/Black freedom organizations, 56; commentary by, 48, 49; and Daytona Normal and Industrial School/Institute for Negro Girls, 57; death of, 48, 57; and education, 56, 57, 58; financial supporters of, 68n24; and Franklin D. Roosevelt, 41, 57–58; and Harlem YWCA, 43; and Harry S. Truman, 58; impact of, 49–50, 56; and labor unions, 58; and National Association of Colored Women's Clubs, 57; and National Commission for Child Welfare, 57; and National Council of Negro Women, 41, 47–48, 49, 56, 60; and National Youth Administration, 41, 57, 58; and philosophies and network of W.E.B. Du Bois, 56, 57, 68n24; and San Francisco UN Conference, 58; vision of, 47–48, 49, 56; on women's role in creating change, 66
Bethune-Cookman College, 57
Biden, Joseph R., 1, 5, 35
"Bigger Than a Hamburger" (Baker), 42
Birney, James G., 127
Birth of a Nation, 19, 133
Black Americans: and 2020 presidential election, 1–2; as abolitionists, 37; and accusations against Black males of raping white women, 130; and antisemitism, 171; and businesses, 18, 53; calls for federal protection of, 172; and churches, 18, 91, 127; and citizenship, 17–18, 20, 92; and civil rights/Black freedom movement, 12, 20–27; and class, 38, 42, 50, 53, 55, 62, 72, 92, 93–94, 96, 98, 107, 116, 136; conservatives and, 12, 13, 15–16; and COVID-19 pandemic, 1; and criminal justice system, 182; and democracy, 2, 5, 7, 15, 16, 17, 19, 20, 21, 25–26, 29, 179–80; and Democrats, 183; and drug abuse, 67; and economic resilience, 162; and education, 24, 25, 53, 58, 59, 60, 92–93, 98; and employment, 41, 91, 131, 171, 180, 181; and family disassociation, 67; formerly enslaved, 38, 39, 41, 45n2; as free Blacks during slavery, 36, 45n2, 126, 127, 128; and freedom schools, 21, 135; and health care, 180; and housing, 131; justifications for mistreating, 90; as legislators, 16, 17, 19; and the Lie, 90–91; and McCarthyism, 133–34, 151n32; and migration, 12, 55, 130, 131, 180; as ministers, 75, 98, 127; and morality, 98; and mutual aid societies, 18; and national celebrations, 91; and New Deal, 58, 167; omission of, from US history narrative, 125; as part of African diaspora, 91; and patriarchy, 48; and patriotism, 7, 179; and political activism, 130; political

leanings of, 134; population figures for, 180; potential white allies for, 183; and protest and dissent, 2, 4, 7, 26, 27–28, 32n28, 79, 80, 81, 112, 117, 130, 133, 134, 142, 143, 144, 146, 179, 180, 182, 184; as public servants, 17, 18–19, 53; during Reconstruction era, 16–20, 94, 108, 172; and Republican Party, 57, 166, 183, 184; and schools, 18, 130; strategies of, 180–82; and unequal pay, 53; and US military, 12, 47, 91, 132; and voting, 17, 18, 19, 21–23, 25, 38, 41, 71–74, 116, 179; and wealth, 31n20, 108, 180; and white allies, 180; white desires to "civilize," 98; white perceptions of, 162; and World War I, 131, 183; and World War II, 110; and worship, 126. *See also* Black women

Black Americans, intimidation of and violence against: beatings and physical violence, 23, 61; Black men and, 63; calls for federal protection against, 172; death threats, 22, 23; efforts to end, 61; gunshots fired into homes of, 22, 23; mob violence, 59, 127, 128, 129; murder, 1, 28, 91, 103n2, 126–27, 142, 173; NAACP opposition to, 166; personal harassment, 22; by police, 21, 23, 27, 28, 32n28, 64, 65, 76, 79–80, 91, 103n2, 125, 182, 184; during Reconstruction, 18–19; sexual assault, 21, 61, 65; in Upper South, 162; white justification for, 129; by white male bus drivers, 64; after World War I, 53, 132, 183. *See also* Featherstone, Ralph: death of; Lynching

BLACKARTSOUTH, 136

Blackburn, Robin, 126

Black Lives Matter, 32n28, 45, 180

Black Manifesto, 138

Black Muslims, 64, 181

Black Panthers: and economic justice, 138; and FBI, 139; goals and programs of, 66, 181; importance of, 180; and murder of Fred Hampton, 49, 124, 139, 142; strategies of, 66; women as, 66, 181

Black Power, 16

Black Student Movement, 137

Black Woman's History of the United States, A (Berry and Gross), 45n2

Black women: activist tradition of, 2, 25, 35–40, 47–48, 50–52; and Barack Obama, 4; and Black culture, 53; as Black Panthers, 66, 181; and bus transportation, 61, 64; and churches, 50, 51, 52, 62, 66; and civil rights/Black freedom movement, 39, 40–44, 47, 48–49, 51, 61; and class, 50, 58, 62, 66; collective power of, 56; and Democratic Party, 62; and desegregation, 59, 61; disrespect for, 35; and education, 24, 25, 50, 51, 53, 55, 61, 66, 67; enslaved and formerly enslaved, 36, 39, 41, 55; and equality, 36, 37, 38, 39, 40, 41, 47–48, 50; as free persons during slavery, 36, 45n2; and gender, 39, 40, 41, 49, 50, 51, 52; as government leaders, 44–45, 58; and historically Black colleges and universities, 102; and image of Black Americans, 66; and Joe Biden, 5; Malcolm X on, 35; and March on Washington, 43–44, 144; and Montgomery bus boycott, 61–62, 63–64; and moral support for Black men, 51; and NAACP, 39, 40, 41–42, 44, 47, 49, 52, 53–55, 66; neglect of, 35; as opponents of lynching, 43, 55, 57, 59, 66, 130–31; organizations founded or co-founded by, 39–40, 41, 43, 44, 51, 52, 57, 62, 64; and protest and dissent, 21, 24, 48, 50, 54, 55, 58, 63, 65, 112, 117, 130, 181; and sexism, 41, 42–43, 44, 48, 49, 52, 60, 62–63, 65, 181; social causes of, 39, 51, 61, 66; and Southern Christian Leadership Conference, 24, 42, 49; strategies of, 59, 61, 64, 65, 66; and Student Nonviolent Coordinating Committee, 21, 22, 24, 42–43, 49, 60, 62–63; treatment of, 36; and US military, 59; and violence, 21, 23, 61, 64; and voting, 38–39, 40, 44, 50, 56, 61; vulnerability of, 35; white men on, 36; and women's rights, 36–37. *See also* Black Americans

"Black Women and Reform" (Burroughs), 40

Bloody Sunday, 112

Bloxham, William D., 94, 95

Bond, Julian, 141

Booker T. Washington High School, 112, 113, 114

Boston, MA, 36, 107, 127

Brazil, 128

Breasted, David, 144–45, 156n63

Breeden, Edward, 112, 114
Brooklyn Law School, 112
Brooks, Gwendolyn, 137
Brotherhood of Sleeping Car Porters and Maids (BSCP), 53, 55, 64, 180, 181
Brown, Alison W., 116
Brown, H. Rap: attempts to kill, 4, 123, 124, 135; and FBI, 139; media coverage of, 151n31; and Student Nonviolent Coordinating Committee (SNCC), 156n66; trial of, 123, 139, 140, 141, 143, 144
Brown v. Board of Education of Topeka, Kansas, 60, 61, 63, 110, 117
Bryan, Albert, 114, 115
Buckley, William F., 26
Burrell, Kristopher, 2
Burroughs, Charles, 134
Burroughs, Nannie Helen, 36, 39–40, 43
Bush, George H. W.: and election to Congress, 3, 71; as Republican, 71; and War on Poverty and Project Freedom, 3, 71, 72, 78, 79–81, 82, 83, 85–86
Button, Robert Y., 115
Butts, Charles Herbert, 113, 117
Butts, Evelyn Thomas: as advisory commission member, 120; background of, 113, 120; as civil rights figure, 61; and employment rights, 117; finances of, 113, 114, 120; as housewife, 106, 112; and housing, 120; impact of, 106, 119, 120; and Joseph Jordan Jr., 106, 113, 114, 120; and Norfolk, VA, schools, 113–14, 117; and opposition to Douglas MacArthur memorial, 117; as plaintiff, 114, 115, 116, 117; as politician, 120; and public accommodation rights, 117; as seamstress, 106, 113; and veterans' services, 113; and voting rights, 4, 106, 107, 112, 113, 114, 115, 117
Butzner, John D., 114, 115, 116
Buy Where You Can Work campaign, 171
Byrd, Harry F., Sr., 110, 111, 114

Calhoun Christian Church/Christian Temple, 164
California, 141, 169
Cambridge, MD, 123, 139, 143, 144
Cambridge Nonviolent Action Committee, 44
Cambridge University, 26
Canada, 37, 126, 127
Carey, Margaret, 170
Carlson, Tucker, 10
Carmichael, Stokely, 136, 139
Carnegie, Andrew, 164
Carver, George Washington, 135
Cary, Mary Ann Shadd, 36, 37–38, 39
Castro, Fidel, 156n66
Catherine Street Baptist Church, 107
CBS, 101
Center for Black Education, 136, 137
Centers for Disease Control, 90
Chaney State University, 104n3
Charlotte, NC, 99
Charlottesville, VA, 1
Charron, Katherine Mellen, 25
Chauvin, Derek, 28, 90, 91, 103n2
Chavis, Charles L., Jr., 4
Cheney, PA, 92
Chicago, IL: anti-Black violence in, 132, 139, 142; founding of National Negro Congress in, 167; Ida B. Wells-Barnett in, 131; NAACP in, 53–54, 181; National Association of Colored Women conference in, 54; YWCA in, 55
Chicago Defender, 131
Chicago Police Department (CPD), 132
Chicago Tribune, 143
Chisholm, Shirley, 44
Choctaw County, AL, 130
Christian Church/Disciples of Christ, 164
Christian Temple/Calhoun Christian Church, 164
Churches: Black Americans and, 18, 91, 127; Black women and, 50, 51, 52, 62, 66; and education, 99
Church Peace Union, 164
Church Women United, 65
Cincinnati, OH, 127, 138, 167
Citizens' Advisory Commissions, 120
Citizenship Education Program, 25
Citizenship/freedom schools. *See* Freedom/citizenship schools
City-Wide Young People's Forum, 171

Civil Rights Act of 1964, 65, 112, 117, 178n47, 184
Civil rights/Black freedom movement: audiences for, 43–44; Black Americans' activities during, 20–27; Black women and, 39, 40–44, 47, 48–49, 51, 61; and class, 62; conservatives and, 11, 12–13, 16, 26; divided nature of, 65–66; and economic independence, 53; focuses of, 182; during McCarthyism, 132–34; media coverage of, 151n31; narratives of, 112; opponents of and resistance to, 13, 62; rolling back of protections achieved by, 8; scholarship on, 107; sexism in, 41, 42–43, 44, 48, 49, 62–63, 65; strategies of, 53, 62, 63, 137; teaching of, 11, 12; threats to, 67; and voting, 39, 41; white Americans and, 20–21, 43, 53, 54, 60, 65, 182–83; youth recruitment for, 42
Civil Rights Commission, 58
Civil Rights Congress (CRC), 133, 167
Civil Rights Division, US Department of Justice, 142
Civil War: aftermath of, 108; Black veterans of, 94; as demarcation point, 17, 38, 50, 128, 129; and end of slavery, 128; occupation of Norfolk, VA, during, 107; rewriting of history of, 11–12; and states' rights rhetoric, 172; voting rights during, 107–8; white veterans of, 94, 108, 128. *See also* Reconstruction era
Clark, John, 52
Clark, Laura, 95, 96
Clark, Septima, 16, 21, 24–25, 27, 29
Clawson, Rosalee, 52
Cobb, Charlie, 136
Cocking v. Wade, 163
Colfax massacre, 128–29, 149n15
Colorado, 170
Colored State Convention, 108
Colored State Teachers Association, 96
Colored Women's League, 52
Colored Women's Suffrage Club, 168
Color of Change, 28
Columbia, SC, 24
Commission on Interracial Cooperation (CIC), 59

Committee, The (Goodman), 134
Committee on Un-American Activities/Dies Committee, US House of Representatives, 133–34, 151n30
Community Action Programs (CAPs). *See* War on Poverty
Congress of Racial Equality, 64, 75
Convocation on Hunger, 66
Conyers, John, 141
Cook, George, 108
Cookman Institute, 57
Coolidge, Calvin, 57
Cooper, Anna Julia, 52
Costigan, Edward, 170
Costigan-Wagner anti-lynching bill and Senate hearing, 159, 170–72, 173
Council of United Civil Rights Leadership (CUCRL), 43
COVID-19 pandemic, 1, 28, 90
Covington, KY, 138
Cox, Courtland, 136, 145
Crenshaw, Kimberlé, 14
Crisis, 40, 90
Critical race theory (CRT), 9, 10–11, 14–15, 146
Crockett, George, 133
Cuba, 139, 140, 156n66
Cullors, Patrisse, 29, 45
Culture of poverty thesis, 14, 31n20
Currier, Stephen, 64

Dagbovie, Pero, 134
Daily Commercial, 130, 131
Dallas, TX, 75
Dallas County, AL, 135
Davis, Clarence, 143
Davis, Ossie, 136
Davis, W. E., 109–10
Daytona Beach, FL, 57
Daytona Normal and Industrial School/Institute for Negro Girls, 57
Dean, Max, 115
"Death to America" (allegedly by Featherstone), 123, 145–46, 156n66
Declaration of Independence, 20, 91, 92
Delaware, 37

Dellums, Ronald, 141, 142
Democracy: Black Americans' role in, 2, 5, 7, 15, 16, 17, 19, 20, 21, 25–26, 29, 179–80; after Civil War, 17; conflicts over, 179; conservatives and, 8, 14, 29; and economic justice, 3, 179; and education, 8, 14, 25, 93; and employment, 180; and equality, 7, 20; historically Black colleges and universities and, 91–92, 93, 103; immigrants and, 18; and individual rights, 86; and interracial marriage, 179; and medical care, 179; and meritocracy, 7; multiracial, 7, 8, 11, 13, 14, 16, 20, 23, 24, 26, 28, 29, 179, 183, 185; and protest, 7, 8, 28, 180; as radical concept, 26; and school integration, 179; threats to, 7–8, 19–20, 21, 28; and voting rights, 3, 179; and War on Poverty, 72; and wealth, 18; and white supremacy, 20
Democratic National Conventions, 22–23, 24
Democrats: and 2020 presidential election, 5; and abolitionists, 127; and anti-lynching bills, 170; Black voters and, 57; Black women and, 62; and economic justice, 183; and fair housing, 183; George Murphy and, 166; Jacksonian, 127; in Maryland, 169; during post-Reconstruction period, 109, 129; as potential allies for Black Americans, 183; and racism, 166; during Reconstruction era, 17; and Republican Party, 183–84; southern, 71, 172, 178n47; and states' rights, 178n47; in Texas, 71, 72, 73; in Virginia, 109, 110; and voting rights, 72, 73, 109; and white supremacy, 110
Denston, Mary, 161
DeSantis, Ron, 5, 10, 13
Detroit, MI, 1, 138
Dickerson University, 166
Dies, Martin, 134
Dies Committee/Committee on Un-American Activities, US House of Representatives, 133–34, 151n30
Dillard University/Straight College, 93
Di Maio, Vincent, 156n66
Disciples of Christ/Christian Church, 164
Discrimination: conservatives and, 9; economic, 12; elimination of discussion of, 28; employment, 41; gender, 12, 35, 66, 128; and housing, 59–60; opposition to teaching history of, 9; racial, 52; sexual, 12, 14; structural, 28. *See also* Racial discrimination
Dissent. *See* Protest and dissent
District of Columbia Teacher's College, 134
Dittmer, John, 106
Division of Negro Affairs/Office of Minority Affairs, National Youth Administration, 57, 58
Division of Social Services, New York City Department of Welfare, 58
Dixiecrats, 172
Domestic and Foreign Missionary Society, 137
Dorchester County Courthouse, 143
Douglas, William O., 116
Douglass, Frederick, 2, 126
Drum and Spear bookstore, 135, 136–37, 153n42
Du Bois, Shirley Graham, 167
Du Bois, W.E.B.: on Black universities, 90; education of, 3, 92; and George Murphy, 167; on histories of Reconstruction, 19, 149n15; and James Edward Shepard, 97; and Mary McLeod Bethune, 56, 68n24; philosophy of, 2, 182; as signatory to "We Charge Genocide" UN petition, 133; and Talented Tenth, 39; on white narrative on US history, 8
Dudley, James B., 100
Dudley, Miss, 111, 112
Duer, Judge, 161
Dunning, William, 11, 19
Dunnsville, VA, 164
Durham, NC, 98, 100
Durham State Normal School/National Religious Training Institute and Chautauqua (NRTIC)/National Training School, 98–100
Duster, Michelle, 173
Dyer, Leonidas C., 172, 177n44
Dyer anti-lynching bill, 173, 177n44

Eastern Shore, MD: anti-Black violence in, 161–62; Asbury Smith in, 165–66; Black economic resilience in, 162; lynchings in, 4, 159, 162, 165, 171, 172, 174; racist beliefs in, 162, 166; slavery in, 159
Eastern Virginia District Court in, 114, 115
East Saint Louis, MO, 132

Economic justice: and democracy, 179; and predatory lending, 184; and protest, 7; and redlining, 184; and voting rights, 2, 3, 71, 79. *See also* War on Poverty

Education: adult literacy, 24; and African American history, 30n4, 40; Black Americans and, 24, 25, 53, 59, 60, 98; Black churches and, 99; and Black citizenship, 92; Black girls and, 40; and Black history, 135; and Black political activism, 130; Black women and, 24, 25, 40, 50, 51, 53, 55, 61, 66, 67; and civil rights/Black freedom movement, 53, 54; conservatives and, 8, 9, 13–15, 27, 100; curricula for, 100, 104n10; and democracy, 25, 93; and desegregation, 127; discrimination in, 24; enslaved and formerly enslaved persons and, 92, 95, 125, 127; impact of World War I on, 99; industrial, 95; and inequality, 16; liberal arts, 57; as means to combat lynching, 163; and model departments, 97, 104n16; and morality, 98; National Council of Negro Women and, 64, 66; post-secondary, 58; for professionals, 56; racial discrimination in, 128; and segregation, 61; Taconic Foundation and, 64; and teachers' pay, 53, 54; vocational, 56, 57, 95; and white supremacy, 8, 16. *See also* Freedom/citizenship schools; Historically Black colleges and universities (HCBUs)

Eisenhower, Dwight D., 43
Elliot, Daniel, 160
Elliott, Bill, 77
Ellis, Reginald, 3
El Paso, TX, 72
Emmett Till Antilynching Act (US), 171, 173, 177n44
England, 125
Enslaved persons: Black women as, 36, 55; conservative education on, 11; and education and literacy, 92, 125, 127; and emancipation, 16, 125; escaped, 107; families of, 18; and Founding Fathers, 184; and manumission, 125, 126; and resistance, 125, 149n13; during Revolutionary era, 91; scholarship on, 148n7; and slave codes, 125, 127

Episcopal Church, 137, 139, 153n42, 183
Episcopal Diocese of East Carolina, 99
Equality: Black women and, 36; conservatives and, 8, 15; and democracy, 7, 20; economic, 7, 8, 27; gender, 27, 41; and patriotism, 7; racial, 27, 41; sexual, 27; social, 7
Equal Justice Initiative (EJI), 130
Equal Suffrage Address, 107–8
Evening Sun, 165
Evers, Medgar, 126
Evers, Myrlie, 44
Exodusters, 130

Fair Deal, 110
Fair Employment Practices Commission, 165–66
Fairfax County, VA, 116
Faith and Order movement, 164
"Faith Can Move a Damp Heap" (Bethune), 48
Farmer, James, 64
Farm Security Administration, 59
Faulkner, William, 146
Favors, Jelani, 3, 92
Featherstone, Ralph: and 1967 National Black Power Conference, 139; background of, 134, 139; and Black education, 137; and Black history, 125, 134–35; and Black Student Movement, 137; characteristics of, 135, 140; in Cuba, 139, 156n66; death of, 4, 123–24, 127, 135, 136, 139, 140–43, 146, 155n58, 183; and Drum and Spear bookstore, 135, 136, 137–38, 139, 141, 183; and economic and community development, 136, 137; and FBI, 124, 135, 137, 138, 139, 146, 183; and Freedom Schools, 135, 139, 183; and H. Rap Brown, 139; jailing of, 135–36; media coverage of, 123–24, 127, 134, 135, 140, 143–45, 183; memorial service for, 144–45; and Stokely Carmichael, 136, 139; and Student Nonviolent Coordinating Committee, 135, 136, 139, 156n66; and Students for a Democratic Society, 144; and Vietnam War, 139; and voting rights, 139; wife of, 124, 135, 145

Featherstone Black Arts Festival, 136
Federal Bureau of Investigation (FBI): and arson at Houston community action agency, 78; and Black Panther Party, 139; Counterintelligence Black National Hate Group program (COINTELPRO) of, 138–39, 140, 141, 142, 145–46; and Drum and Spear bookstore, 153n42; and Fred Hampton, 124, 139, 142; and H. Rap Brown, 139; J. Edgar Hoover as director of, 125, 131; and Martin Luther King Jr., 139; and Maryland State Police, 143; and National Black Economic Development Conference attendees, 138; and Ralph Featherstone, 124, 135, 137, 138, 139–40, 142, 143, 146, 183; and Stokely Carmichael, 139
Federal City College, 137
Federal Council on Negro Affairs, 58
Federation of Colored Women's Clubs, 55
Federation of Labor, 168–69
Fields, Barbara Jeanne, 163
First Colored Professional, Clerical and Business Directory of Baltimore City, The, 165
Fisk University, 92
Flint, MI, 115
Florida: 1885 Constitutional Convention in, 94; Black middle class in, 93–94; capital of, 95, 96; college instructor compensation in, 104n12; governors of, 94; higher education for Black persons in, 57, 94; public school education in, 5, 10, 12, 30n4; reversing of Reconstruction-era policies in, 94
Florida Agricultural and Mechanical University, 93
Florida Social Studies Standards for African American History, 11, 12
Florida State Federation of Colored Women's Clubs, 57
Florida State Normal and Industrial School for Colored Students (FSNIS): admission standards of, 95; and Colored State Teachers Association, 96; curriculum of, 93, 95, 96, 97, 104n10; founding of, 94; funding of, 93, 96, 101; impact of, 97; location of, 95; staff of, 95–96; student population of, 95; Thomas Tucker as first president of, 95; white support for, 97

Floyd, George, 1, 28, 90, 91, 103n2, 173
Foner, Eric, 17, 128
Ford, Charles, 3, 4
Ford Foundation, 137
Forman, James, 64, 138
"Form Human Shield Between Cops and Crooks" (Breasted), 156n63
Forrest, Nathan Bedford, 128
4th Circuit Court of Appeals, 114, 115
Fox News Channel, 10
Franklin, Ben, 91
Franklin, John Hope, 3, 92
Fredericksburg, VA, 114
Free Blacks, 37, 45n2, 126, 127, 128. *See also* Black Americans; Enslaved persons
Freedom/citizenship schools: Black women and, 25, 66–67; at Drum and Spear bookstore, 136; Fannie Lou Hamer and, 22, 24; as grassroots effort, 180; Ralph Featherstone and, 135, 136, 183; Septima Clark and, 21, 24, 25; spread of, 25
Freedom Democratic Party (FDP), 22, 23–24
Freedom Rides, 42
Freedom Summer, 134–35
Freedomways, 134
Free Southern Theater, 136
Free Speech, 131
Fugitive Slave Act, 37, 127

Gage, Francis, 45n3
Gainesville, FL, 94
Gallegos, Mario, 82, 85
Gamble, James, 57
Garnet, Henry Highland, 126
Garrison, William Lloyd, 92, 126, 168
Garvey, Marcus, 53, 131, 134, 181
Gary, IN, 141
Garza, Alicia, 29, 45
Gender: Black women and, 39, 40, 41, 49, 50, 51, 52; and citizenship, 17–18; and discrimination, 12, 35, 66, 128; and equality and inequality, 2, 3, 8, 41
Gentry, Betty, 79–80, 81
Georgetown district, Salisbury, MD, 160
Georgia, 17, 110, 141
Germany, 168, 169
Gibbs, Thomas Van Renssalaer, 94, 95, 96

Gillard, John T., 170
Gillum, Andrew, 103
Gilman, Daniel C., 168, 170
Gilman, Elizabeth, 159, 162, 164, 168, 170
Glass, Carter, 109
Glenn, Susan, 133
Gold, Ted, 144
Goodman, Walter, 133, 134, 151n31
Gorman, Amanda, 5
Goucher College, 170
Great Depression, 4, 24, 54, 162, 170
Great Society, 110. *See also* War on Poverty
Great Uprising, 127
Green, Asbury, 169–70
Greenberg, Jack, 64
Greene, James, 16–17, 29
Greensboro, NC, 100
Greenwood, MS, 65
Griffith, D. W., 19

Haas, Jeffrey, 142
Hague Conference of the World Alliance for International Friendship, 164
Hahn, Steven, 129, 130
Haitian Revolution, 125–26
Hamer, Fannie Lou: background of, 21; as civil rights activist, 16, 29, 61, 62, 136; and Democratic National Conventions, 22–23; and freedom schools, 22; issues tackled by, 21–24; and Loyalty Democrats, 24; and Mississippi Freedom Democratic Party, 22–24; police violence against, 21, 65; as political candidate, 22, 24; and sexism, 62; and Student Nonviolent Coordinating Committee, 22
Hammond, James Henry, 127
Hampton, Fred, 124, 127, 139, 142
Hampton, VA, 94, 109
Hannah-Jones, Nikole, 15
Harambee Singers, 136
Harding, Vincent, 124
Harlem, NY, 43
Harper, Annie E., 115
Harper v. Virginia Board of Elections, 74
Harris, Kamala, 2–3, 35, 45, 103, 173
Harris County, TX, 73, 77
Harris County Hospital District, 76

Harris County Tax Assessor-Collector, 77
Harrison, Albertis, 114, 115
Har Sinai Congregation, 167
Hart, Brooke, 169
Hatch Act, 77
Hatcher, Richard, 141
Hayes, Curtis, 136
Haynesworth, Clement F., 114
Height, Dorothy I.: as activist, 2; background of, 43; and civil rights/Black freedom movement, 36, 41; and Council of United Civil Rights Leadership, 43; and Dwight Eisenhower, 43; and Harlem YWCA, 43; and Lyndon Johnson, 43; and March on Washington, 43–44, 65, 112, 114, 144, 145, 181; and memorial service for Ralph Featherstone, 144, 146; and NAACP, 64; and National Council of Negro Women, 43, 44, 64–65, 66; and racism, 44; and sexism, 41, 43–44, 65; on sexual and physical violence against Black women, 65; and Taconic Foundation, 64, 65; and YWCA, 64
Hemmingway, Grace, 99
Highlander Folk School, 24–25, 63, 67
"Hill We Climb, The" (Gorman), 5
Hinojosa, Mrs. Joel, 82, 85
Hiss, Alger, 133
Historically Black colleges and universities (HCBUs): Ashmun Institute as first degree-granting US Black college, 92; Black women and, 102; curricula of, 97, 104n10; and democracy, 91–92, 93, 103; disrepair of, 101–2; faculty compensation at, 104n12; funding of, 93, 101–2, 103, 183, 184; impact of, 2, 3, 92, 101, 102, 103; opposition to, 92, 93; and societal change, 180; and white supremacy, 93
Hitler, Adolf, 169
Hoffman, Walter E., 114, 115
Holly Springs, OH, 135
Hollywood Ten, 133
Holt, Leonard, 114, 115
Homewood Friends Meeting, 169
Hooks, Benjamin, 52, 67
Hoover, Herbert, 57
Hoover, J. Edgar: and Black bookstores, 137, 138, 139; and Black challenging of excep-

tionalist narrative of US history, 125; and Black dissenters, 131; and civil rights/Black freedom movement, 58, 131, 156n63, 182; and death of Ralph Featherstone, 140, 143; and investigation of possible links between Communism and Black persons and organizations, 132
"Hoover Warns U.S. of Extremism Peril," 156n63
Hope, John, 59, 101
Hope, Lugenia Burns, 59
Horne, Gerald, 134, 151n32
Houston, Charles Hamilton, 53, 167
Houston, TX: and city services for poor neighborhoods, 75; civil rights/Black freedom movement in, 75; Democratic Party in, 72; economic justice in, 85, 86; health care in, 75, 76; housing in, 75; mayor of, 74, 76, 78, 79, 80–81, 83; police intimidation and brutality in, 76, 79–80; poor in, 86; sanitation services in, 76, 79; Settegast neighborhood of, 76, 77–78, 79–80; voting rights in, 71, 72, 73, 75, 76–79, 82, 84–85, 86, 183; War on Poverty and Project Freedom in, 3, 71, 72, 74–82, 84–86; water quality in, 76, 79
Houston Chronicle, 78, 83
Houston Post, 76
Howard University Law School, 38, 101, 166
Howell, Henry, Jr., 111, 112
HUAC. *See* Committee on Un-American Activities
Human Organizational, Political, and Economic Development, Incorporated (HOPE), 83, 84, 85
Hume, Brit, 10
Hunter-Gault, Charlayne, 145
Hurburt, Jess, 99

"I Have a Dream" (King), 10
Illinois, 55
Indigenous peoples, 2, 29
Inequality: and civil rights/Black freedom movement, 26; conservatives and, 7, 8, 14–15; economic, 8; and education, 16; racial, 8, 35; structural, 26
In Friendship, 42
International Labor Defense (ILD), 166

International Ladies' Garment Workers' Union, 168
International Sunday School Association, 98
Israel, Edward, 162, 164, 166, 167–68, 170, 171

Jackson, Juanita, 159, 170, 171–73
Jackson, Lillie May Carroll, 171
Jackson, MS, 126
Jacobs, Clyde H., 111
January 6, 2021, insurrection, 1, 5, 19–20, 28
Japan, 169
Jefferson, Thomas, 91, 126
Jeffries, Hasan Kwame, 11
Jews, 171
Jim Crow: Black college presidents and, 97, 101; Black economic resilience during, 162; civil rights/Black freedom movement and, 53, 56, 57, 131; definition of, 20; and employment, 131; FBI surveillance of organizations opposed to, 132; and housing, 131; inclusion of, in Florida history curricula, 12; in Northern United States, 131; and school desegregation, 114; and voting rights, 114, 183. *See also* Racial discrimination; Racism, systemic/structural
Johns Hopkins University, 158, 168, 170
Johns Hopkins University Liberal Club, 168
Johns Island, SC, 24
Johnson, Andrew, 128
Johnson, Lyndon B.: and 1964 Democratic Convention, 23; and civil rights, 43; and Dorothy I. Height, 43; and Fannie Lou Hamer, 23; and Great Society initiative, 110; and Louie Welch, 80; and response to Selma, AL, demonstrations, 106; and War on Poverty, 71, 74
Johnson, Mordecai, 101
Johnson, Patsy, 161
Johnson, Walter, 148n7
Johnson C. Smith University, 99
Jones, Leroi (Amiri Baraka), 134
Jones, Lillie, 136
Jones, Martha, 56
Jordan, Joseph, Jr.: background of, 112–13; cocounsels of, 114, 115; contempories' opinion of, 107; and employment rights, 117; and Evelyn T. Butts, 106, 113, 114, 116,

120; impact of, 106, 119–20; and *Journal and Guide* newspaper, 117; as judge, 120; and Martin Luther King memorial in Norfolk, 120; and NAACP, 112, 117; and opposition to Douglas MacArthur memorial, 117; as politician, 117–19; and public accommodation rights, 117; strategies of, 118; and US Supreme Court, 116, 118; and Virginia public school desegregation, 113, 117; and voting rights in Virginia, 4, 112, 113, 114, 115, 116, 117, 120
Jordan, Winthrop, 126
Journal and Guide, 117
Joyner, Tom, 103

Kaepernick, Colin, 27, 28, 29, 32n28
Kansas, 130
Keith, LeeAnna, 128–29, 149n15
Kennedy, Robert F., 118
Kenyatta, Muhammad, 138, 146
Kern, Jerome, 119
King, Martin Luther, Jr.: assassination of, 118, 127, 137; authoritarian style of, 42; challenge to America by, 2; conservatives' quoting of, 10; education of, 3, 92; and Ella Baker, 42; FBI surveillance of, 139; independent employment of, 62; and March on Washington, 144, 145; and mobilization of Black persons of all walks of life, 42; and Montgomery bus boycott, 64; and Montgomery Improvement Association, 42; on need for tension to bring about justice, 27; as patriot, 29; as possible political candidate, 151n31; public perceptions of, 181; and sexism, 42; and Southern Christian Leadership Conference, 42, 64, 141; speeches and writings of, 10, 135; and Taconic Foundation, 64; on white moderates, 20–21
Kipling, Rudyard, 98
Kornweibel, Theodore, 131
Ku Klux Klan, 19, 124, 128, 129–30, 139
Kunstler, William, 124, 139, 140

La Guardia, Fiorello Henry, 58
Lally, Col., 143
Lamb, William, 108

Lampkin, Daisy, 54
Lane, W. Preston, 161, 170
Latino people, 27
League for Industrial Democracy, 168
League of Women Voters, 47, 56
Legal cases: *Breedlove v. Suttles,* 110; *Brown v. Board of Education of Topeka, Kansas,* 60, 61, 63, 110, 117; *Cocking v. Wade,* 163; *Harper v. Virginia Board of Elections,* 74; *Plessy v. Ferguson,* 104n12; *Smith v. Allwright,* 73
Legal Defense Fund, NAACP, 53, 64, 73
Legislation: Anderson-McCormick Act of 1884 (VA), 109; antebellum slave codes, 125, 126, 127; anti-lynching (VA), 163; anti-miscengenation laws, 128; Civil Rights Act of 1964 (US), 65, 112, 117, 178n47, 184; Costigan-Wagner anti-lynching bill (US), 170; Emmett Till Antilynching Act (US), 171, 173, 177n44; Fugitive Slave Act (US), 37, 127; Hatch Act (US), 77; post-Civil War Black codes, 128; in response to Haitian Revolution, 126; Stop the Wrongs to Our Kids and Employees Act/Stope WOKE Act (FL), 10. *See also* Voting Rights Act of 1965 (US)
Leonard, Jerris, 142
Leon County, FL, 94
"Letter from a Birmingham Jail" (King), 135
Levison, Stanley, 42
Levy, Peter, 4
Lewis, Earl, 107
Lewis, Edward S., 169
Lewis, John, 64, 144
Lewis, Oren R., 115
Lewis, Rufus, 48
Liberation, 134
Liberator, The, 126, 134
Lie, the, 90–91, 92
Lincoln, Abraham, 128
Lincoln, C. Eric, 64
Lincoln, PA, 92
Lincoln-Grant High School, 138
Lincoln University, 92
Littlejohn, Jeffrey, 3, 4
Little Rock, AR, 127
Little Rock Central High School, 44

Litwack, Leon, 129
Local People: The Struggle for Civil Rights in Mississippi (Dittmer), 106
Logan, Trevor, 18
Lost Cause, 108–9
Louisiana, 50, 93
Louisville, KY, 91
Lovejoy, Elijah, 127
Lowndes County, AL, 136
Loyalty Democrats, 24
Lusk Commission, 132
Lynching: Black women as opponents of, 43, 55, 57, 59, 66, 130–31; in California, 169; and defense of slavery, 127; definition of, 130; efforts to pass legislation against, 159, 170–72, 173; Eleanor Roosevelt as opponent of, 167; federal goverment programs against, 41; Franklin D. Roosevelt's response to, 167; investigations of, 158, 161; lack of consequences for perpetrators of, 90, 131, 159, 161, 163, 171–72; in Maryland, 4, 158, 159, 160–61, 162, 163, 164, 165, 166, 171–72; in Missouri, 169; myths about, 159; NAACP opposition to, 54, 166; pervasiveness of, 182; by police, 90; post-World War I upsurge in, 132, 170; proposed legislation on, 170–73, 177n44; purposes of, 130, 159; scholarship on, 175n5, 175n12; statistics on, 130; strategies for ending, 163, 166; systematic support of, 131; US law against, 173; US Senate hearing on, 159, 170–72; and victims' families, 159, 174; white defenses of, 131; white response to opponents of, 130–31, 172, 178n47. *See also* Maryland Anti-Lynching Federation (MALF)

MacArthur, Douglas, 117
MacNeal, A. Clement, 53–54, 181
Madison, James, 91
Mahone, William, 108
Malcolm X, 35, 127, 134
Mallory, Tamika, 29
Manchuria, 169
Mandel, Marvin, 140, 143
Manhattan Institute for Policy Research, 14
Many Thousands Gone: The First Two Centuries of Slavery in North America (Berlin), 148n7

Mao Tse-tung, 129
March on Washington: aftermath of, 114; Bayard Rustin and, 43, 65; Black women and, 43–44, 144; and Civil Rights Act of 1964, 112; Dorothy I. Height and, 43–44, 65, 144, 145, 181; Martin Luther King Jr. and, 144, 145; National Council of Negro Women and, 44, 65; organizers of, at Ralph Featherstone's memorial service, 145
March on Washington Movement, 132
Markle, Seth, 137
Marshall, Thurgood, 3, 73, 92, 167
Martin, Roy, 118, 119
Maryland: civil rights organizations in, 44; during Civil War, 163; and death of Ralph Featherstone, 142–43; governors of, 140, 143, 159, 160–61, 163, 172, 183; gubernatorial candidates in, 168; and historically Black colleges and universities, 101; history of civil rights in, 163–64; interracial advocacy in, 163, 176n19; lynchings in, 4, 158, 159, 160–61, 162, 163, 164, 165, 166, 171–72; Lynching Truth and Reconciliation Commission in, 174, 178n54; officials of, 161; racism in, 169; slavery in, 159. *See also* Maryland Anti-Lynching Federation (MALF)
Maryland Annotated Code of the Public General Laws, 163
Maryland Anti-Lynching Federation (MALF): Congressional testimony on behalf of, 159; creation of, 4, 162; founders, leaders, and membership of, 4, 159, 162–63, 164, 165, 168–69, 170, 174; goals and activities of, 159–60, 162, 163, 169–70, 173; impact of, 4, 162; scholarship on, 159; strategies of, 168, 169
Maryland Civil Liberties Committee, 168
Maryland Department of Public Safety and Corrections, 143
Maryland Interracial Commission, 165
Maryland Lynching Truth and Reconciliation Commission, 174, 178n54
Maryland State Police, 143
Mary S. Peak School, 94
Mason, Vivian Carter, 47, 58–59, 60

Mathews, Donald G., 160, 175n12
Matthews, Jack, 76–77
Mayor, Jim, 78
Mays, Benjamin E., 101
McCarthyism, 132–34, 151n30, 151n32
McGuire, Danielle, 63
McKendree/Arlington congregation, 165
McKinley, William, 177n44
McKissick, Floyd, 142
McWhirter, Cameron, 132
McWorter, Thelma, 55
Memphis, TN, 131
Menard, John Willis, 94
Mexicans, 2, 29
Michigan, 116, 141
Mississippi, 21–23, 24, 134, 139, 183
Mississippi Democratic Party, 22
Mississippi Freedom Democratic Party (FDP), 22, 23–24
Mississippi Gulf, 136
Mississippi River, 130
Missouri, 169, 172, 177n44
Mitchell, Broadus, 158–59, 170
Mitchell, Clarence, 170
Mitchell, Juanita Jackson, 159, 170, 171–73
Model Cities Advisory Commission, 120
Moffitt, Franklin, 78
Moms for Liberty, 9, 13
Monteagle, TN, 24
Montgomery, AL, 61, 62, 63, 64
Montgomery bus boycott, 42, 48, 60, 61–62, 63, 181
Montgomery Bus Boycott and the Women Who Started It, The (Robinson), 48
Montgomery Improvement Association (MIA), 42, 62
Moore, Howard, 155n58
Morehouse College, 59, 92, 101
Morgan, Patricia, 7, 13
Movement for Black Lives, 28
Moynihan, Daniel Patrick, 31n20, 136, 142
M Street High School, 39, 40
Murphy, George B., 159, 162, 164, 166–67, 171
Murphy, John H., 166
Murray, Pauli, 61
Muse, Daphne, 135
Mutual aid societies, 18

Nash, Diane, 42
Nation, 169
National Advisory Council, Office of Economic Opportunity, 80
National Association for the Advancement of Colored People (NAACP): and anti-Black violence and murder, 54, 166; Baltimore chapter of, 171; Black women and, 39, 40, 41–42, 44, 47, 49, 52, 53–55, 66; and *Brown v. Board of Education of Topeka, Kansas,* 60; Charles Hamilton Houston and, 166; in Chicago, 53–54, 181; and conflict with other civil rights/Black freedom organizations, 53–54; Dorothy I. Height and, 64; and education, 53; Edward Israel and, 171; Eleanor Roosevelt and, 167; Elisabeth Gilman and, 168; founding of, 39, 52; funding for, 54; George Murphy and, 166; importance of, 180; as integrated organization, 180; and Jim Crow, 53; Joseph Jordan Jr. and, 112, 117; leaders of, 42, 44, 52, 53–54, 67, 169; Legal Defense Fund of, 53, 64, 73; Mary McLeod Bethune and, 56; and National Council of Negro Women, 60, 64; partner organizations of, 47, 67; and policy disagreements, 166; Rosa Parks and, 63, 181; sexism in, 42, 44, 49; strategies of, 42, 53–54, 180–81; and voting rights, 39, 74; white opposition to, 131; white support for, 53, 54; Youth Council of, 63
National Association of Colored Women (NACW), 39, 40, 52–53, 54, 55
National Association of Colored Women's Clubs, 57
National Baptist Convention, 39
National Black Economic Development Conference (NBEDC), 138
National Black Power Conference, 139
National Commission for Child Welfare, 57
National Committee to Abolish the Poll Tax, 110
National Conference for New Politics, 151n31
National Council of Catholic Women, 65
National Council of Churches, 137
National Council of Jewish Women, 65
National Council of Negro Women (NCNW): and activism, 58–59; and Convoca-

tion on Hunger, 66; on deaths of Ralph Featherstone and William "Che" Payne, 141; focuses of, 3, 47, 58–59, 60, 64, 65, 66; founding of, 41, 49, 57; as grassroots organization, 3; impact and importance of, 49, 64, 67, 180; international perspective of, 47, 49, 60; leaders of, 41, 43, 44, 47–48, 58, 60, 64, 65, 141; and March on Washington, 65; membership of, 59, 64; and partner organizations, 47, 59, 60, 64, 66; programs of, 41, 47; and Project Womanpower, 66; role of, 41, 49–50; and sexism, 44; strategies of, 60, 66; vision of, 3
National Football League, 27
National Guard, 161
National Negro Congress (NNC), 132, 133, 167
National Religious Training Institute and Chautauqua (NRTIC)/National Training School/Durham State Normal School, 98–100
National Training School for Women and Girls, 39–40
National Urban League, 52, 64, 166, 171
National Women Suffrage Association (NWSA), 39
National Youth Administration, 41
Nation of Islam, 35
Nation under Our Feet, A (Hahn), 129
Nat Turner's rebellion, 126
NBC Nightly News, 123
"Negro College, The" (Du Bois), 90
Nesoba County, MS, 136
New Amsterdam News, 142
Newark, NJ, 99, 139
Newby-Alexander, Cassandra, 3, 4
New Deal, 58, 107, 110, 114, 167, 183
New Mob, 156n63
Newport News, VA, 117, 164
New York, NY, 43, 58, 127, 131, 138, 144
New York City Department of Welfare, 58
New York Daily News, 144, 156n63
New York Independent, 45n3
New York State, 132, 170
New York Sunday Times Magazine, 151n31
New York Times, 133, 143

New York University, 43
Neyland, Leedell, 95
Nixon, E. D., 48
Nixon, Lawrence A., 72–73
Nixon, Richard M., 138, 142
Norfolk, VA: Black and white female activists in, 50, 59; Black newspaper in, 117; Black political participation in, 108; Black population of, 119; city officials in, 108, 118, 119–20; during Civil War, 107; class in, 107; court officials in, 114; Democratic Party/Harry F. Byrd machine in, 114; division of Virginia State College in, 117; Eastern Virginia District Court in, 114, 115; Ella Baker in, 41; Evelyn T. Butts in, 106, 113–14, 117; General Assembly delegates from, 114; housing in, 59, 60; Joseph Jordan Jr. in, 106, 112–13, 117–20; Martin Luther King memorial in, 120; Poor People's March in, 118; public schools in, 60, 113–14, 119; racial discrimination in, 59; racial tensions in, 118; reputation of, 108; Vivian Carter Mason in, 59, 60; voting rights in, 50, 106, 107–8, 111–12, 113, 114; Women's Council for Interracial Cooperation in, 59–60
Norfolk Alliance of Political Action Committees, 113
Norfolk Division, Virginia State College, 117
Norfolk Electoral Board, 111
Norfolk Housing and Redevelopment Administration (NHRA), 60
North Carolina, 97, 99, 100, 110, 130, 177n44
North Carolina A&M College, 100
North Carolina College for Negroes/North Carolina Central University, 97, 98–100, 101

Oakwood Parents Teacher Association, 113
Obama, Barack, 4, 11
Oberlin College, 38, 93
Oblate Sisters of Providence, 170
O'Brien, Soledad, 63
Observer, 127
Ocasio-Cortez, Alexandria, 28, 29
Office of Economic Opportunity (OEO), 74, 77, 79, 80–81

Office of Minority Affairs/Division of Negro Affairs, National Youth Administration, 57, 58
Office of the Chief Examiner of Maryland, 156n66
Ohio State University, 11
Olvera, Isabel de, 45n2
Omar, Ilhan, 28, 29
Orange-Featherstone, Charlotte, 124, 135, 145
O'Reilly, Kenneth, 131
Owens, Jesse, 132
"Own Bomb Slew Rap's Pals," 144

Page, Walter A., 114
Panthers, Black, 60
Park Avenue Friends Meeting, 168
Parks, Rosa, 61, 62, 63, 64, 181
Patriotism: Black Americans and, 7, 179; and Christianity, 15; conservatives and, 9, 13, 14, 15, 29; definitions of, 7, 9, 13, 15, 16, 20, 27, 28, 29; and obedience, 27; and protest, 7; and US history, 7; and white supremacy, 15–16
Paul, Alice, 38
Paul, Rand, 173
Payne, William "Che": background of, 138; death of, 123–24, 135, 138, 140, 141, 144; and FBI, 140, 142, 144; media coverage of, 123, 140; and Muhammad Kenyatta, 138, 146; and Student Nonviolent Coordinating Committee, 123, 138
Peabody Education Fund, 54
Peninsula General Hospital, 160
Pensacola, FL, 93, 94, 95
People's Unemployment League of Maryland, 168
Perry, Edward A., 94
Phelps, Wesley, 3, 4
Philadelphia, PA, 1, 91, 92
Philanthropist, 127
Phillips, Ulrich B., 11
Phoenix, AZ, 1
Phyllis Wheatley House for Girls, 55
Phyllis Wheatley YWCAs, 55–56
Pinkerton National Detective Agency, 161
Pittsburgh Courier, 124

Poland, 169
Police brutality. *See* Black Americans, intimidation of and violence against: by police
Poor People's Campaign, 28
Poor People's March, 118
Populist Party, 183
Portsmouth, VA, 117
Post-Reconstruction period: Black disenfranchisement during, 129; Black strategies during, 129; citizenship during, 17; Democrats during, 109, 129; police and criminal justice system during, 129; racial violence during, 129; Republican Party during, 128; rewriting of history of, 129; segregation during, 129; systemic/structural racism during, 50; white Americans during, 129–30; white supremacy during, 129
Presbyterian Church, 99
President's Committee on Civil Rights, 40
Pressley, Ayanna, 28, 29
Prieur, William "Billy," 114
Princess Anne, MD, 159, 161
Progressive movement, 52
Project Freedom, Houston, TX, 76–78
Project Womanpower, National Council of Negro Women (NCNW), 66
"Protest and Death," 144
Protest and dissent: Black Americans and, 4, 7, 26, 27–28, 32n28, 79, 80, 81, 112, 117, 130, 133, 134, 142, 143, 144, 146, 179, 180, 182, 184; Black women and, 21, 24, 48, 50, 54, 55, 58, 63, 65, 112, 117, 130, 181; and citizenship, 28, 179; and democracy, 7, 8, 28, 180; inclusion of, in US history and curricula, 4, 7, 8, 29, 125, 134, 135, 184; after murder of George Floyd, 1, 28; NAACP and, 54, 180–81; opposition to, 1, 2, 4, 8, 15, 27–28, 32n28, 131, 132, 136, 146, 173, 182; and patriotism, 7; white Americans and, 165, 169; against white supremacy, 8
Provincial Freeman, 37
Public schools: bans on teaching critical race theory in, 10–11; conservatives and, 9, 13; development of, 17; in Florida, 5, 10, 11, 12, 30n4; in Virginia, 10–11, 117, 119
Purnell, Brian, 31n20

Quakers, 170

Racial discrimination: among Jews, 171; Black women and, 66; and civil rights/Black freedom movement, 124; conservatives and, 8, 13; and education, 14, 24, 128; inclusion and exclusion of, in US history, 8, 9, 13; increases in, 53; and repression of Black dissidents, 124; rewriting of history of, 124–25; and segregation, 41, 47, 62; and status quo, 14; in US military, 12, 59, 128
Racism, anti-white, 12, 13
Racism, systemic/structural: and civil rights/Black freedom movement, 20; conservatives and, 11, 12–13, 26; and critical race theory, 14; education on, 11; in post-Reconstruction era, 50; protests against, 27–28; and segregation, 50; structural barriers in, 12; teaching about, 9, 12, 124, 146; and US history, 184
Raleigh, NC, 97, 99
Randolph, A. Philip, 64
Readjuster Party, 108–9, 183
Reagan, Ronald, 67
Reagon, Bernice, 136
Rebellious Life of Mrs. Rosa Parks, The (book, Theoharis), 63
Rebellious Life of Mrs. Rosa Parks, The (documentary), 63
Reconstruction era: Black Americans during, 16–17, 94, 108, 172; citizenship during, 17–18; end of, 129; Northern elites and, 18; and public infrastructure, 18; rewriting of history of, 11–12, 15–16, 17, 19, 128–29, 184; and social safety nets, 17; and tax codes, 17, 18; in Virginia, 108; white against Black violence during, 129–30; and white supremacy, 18, 20, 128
Recorder of Deeds office, 97
Redemption movement, 109
Rehnquist, William H., 67
Reid, Milton, 118
Report of the 1776 Commission, 14, 184
Republican Party: Black Americans and, 57, 166, 183, 184; civil rights opponents and, 62; and Democratic Party, 183–84; George H. W. Bush and, 71; in Harris County, TX, 78; during Reconstruction and post-Reconstruction eras, 128, 129; in Virginia, 108, 115; and voting rights, 108; and working-class voters, 183–84
Republicans: and anti-lynching efforts, 172; Black, 17, 18; and Black colleges and universities, 100; and January 6, 2021, insurrection, 28; murder of, by white supremacists, 130; in North Carolina, 100; and race education, 16; and US history, 8; white, 8, 18, 28, 130
Resettlement Administration, 59
Rhode Island, 13–14
Richardson, Gloria, 44
Richardson, Judy, 136
Richmond, VA, 43, 111, 112
Ritchie, Albert C., 159, 160–61, 163, 172, 178n47
River of Dark Dreams: Slavery and the Empire of the Cotton Kingdom (Johnson), 148n7
Riverside Church, 138
Robeson, Paul, 133, 167
Robins, John, 161
Robinson, Jo Ann Gibson, 48, 61–62, 64, 181
Robinson, William P., Sr., 117–18
Roosevelt, Eleanor, 57, 167
Roosevelt, Franklin D.: "Black Cabinet" of, 41, 58; cabinet officers under, 132; and Edward L. Israel, 168; and Mary McLeod Bethune, 58; and New Deal, 59, 110; political challengers to, 160; response of, to lynching, 167, 173; and surveillance of possible Communist Party members, 132; and Vivian Carter Mason, 47
Roosevelt, Theodore, 98
Roosevelt High School, 134
Rosenbergs, 133
Rosenwald, Julius, 54
Rosenwald, William, 54
Rosenwald Fund, 54
Rovere, Richard, 133
Ruffin, Josephine St. Pierre, 61
Rufo, Christopher, 14
Ruleville, MS, 21
Rustin, Bayard, 42, 43, 65

Saint-Domingue/Haiti, 125–26
Salisbury, MD, 158, 159, 160, 161, 164, 165
San Francisco [UN] Conference, 58
San Francisco 49ers, 27
San Jose, California, 169
Schweitzer, Paul, 119
Scottsboro Boys, 133, 166
Sears and Roebuck, 54, 181
Segar, Robert L., 115, 116
Selma, AL, 106, 112, 135, 138
Senator Joe McCarthy (Rovere), 133
Settegast neighborhood, Houston, TX, 76, 77–78, 79–80
1776 Commission, 14, 184
Shaw University, 42, 97, 99
Shepard, James Edward, 97–101
Sherbro, Sierra Leone, 93
Shiloh Institute, 97
Showboat (Kern), 119
Sinegal-DeCuir, Sharlene, 2, 3, 48
Sinha, Manisha, 149n13
1619 Project, 146
Skeen, John Henry, 169
Slave codes, 125
Slavery: Black families during, 18; duration of, 128; education on, 11; and federal government expansion, 127–28; higher education as means to end, 92; justifications for, 90; in Maryland, 159, 163; opposition to, 126–28; racial basis of, 52; scholarship on, 148n7; violence in defense of, 127. *See also* Black Americans: formerly enslaved; Black women: enslaved and formerly enslaved; Enslaved persons
Smalls, Chris, 29
Smith, Asbury, 159, 162, 164, 165–66, 168, 170
Smith, Florine, 111
Smith, J. Douglas, 110
Smith, Lonnie, 73
Smith, Thomas, 142–43
Smithsonian National Museum of African American History and Culture, 160
Smith v. Allwright, 73
Soboloff, Simon E., 115, 171
Social Gospel, 166
Socialist Party, 168

Some Experiments in Living (Ainslie), 164
Somerset County, MD, 159, 161
South Africa, 129
South Carolina, 18, 24, 25, 98, 166
Southern Christian Leadership Conference (SCLC): Black women and, 24, 42, 49; creation of, 42; and freedom schools, 24; leaders of, 141; Martin Luther King Jr. and, 42, 64, 141; strategies of, 42; as top-down organization, 181
Southern Hotel, 168
Southern Manifesto, 110
Southern Methodist University, 75
Spelman College, 124
Spock, Benjamin, 151n31
Stalin, Joseph, 129
Stant, Frederick, 119
Stanton, Elizabeth Cady, 51
State Conference of the Colored Men of Florida, 94
Stewart, Maria, 2, 36, 37
Still a Brother, 136
St. Joseph, MO, 169
Stone, I. F., 135
Stop the Wrongs to Our Kids and Employees Act/Stop WOKE Act (FL), 10
Straight College/Dillard University, 93
Strange, Robert, 99
Student Nonviolent Coordinating Committee (SNCC): Black women and, 21, 22, 24, 42–43, 49, 60, 62–63; creation of, 42, 62, 63; Diane Nash and, 42; Ella Jo Baker and, 42, 62–63; Fannie Lou Hamer and, 21, 22, 24; and freedom schools, 22, 24, 135; H. Rap Brown and, 139, 156n66; importance of, 180; James Forman and, 64; John Lewis and, 64; Julian Bond and, 141; leaders of, 138; murders of members of, 123; Ralph Featherstone and, 123, 135, 136, 139, 156n66; sexism in, 42–43, 49; Stokely Carmichael and, 139; strategies of, 42, 181; at Texas Southern University, 80; and voting rights, 22; William "Che" Payne and, 123, 138
Students for a Democratic Society (SDS), 144
Synagogue Youth, 168

Taconic Foundation, 64, 65
Tallahassee, FL, 95, 96
Tappan, Lewis, 127
Taylor, Breonna, 91
Taylor, Flint, 142
Taylor-Burroughs, Margaret, 134
Tennessee, 183
Tennessee State University, 101, 102
Terrell, Mary Church: background of, 38; and gender equality, 40; and Harlem YWCA, 43; impact of, 36; and M Street School, Washington, DC, 40; and NAACP, 39; and Nannie Burroughs, 39; and National Association of Colored Women, 39, 52–53, 55; philosophies of, 39; and racial equality, 40; as signatory of "We Charge Genocide" UN petition, 133; and Susan B. Anthony, 39; and voting rights, 38–39
Texas, 71–74, 76–77
Texas Southern University (TSU), 75, 80
Theoharis, Jeanne, 12, 31n20, 63
Thompson, J. D., 93
Tidewater Voter Registration Project (TVRP), 111
Till, Emmett, 60, 171, 173, 177n44
Tillman, Ben, 98
Time, 123, 144
Tlaib, Rashida, 28, 29
Tometi, Ayọ, 29, 45
To Secure These Rights: The Report of the President's Committee on Civil Rights, 40–41
Toussaint-Louverture, 126
Truman, Harry S., 40, 58, 110
Trump, Donald J.: and 1776 Commission, 14; and 2020 presidential election, 1, 5; and critical race theory, 9; and diversity, equity, and inclusion training, 9–10; and immigration, 1; and January 6, 2021, insurrection, 1, 5, 28; and "patriotic education," 16; and race, 1; response of, to protests, 1, 27–28, 32n28, 127
Truth, Sojourner, 2, 36–37, 38, 45n3, 126
Tubman, Harriet, 126
Tucker, Charity, 95
Tucker, Thomas DeSaille, 93–97, 101, 104n10
Tulsa, OK, 132

Turner, Jack, 130
Tuskegee University, 103

Underground Railroad, 37, 107
UN Genocide Convention, 133
Union Leagues, 129, 130
Union Safety Committees, 128
United Daughters of the Confederacy (UDC), 9, 11–12
United Methodist Church, 166
United National Declaration of Human Rights, 25
United Nations, 58, 133, 167
United Negro College Fund, 102
United States, 91, 126, 131, 132. *See also* US history
Universal Negro Improvement Association (UNIA), 53, 131, 181
University of California, Berkeley, 156n63
University of Georgia, 145
University of Pennsylvania Law School, 40
Urban League, 56, 67, 168, 169, 180
US Congress: anti-democratic tendencies of, 182; election of Shirley Chisholm to, 44; and Hatch Act, 77; and House of Representatives Dies Committee/Committee on Un-American Activities, 133–34, 151n30; and opposition to lynching, 170; race of members of, 17; and Voting Rights Act of 1965, 72, 74; and War on Poverty, 74
US Constitution: 1st Amendment of, 116–17; 2nd Amendment of, 66; 13th Amendment of, 16, 128; 14th Amendment of, 16–17, 74, 107, 110, 116, 129; 15th Amendment of, 16, 18, 38, 73, 108, 110, 116, 129; 19th Amendment of, 40, 50, 110; 24th Amendment of, 74, 106, 114, 115; Black Americans and, 5; Black women and, 36; definition of "the people" referenced in, 92; and enactment of Bill of Rights, 126
US Department of Justice, 41, 142
US District Courts, 114, 115
US history: as basis for legislation and policy, 7; Black movement leaders in, 29; and Black protest and dissent, 7, 8, 29, 125, 134, 135, 184; and Christian nationalism, 9; and civil rights/Black freedom movement, 11–12,

133–34; and Civil War, 11–12; conservatives and, 8, 9, 11, 12–15, 19–20, 28–29; control over narrative of, 184; and critical race theory, 9, 10, 14, 146; and equality and inequality, 7, 184; and Eurocentrisim, 9; exclusion of Black Americans from, 125; exclusion of Black women from, 51; and McCarthyism, 133–34; and patriotism, 7; post-racial narrative of, 12–13; progressive/exceptionalist narrative of, 2, 28–29, 125, 134, 135, 184; and racial status quo, 11; and racism and discrimination, 8, 9, 10, 11, 13–15, 146, 184; rewriting of, 4, 14; and slavery, 10, 11; teaching of, 9; white focus of, 8; white nationalist interpretation of, 2, 28–29; and white supremacy, 184. *See also* Reconstruction era

US House of Representatives, 171, 172
US Naval Reserves, 138
US presidency, 182
US Senate, 108, 110, 159, 170–72
US Supreme Court: anti-democratic tendencies of, 182; and *Breedlove vs. Suttles*, 110; and *Brown v. Board of Education of Topeka, Kansas*, 60, 110; Earl Warren as chief justice of, 107, 116, 182; and *Harper v. Virginia Board of Elections*, 74; justices of, 116; and *Plessy v. Ferguson*, 104n12; and poll taxes, 110; Ronald Reagan and, 67; and segregation, 182; and slavery, 182; and *Smith v. Allwright*, 73; and voting rights, 4, 73, 74, 107, 116–17, 182

Vanguard, 56
Vicksburg, MS, 18
Victoria, Sherbro, Sierra Leone, 93
Vietnam War, 138
Villard, Oswald Garrison, 168, 169
Virginia: 2022 gubernatorial election in, 10; anti-lynching legislation in, 163; class in, 116; constitutions of, 107, 111, 114, 116; Democratic Party in, 110; desegregation in, 110, 114, 117; General Assembly of, 114–15; governor of, 110; public schools in, 10–11, 114, 117; racism in, 164; during Reconstruction, 108; Redemption movement in, 109; Republican Party in, 115;
voting rights in, 4, 106, 107–8, 109–12, 113, 114–17, 183; wealth in, 115
Virginia Beach, VA, 117
Virginia House of Delegates, 117, 118
Virginian-Pilot, 111, 118, 119
Virginia State College, 117
Virginia Supreme Court, 109
Virginia Union University, 112
Voting rights: as catalyst for other change, 72; during Civil War, 107–8; connections of, to other civil rights issues, 2, 3; Democratic Party and, 72, 73; and economic justice, 71, 79, 86; in Georgia, 110; grassroots efforts to secure, 180; in Houston, TX, 71, 76–79, 82–83; New Deal and, 107; in North Carolina, 110; during Reconstruction era, 18; strategies for achieving, 76–77, 82–83, 108; suppression of, 182; in Virginia, 4, 106, 107–8, 109–12, 113, 114–17, 183; and War on Poverty, 71, 72, 75, 183
Voting Rights Act of 1965 (US): aftermath of, 113, 184; as catalyst for change, 3, 72; as civil rights victory, 65; impact of, in Texas, 71, 72, 74, 86; impact of, on Black women, 44; impact of, on civil rights organizations, 74–75; NAACP and, 39; opposition to, 178n47; provisions of, 23; in Virginia, 106

Wagner, Robert F., 170
Walker, David, 126
Wallace, George, 127
Wallace, John, 94–95
Walls, Josiah T., 94–95
Wang, Arthur, 135
Warner, Joseph, 169
War on Poverty, 71, 72, 74, 75–77, 82–83, 183
Warren, Earl, 107, 116, 182
Warrenton, NC, 97
Washington, Booker T.: inclusion of, in public school curricula, 135; and James Edward Shepard, 97; and Mary McLeon Bethune, 56–57, 68n24; philosophies of, 56, 96, 97, 99, 182; prominence of, 93, 96; speeches of, 96, 97, 104n12; white perceptions of, 132; wife of, 56
Washington, DC: antiwar rallies in, 156n63; Center for Black Education in, 137; display

of Freedom School artwork in, 135; Drum and Spear bookstore in, 136, 137, 183; James Edward Shepard in, 97; Louie Welch in, 80; Mary Church Terrell in, 39, 40; M Street High School in, 39, 40; Nannie Helen Burroughs in, 39, 40; National Training School for Women and Girls in, 39–40; race riots in, 137; Ralph Featherstone in, 134, 135, 136–38, 139; Recorder of Deeds office in, 97; Sadie T. M. Alexander in, 40; segregation in, 134
Washington, Margaret, 56
Washington Post, 123
Watkins, Francis, 126
Weathermen, 144
"We Charge Genocide" (CRC), 133, 167
Wednesdays in Mississippi, 65
Welch, Louie: and Black voters, 79; and George H. W. Bush, 79, 80–81, 82, 83, 85–86; and Lyndon B. Johnson, 80; and National Advisory Council, Office of Economic Opportunity, 80; and War on Poverty and Project Freedom, 74–75, 76, 78, 79, 80–81, 82, 83, 85, 86
Wells-Barnett, Ida B., 52, 55, 130–31, 173, 177n44
Westminster Presbyterian Church, 169
"We Want the Voice of Black Women to Be Heard" (Height), 43
Wheatley, Phyllis, 55
White, George Henry, 177n44
White, Walter, 53, 54, 169
White Americans: and 2020 presidential election, 1; as abolitionists, 37; and accusations of rape of white women by Black men, 130; and Black protest, 182–83; and class, 116; and criminal justice system, 182; and desire to "civilize" nonwhites, 98; and Haitian Revolution, 125–26; and immigrants, 18; as opponents of civil rights/Black freedom movement, 62; during Reconstruction and post-Reconstruction periods, 18, 129–30; support for civil rights organizations by, 43, 53, 54; and taxes, 18; and US history, 2; and violence against Black Americans, 18–19; voting rights for, 112, 116; and wealth, 18, 108, 112, 115

"White Man's Burden, The" (Kipling), 98
Whiteside, Charles, 92
White supremacy: Black resistance to, 129, 179; and democracy, 20; and education, 8, 13–15, 16, 19; elimination of discussions of, 28; J. Edgar Hoover and, 131; and patriotism, 15–16; protest against, 8, 32n28; during Reconstruction and post-Reconstruction periods, 128, 129; as replacement for slavery, 172; and status quo, 14; Tucker Carlson and, 10; and US history, 184; and US laws, 14; and violence, 1; after World War II, 151n32
White women, 36, 38–39, 51–52, 60, 65. *See also* Black women
Wicomico County, MD, 159
Wilberforce College, 95
Wilkerson, Cathy, 144
Wilkins, Roy, 54
Williams, Matthew: failure to punish murders of, 159, 172; family of, 158, 159; lynching of, 4, 158, 159, 160–61, 162, 164, 165, 171–72, 174
Williams, Peter, 127
Williams, Wilbert, 82, 85
Williamson, Vanessa, 18
Wilmington, NC, 129
Wilson, Mary, 52
Wilson, Woodrow, 53
Wise, Stephen, 167
WNEW radio station, 65
Wolcott, James M., 111, 112
Women's Convention (WC), 39, 40
Women's Council for Interracial Cooperation (WCIC), 59–60
Women's International League for Peace and Freedom, 168
Women's Political Council (WPC), 48, 61–62, 64
Women's rights, 36–37
Women's Rights Convention, 45n3
Woodson, Carter G., 92, 135
Workmen's Circle, 169
World Council of Churches, 164
World War I, 99, 131
World War II, 132, 151n32
Wyatt, Vincent, 119

Xavier University, 138

Young, P. B., Sr., 117
Young, Whitney, 64
Young Democrats, 118
Youngkin, Glenn, 10–11
Young Men's Christian Association, 168
Young People's City-Wide Forum, 168
Young Women's Christian Association (YWCA): activities of, 55–56; Dorothy I. Height and, 43, 64, 65, 181; Ella Jo Baker and, 43; Harlem branch of, 43; Mary Church Terrell and, 43; Mary McLeod Bethune and, 43, 56; Nannie Helen Burroughs and, 43; and National Association of Colored Women, 55; and National Council of Negro Women, 47, 56, 60; Phyllis Wheatley branches of, 55–56, 66; and segregation, 55–56; South Parkway, Chicago, branch of, 55; Thelma McWorter and, 55; Vivian Carter Mason and, 60

Yugoslavia, 169

Zimmerman, George, 91, 156n66

www.ingramcontent.com/pod-product-compliance
Lightning Source LLC
Chambersburg PA
CBHW030623230426
43661CB00053B/2112